Praise for *The Interior Circuit*

"*The Interior Circuit* energetically covers so much of the city ground, from its traffic and politics to its bars and streetwalkers . . . Goldman brings something new to the [chronicle] form. He is intimate with the city in a way travel writers so often are not; but he is also intimate with the reader in a fashion that feels unusual to the form as well."
—John Freeman, *Boston Globe*

"Part travelogue, part memoir, part reportage on Mexican politics and the scourge of narco-terrorism, it is also, in the finest sense, a book that creates its own form . . . The genius of *The Interior Circuit* [is that it] link[s] Goldman's grief for Aura to the grief of all these families and indeed of Mexico. It's an audacious move, but it works because of the offhand beauty of the writing, which shifts from individual to collective with the fluid grace of circumstance."
—David Ulin, *Los Angeles Times*

"An indispensable contribution to the growing body of artistic representations of Mexico's most recent years of darkness . . . there is an urgent, raw beauty in Frank's prose, as if we are plugged into an only slightly edited version of his journals, and it is full of 'cortos': journal gives way to reportage, reportage to lament, lament to polemic, polemic to erudite rumination . . . Here Frank joins a growing crew of writers . . . who undertake dogged investigative journalism—the kind there is precious little support for in the digital age, and which in the Latin American context can get you killed—and dedicate themselves to revealing the victims, itself an eminently political (and also spiritual) task that is the heart of Javier Sicilia's movement . . . *The Interior Circuit* confronts the corto, the short-circuit, as in too-brief-is-our-time, by recognizing the absurdity of both 'freakish' and politicized death, and of the necessity of mourning both intimately and in community—of reconnecting the broken circuit with the language of pain itself."

—Rubén Martínez, *Los Angeles Review of Books*

"Though much can be said about the elegance of Goldman's writing and the piercing quality of his reportage, it's really the emotion-driven moments—his identification with those seeking to improve the city's living conditions and with those affected by the Tepito victims' deaths—that take *The Interior Circuit* to a commendable height that even crónica doesn't set out to reach . . . Altogether moving and eye-opening, *The Interior Circuit* is as much a love letter to Mexico City as it is to his late wife."

—Rigoberto González, *San Francisco Chronicle*

"Francisco Goldman, whom I never read before this year, has quickly become one of my favorite contemporary authors. This great work of literary nonfiction begins after the tragic death of its author's wife and moves forward as a variegated chronicle of Mexico City."

—Jonathon Sturgeon, Flavorwire

"*The Interior Circuit* is a marvel, and if you've been reading [Goldman's] incredible reporting from Mexico for *The New Yorker*, you know that Goldman knows the country well: its moods, its culture, its history. This particular book is almost unclassifiable . . . Part memoir, part reportage, part homage to Mexico City . . . marvelous."

—Daniel Alarcón, Gawker

"Goldman transcends the personal, transmuting the role of memoirist into that of city chronicler . . . Goldman's surrealistic portrait of the DF gives due weight to the city's layered complexities . . . In searching for some essence in the city Goldman finds an inner territory beyond personal grief."

—Daily Beast

"Suddenly, thanks to the keen eye and sympathetic imagination of the journalist and novelist Francisco Goldman, I care about the place that locals call the DF . . . Goldman is by turns impassioned and detached, loving his adopted city while by no means blind to its many faults . . . Goldman made me care. That's what the best writers do."   —Chris Tucker, *Dallas Morning News*

"Incisive observation, flashing wit, intense curiosity . . . vivid prose . . . The vibrant life of Mexico City makes for a compelling story in its own right, and not merely as the backdrop for Goldman's personal quest, as absorbing as that continues to be. In either of its incarnations, this is a story about love, whether for a person or for a city, in all the complicated, rewarding, and painful messiness that emotion entails."

—Harvey Freedenberg, Bookreporter

"Much of the pleasure of *The Interior Circuit* builds on Goldman's knowledge and love of Mexico City and his unabashed personalization of its streets and student dives . . . If *The Interior Circuit* is partly Goldman's chronicle of overcoming personal sorrow, it is even more his take on the politics, complexity, romance, and vibrancy of one of the great megacities of the world."   —Shelf Awareness

The Interior Circuit

The Interior Circuit

A Mexico City Chronicle

Francisco Goldman

Grove Press
New York

Published simultaneously in Canada
Printed in the United States of America

ISBN 978-0-8021-2377-0
eISBN 978-0-8021-9263-9

Grove Press
an imprint of Grove Atlantic
154 West 14th Street
New York, NY 10011

Distributed by Publishers Group West

groveatlantic.com

15 16 17 18   10 9 8 7 6 5 4 3 2 1

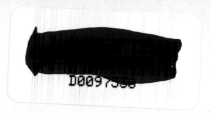

For Jovi

Contents

The Interior Circuit: Summer of 2012

Amor se llama
el circuito, el corto, el cortísimo
circuito interior en que ardemos.
—Efraín Huerta, "Circuito Interior."*

---

* "It's called love, the circuit, the short, the very short, interior circuit in which we burn."

1

The Student Driver

FROM 1998 TO 2003 I rented an apartment on Avenida Amsterdam in the Mexico City neighborhood La Condesa, dividing my time between there and Brooklyn, where I also had a rented apartment, sometimes spending at least most of the year in one city or the other, and sometimes, during especially hectic periods—teaching job, some other paying commitment up north, love interest in Mexico—moving between the two cities almost weekly. Avenida Amsterdam encircles lush Parque México and the narrow one-way avenue that rings it. On both sidewalks and down its median runs a stately procession of jacaranda, elm, ash, palm, rubber, and *trueno*—thunder—trees, among others. The median is a stone-paved walkway flanked by packed dirt where people exercise their dogs, by shrubbery and flower beds, and inside the curb at many intersections stand windowed shrines to the Virgin of Guadalupe. In the daytime the avenue is a canopied green tunnel from which you emerge into the Glorieta Citlaltépetl, a traffic roundabout with a fountain in the middle, as if into a sunny jungle clearing.

As Mexico City roundabouts go the Glorieta Citlaltépetl is a tranquil one, with only two streets feeding in and out, Amsterdam and Calle Citlaltépetl, the latter just a few blocks long, also with a tree-lined median. But during the rush hours even this circle gets hectic, as the Condesa fills with traffic, horns blaring and jabbing, cutting through the neighborhood to and from the major thoroughfares that border it. That's when drivers circling the roundabout from the direction of Parque México and busy Avenida Nuevo León routinely invade Calle Citlaltépetl's opposite traffic lane for a shortcut left onto Calle Culiacán, about thirty yards down. Whenever one car seizes an opening, making a break for that lane, others, speeding up, follow, in almost festively paraded outbursts of banal traffic delinquency. Many times, before it became automatic to look to my right before crossing, I had to hurl myself back onto the curb.

One late morning, ten or so years ago—the traffic, as usual at that hour, light—as I was walking across the Glorieta Citlaltépetl, I noticed a dark-colored Volkswagen Beetle going around and around it. Probably it was nothing more than that repeated circling that made me stop and watch. Or else maybe, for a moment, I semiconsciously wondered why a taxi—because back then, most of the VW Beetles you saw in Mexico City were taxis—would be going around and around as if the driver were lost in a manner that just circling the roundabout was unlikely to solve, or couldn't find the exact address on the *glorieta* that his passenger was stubbornly insisting on, or else was running up the fare on a sleeping or passed-out passenger in this demented way. But I must have quickly noticed that it wasn't a taxi. Lettering on the VW's doors identified it as a driving school car. When it went past again I saw that the student driver, his instructor alongside in the passenger seat, was a silver-haired man with a mustache, well into his seventies at least, dressed in white shirt, tie, and suit jacket. The student driver sat erect behind the wheel, grasping it with both hands at ten and two o'clock, his posture, his protruding neck above the tie, giving an impression of elegant lankiness. My memory of his face seems vivid, except the face I recall exactly resembles that of Jed Clampett, the *Beverly Hillbillies* patriarch, though with a brown complexion. What, I wondered, had inspired this man to learn to drive at his age? His attire suggested that the driving lesson was a pretty momentous occasion for him, or maybe he was just that sort of old Mexican who never went out anywhere unless in suit and tie. I imagined the scene at his home earlier that morning when he was leaving for his lesson, an affectionate and proud send-off from his wife, or maybe an affectionately teasing or ironic one. Or maybe he lived with a daughter. Or maybe it was one of those inertia-defying widowerhood decisions, that he would finally learn to drive, which is almost precisely what, in the summer of 2012, it would be for me. July 25 would mark the fifth anniversary of my wife Aura Estrada's death. Aura died in Mexico City, in the Ángeles de Pedregal hospital in the city's south, twenty-four hours after severely breaking her spine while bodysurfing at Mazunte, on the Pacific coast of Oaxaca. She was thirty years old, and we'd been married a month short of two years.

Unlike the elderly man circling the *glorieta,* I wasn't a beginning driver. I did know how to drive, but I didn't know how to drive in Mexico City, where I mostly depended on taxis and public transportation to get around. I could count on one hand the numbers of times I'd tried to drive there, though I'd been living in the Distrito Federal, the DF, as the city is formally but also popularly called, off and on for twenty years. The DF has a population of about eight million, but during weekdays, with so many commuters pouring in from surrounding metropolitan México State to work, the number swells to twenty million. The seemingly anarchic chaos and confusion of the city's traffic had always intimidated and even terrified me: octopus intersections and roundabouts like wide Demolition Derby arenas; cars densely

crisscrossing simultaneously from all directions and all somehow
missing each other, streaming through each other like ghosts;
busy cross streets without traffic lights or stop signs; one-way
streets that change direction from one block to another; jammed
multi-lane expressways and looping overpasses, where a missed exit
invariably means a miscalculated turn onto another expressway or
avenue heading off in some unknown direction, or a descent into
a bewildering snarl of streets in some neighborhood you've never
been to or even heard of before. My most gripping fear was getting lost on an expressway, on the Anillo Periférico or the Circuito
Interior, during one of the torrential summer rains, thunder and
lightning in the low flat heavy sky like sonic sledgehammers falling on the car roof, and the rain, dense, blinding, trapping you
inside a steady frenetic metallic vibration, and even welting hail
menacing the windshield, and in a panic making for the first near
exit and descending into drain-clogged streets that are suddenly
and swiftly flooding, crap-brown water engulfing stalled cars, the
tide rising to door handles; newspapers publish photographs of
those routine calamities all summer long. Everyone tries, though
it isn't always possible, to keep a distance from the careening
peseros, hulking minibuses whose bashed and scarred exteriors
attest to the Road Warrior aggression of their notorious pilots,
responsible for so many accidents and fatally struck pedestrians
that two consecutive *jefes de gobierno,* or mayors, of the Distrito
Federal have vowed to abolish the fleet entirely. Trucks and buses
crowd and bully traffic. Electrified trolleybuses inexplicably run
down major avenues in the opposite direction from the traffic
in their own not always so clearly marked lanes; you just have to
know that you're on one of those avenues and watch out.

I didn't see how I could ever know enough to drive in Mexico City, that population-twenty-two-million sprawl covering

and climbing up the sides of the Valley of Mexico, the world's third-largest metropolis, with its seemingly countless jigsaw-puzzle neighborhoods and infinite streets. Every taxi driver I've ever asked about it admits to getting lost. I've ridden in countless taxis that, in fact, were lost, even as we blundered through familiar neighborhoods that I would have guessed the drivers knew too, since I infrequently venture far from the areas of the DF where I and most of my friends live and hang out—neighborhoods, or *colonias*, that cover a small swath in the lower quadrant of the floor-to-ceiling *Guía Roji* Mexico City wall map hanging in the apartment I live in now. In this map the DF, inside its scarcely delineated borders, is dwarfed by the metropolitan Mexico City area, in México State, filling the map's upper two-thirds. Always, when getting into a taxi at the airport, I'm silently dumbfounded, or else kind of awed, by the drivers who seem to have no idea of how to get to colonias Roma or Condesa, the nucleus of my inexhaustible little world, especially since about a quarter of the passengers on my favored evening flight from New York City to Benito Juárez International Airport always at least look like typical residents of those neighborhoods. The taxi drivers have their own horror stories about getting lost (they have other genres of horror stories too), such as dropping passengers off deep inside the maze of a never-before-encountered, poorly lit neighborhood and not being able to find their way out for hours.

There was one night, twelve or so years ago, when I mastered driving in the DF, or at least felt I had, charging a long distance across the city with unself-conscious confidence, effortless control and speed. I'm night-blind and should never drive in the dark without eyeglasses, but I didn't even own a pair back then. I really shouldn't have been driving at all, because I was pretty drunk. The car belonged to a Cuban friend, and we'd been at a wedding party in Desierto de Leones, on the outskirts of the DF. My friend, who'd only recently learned to drive and was proud of it, was such a haltingly haphazard driver that I often felt impatient riding with him, silently comparing him to Mr. Magoo. Maybe I was in a hurry to get somewhere that night, or maybe I was envious because he could now drive himself around the city whenever he wanted—we'd been taxi-bound friends for several years—but as we were getting into his car I insisted that he hand over the keys. What I remember is a euphoric ride, racing down Avenida Insurgentes Sur, passing cars, an impression of lights bursting and streaming past and vanishing behind, going superfast, and thinking, maybe even shouting, that I was driving like Han Solo, rocketing toward the Death Star. Ever since, the thrill of that drive had lodged inside me as a challenge and as a rebuke to the argument that it was too late to learn to drive in Mexico City, or that I could never overcome my fear. It must be in me to do it again, I repeatedly told myself, though next time less recklessly. Then I'd remember that elderly man in his suit and tie circling the Glorieta Citlaltépetl in the driving school car and tell myself that of course it wasn't too late.

Every year, it has seemed to me, grief changes, persisting in shape-shifting ways that, as the years go by, become more furtive. But as that fifth anniversary of Aura's death approached—a year that would mark a period in which I'd now been mourning Aura longer than I'd known her—the intensity of my grief was, unsurprisingly, resurgent, weighing on me in a new and at times even somewhat frightening way that I didn't know how to free myself from. There was maybe not much logic to this, but I felt that there was a problem or riddle I had to solve and that somehow Mexico City, or something in my relationship to the city, held a solution. For example, sometimes I told myself that one logical step would be to leave the city and begin anew somewhere else, a city I'd never lived in before, one free of memories and associations with Aura but also one in which I'd be able to escape my complicated role as private but also rather public widower. But whenever I thought it over, I'd decide that leaving was an inconceivable step and that maybe the solution lay in staying. And not merely staying, but going further in, embracing with more force what I'd been tempted to flee, maybe that was how to find a way to live in Mexico City without Aura. The approaching anniversary had more than a little to do with my decision that this was the summer when I was finally going to learn to drive in Mexico City.

I was living in a newly rented apartment in Colonia Roma, though I still had our place in Brooklyn. Often when Aura and I had taken a trip out of New York City, or when we were in Europe, or were staying at a Mexican beach, we'd rented cars and I'd been happy to drive. But I hadn't driven a car, not once, since Aura's death, and that did seem to symbolize several aspects of grief, its listlessness, loneliness and withdrawal, its grueling duration. Five years without getting behind the wheel of a car suggested a maiming of the spirit but one that should be easy to repair. I just had to start driving again. But I wondered if I even knew how to drive anymore.

One afternoon in early July, I visited my therapist, Nelly Glatt, in her office in Las Lomas. I hadn't seen her in about a year. Before Aura's death I'd never been to a therapist, but within days afterward I was directed by a friend to make an appointment with Nelly, a *tanatologa* or grief specialist, and I obediently went. I remember that first visit well because all I did was sit or slouch or fall over on Nelly's couch and sob. Nelly, a queenly, extremely beautiful middle-aged woman with pale blue lynx eyes, a diaphanously ivory complexion, and a manner at once soothing, warm, and direct, did so much to help me get through those first few years. That afternoon we spoke about what the fifth anniversary would mean for me, and about whether or not I was ready to re-embrace life, maybe even love again. When I told Nelly about my plan to learn to drive in Mexico City, she approved. She said it signified I was ready to reassert control over my life, as opposed to allowing it to be controlled by grief as if by self-imposed obligation. Nelly said that something inside me had decided that I "owed" Aura five years. I'd refused to move or allow myself to be moved off that one square in the vast grid of possibility.

Couldn't learning to drive in Mexico City also be something I was determined to do for its own sake? I wasn't intending to just get into a car and drive around randomly; I'd actually come up with an elaborate, Aura-like method for carrying out my "driving project," as I called it. She was a fan of Oulipo-like experimental writing games of formal restriction and chance, and also of the I Ching, as well as a devoted Borgesian. But what if carrying it out was actually more of the same, yet another conjured grief ritual, a desire to maneuver and explore the streets of Aura's childhood by executing a performance game that she would have liked, all in order to intermingle with her city as I might yearn now to trace with my fingertips the contours of her lips, her eyes, her face? I wasn't sure. But I had formulated a notion that the driving project had something to do with my relationship to Mexico City, Aura's city, the city where she died and the place that held her ashes, and that now, because of this, had become my sacred place, and my home in a way no other place ever had.

From the air, on a flight in, what the eye mostly picks out from the megacity's stunning enormousness is a dense mosaic of flat rooftops, tiny rectangles and squares, and a preponderance of reddish brown, the volcanic *tezontle* stone that has forever been the city's most common construction material, also other shades of brown brick and paint, imposing an underlying coloration scheme. But there are also many concrete and metallic surfaces and many buildings painted in pastel and more vivid hues like bright orange, and rows of trees, and parks and *fútbol* fields, and modern towers rising here and there, in Polanco, Santa Fe, and the august Torre Latinoamericana at the edge of the Centro, and the straight and snaking traffic arteries, beady and silvery in the sunlight, and an infinite swarm of streets. You think, of course, awed, of the millions and millions of lives going on down there. (I reflexively think, as I have for years whenever flying into the city, that she's down there somewhere, living her mysterious life beneath one of those tiny squares, her too, and also her, Chilangas, female residents of the DF, who over the past two decades I've met only once or twice but who left an impression, women who almost surely no longer remember me.) From the air, perhaps because it is such a predominately flat city and almost all the roofs are flat and because so much of it is brown, Mexico City looks like a map of itself, drawn on a scale of 1:1, as in the Borges story "The Exactitude of Science," which refers to "a Map of the Empire that was of the same Scale as the Empire and that coincided with it point for point."

Supposedly the young Józef Teodor Konrad Korzeniowski (Joseph Conrad), seeing a map of Africa, put his finger in its cartographically blank center, the void of an unmapped Congo, and said, "I want to go there." An opposite of that map would be the *Guía Roji*, which evokes Borges's map sliced and bound into an inexhaustible book. My spiral-bound large-format 2012 edition presents Mexico City's streets and neighborhoods in 220 pages of zone-by-zone maps; at its front 178 additional pages of indexes list some 99,100 streets, and 6,400 *colonias*, or neighborhoods. The Mexican writer Alvaro Enrigue told me that when he was a boy an aunt gave him a *Guía Roji* as a Christmas gift, inscribed, "This book contains all roads." The *Guía Roji* also suggests a Borgesian metaphysical limitlessness, a bewildering chaos that is actually possessed of a mysterious order that even those who've spent a lifetime exploring the city can only dimly perceive. The *Guía Roji* may be every taxi driver's bible but he or she needs a microbiologist's eye, quick mind-hand coordination, and a strong, intuitive memory in order to use it effectively—i.e., find the way to an obscure destination—along with, probably, apt patience and interpersonal skills for engaging with querulous, frustrated, drunken, clueless, and otherwise unhelpful passengers. For instance, the first page of the index, under the letter A—which, like all the other index pages, has six vertical columns of street names in tiny bold print, each street's *colonia* listed below each name in infinitesimal print, with map-page number and map quadrant (B-3, for example) to the right—reveals 82 different Mexico City streets named Abasolo. I didn't recognize Abasolo as an iconic Mexican name, like, for example, Juárez or Morelos. I asked some of my friends why there were so many streets named for Abasolo, and no one had any idea, though it turns out Mariano Abasolo was a relatively minor revolutionist in the war of independence from Spain. In an exercise akin to counting grains of sand, I took the time to count 259 streets named Morelos in the *Guía Roji* index; Calle Morelos's columns are followed by several more of Morelos variations: the numerous Morelos that are *avenidas, cerradas* (dead-end streets), *calzadas* (inner-city highways), *privadas*, and so on. Let's not count all the streets named for Benito Juárez, far more numerous than even Morelos. As for Calle Abasolo, two separate *colonias,* both named San Miguel, have streets named Abasolo, one on map-page 246, the other on page 261; so do two distinct Colonia Carmens. There are numbered streets too. Over a hundred Calle 1s; nearly as many Calle 2s. The city has some 6,600 *colonias,* and fourteen of them are named La Palma and five are named Las Palmas. And so on. *Buenas noches, señor,* please take to me to Calle Benito Juárez in Colonia La Palma . . . now the fun begins.

Whenever I flip through the minutely mapped pages of the *Guía Roji*, I like to put my finger down on a randomly chosen page, and then, lifting my fingertip, leaning close, and squinting, discover, in tiny print, the name of the street I've landed on—just now, Calle Metalúrgicos, on map-page 133, in a *colonia* called Trabajadores de Hierro (Ironworkers.) Never heard of it. Though Metallurgists is obviously appropriate for a *colonia* named Ironworkers, it still seems like a pretty weird name for a street. What's it like to be a child, trying to incorporate the fact that you live on Calle Metalúrgicos into your sense of the world's hidden meanings and magic and of your place at the very center of it all? That your street, your *colonia*, is a magnet, pulling the entire universe down toward you? Turning to the index I find that Mexico City has five different Calle Metalúrgicos, in five different *colonias*. I look at the gridded Mexico City map on the back cover of the *Guía Roji* and find the square numbered 133, situated almost in the middle, just within the yellow-shaded northern border of the DF. Green-shaded metropolitan Mexico City, in México State, lies just beyond.

Calle Metalúrgicos, in Colonia Trabajadores de Hierro. What's it like there? That was the driving game I'd come up with. To use the *Guía Roji* almost like the I Ching, open to any page, put my finger down, and try to drive wherever it landed. A game of chance and destination, if not destiny. Of course, first I had to learn to drive around Mexico City. Since, technically, I did know how to drive, it seemed redundant and embarrassing to enroll in a driving school, but doing so also seemed a good way to get used to being behind the wheel again while also learning the city's traffic rules and layout under the instruction of a knowledgeable guide. I'd never learned to drive with a stick shift; I'd driven only with automatic. Learning to drive standard, I decided, would justify enrolling in a driving school, because then I would be overcoming two inhibitions at once. I looked up driving schools on the Internet. I went to the *Guía Roji* store on a gritty street in Colonia San Miguel Chapultepec, and bought the huge map of Mexico City that now hangs on my wall; my 2012 *Guía Roji;* and a small, rectangular illuminated magnifying glass that would surely prove crucial for reading those densely intricate map pages, especially if I found myself lost while driving in the dark. I went with my friend Brenda to Dr. York, a trendy Colonia Roma eyeglass shop that also sells secondhand English books. Brenda picked out for me a pair of eyeglass frames that I had outfitted with bifocal lenses, and I also bought a copy of Halldor Laxness's *Independent People*, a book I'd been meaning to read for years.

I procrastinated on the driving project, but I wore the eyeglasses all the time. Print was now magnified and clearer. By day the world lost its soft blur. My eyeglasses were a cinematographer who'd mastered the noirish expressionism of Mexico City's nighttime streets, shadows starkly outlined; street lamps like glass flowers instead of spreading haze; the rediscovery of one-point linear perspective in long, receding double files of softly gleaming parked cars; the intermittently illuminated facades of old and sometimes very old buildings like glimpses into individual personalities that are hidden by day, revealing scars but not secrets, battered but proud endurance, psychotic earthquake cracks, the maternal curve of a concrete balcony holding out its row of darkened flowerpots.

In the late spring and early summer of 2012 I had to travel a lot: to Poland; back to New York; then to Mexico to set up the new apartment in Colonia Roma that I was renting with my friend Jon Lee, a journalist who needed a base in Mexico; to Paris less than a week later; to Lyon, broiling with summer heat; back to Paris and from there directly to Buenos Aires to teach a workshop, arriving to snow flurries and a deep wet winter cold. Then I touched down for a few days in the DF, before having to fly to Aspen, Colorado, for a literary conference. Among my responsibilities at the conference was to teach a two-day morning-long seminar on Latin American and U.S. Latino fiction. Most of the students were adults, many retired. On the second morning we discussed Roberto Bolaño and a couple of his stories. This led to a long conversation about Mexico. The students wanted to talk about the so-called narco war, and many of them had grisly perceptions of life in Mexico, which were not inaccurate but were certainly incomplete. Yes, vast portions of Mexico were currently enmeshed in the nightmare and bloodbath of the narco war launched by President Felipe Calderón in 2006, when he'd made his disastrous decision, partly at the behest of the U.S. government, to send the military into the streets to fight the cartels, which were already doing battle with each other. But Mexico City, I told them, specifically the DF—which is what most people mean when they say Mexico City—was a different story. The DF had been largely spared the catastrophe of the murderous narco war; in fact its homicide rate was comparable to New York City's, I told them, and lower than that of many other U.S. cities, such as Chicago and Miami. I'd lived there off and on for twenty years, and had witnessed how the city had evolved. A dozen years of fairly progressive and energetic political leadership in the DF, among other factors, I told them, had seen the city become a vibrant, relatively prosperous, uniquely tolerant place, however beset with poverty and other problems, a great world city though entirely idiosyncratic, comparable to no other. People say that Buenos Aires is like a European city, but what other city anywhere is the DF like? It doesn't resemble any other city. In many ways, I told them, Bolaño's depiction of 1970s Mexico City, especially in his novel *The Savage Detectives*, as an inexhaustible, gritty, dangerous, but darkly enchanting and sexy sort of urban paradise for youth, but not only for youth, seemed as true to me now as it must have to him when he'd lived there in his adolescence and early twenties. And I went on in this way, my voice swelling with homesick emotion.

"Oh, come on, what a bunch of bullshit," a student, a middle-aged physician, barked out angrily, cutting me off. "Everyone knows Mexico City is violent, corrupt, overpopulated, and polluted as hell! How can you be talking about it like that?"

*   *   *

For nearly twenty years, since 1995, I've been living off and on in the DF. What living there means now is that I often spend day after day without leaving my block in Colonia Roma, or barely leaving it. In the morning I take the elevator from the sixth floor down to the lobby and say hello and sometimes stop to chat with the doorman, David or Eugenio, and sometimes also the security agents, all drawn from the Mexico City police—that is, the few I've grown friendly with—who protect my downstairs neighbor Marcelo Ebrard, who a few months ago, in December, finished his six-year term as *jefe de gobierno,* or mayor, of the DF. Then I go out the door and cut diagonally across the Plaza Río de Janeiro to the Café Toscano, where I have breakfast— almost always the same, papaya with granola, juice, coffee, or, whenever I'm hungover, *chilaquiles verdes*—and then I stay to work there, often for many hours. Then I go back to my apartment and try to work some more, until evening, when I like to go to the gym. At night I often drop into a cantina, usually the Covadonga, just around the corner on Calle Puebla, though sometimes the nights extend well past the cantina's closing hours, taking me to other places, usually within the neighborhood, or not that far from it. Before, when I lived in the Condesa, my life wasn't so different: going to a café in the morning to start my workday, and then often moving from one café to another— I'm a restless person, too restless, I sometimes think, to have chosen a writing career—counterclockwise all the way around Parque México. Only during the four years that I lived with Aura in Colonia Escandón, where there were no cafés nearby, did this routine vary much. Mostly I worked at home. I didn't go as often to my favorite cantinas. Sometimes in the evenings I went to meet Aura far away in the city's south, when she'd been to the UNAM, the great public autonomous university, or visiting her mother—Aura had studied as an undergraduate at the UNAM and her mother worked there and lived near the Ciudad Universitaria.

I'd first visited Mexico City in the 1980s, when I was mostly earning my living as a freelance journalist in Central America, and two or three times traveled up from there to receive payment from magazines by bank wire that couldn't be sent to Guatemala City banks. I never stayed more than a couple of weeks. I remember, during that first trip, in 1984, attending a clamorous party thrown by the embassy of the Soviet Union in the foreign press club where my friends and I were generously plied with vodka poured from bottles encased in rectangles of ice while being interrogated about our impressions of Central America by cheerfully persistent strangers speaking Boris Badenov Spanish and English. (In Central America I never encountered a Soviet journalist outside Sandinista-ruled Nicaragua, probably because any Soviet journalist who ventured into Guatemala, El Salvador, or Honduras during those years was likely to be arrested and deported or even killed.) I also remember being taken by a journalist friend up to the Reuters office, seeing my first fax machine, and being dumbstruck, dazzled. An unforgettable kiss outside the Museo Tamayo with a really beautiful girl, an art school student with delicate Mayan features whom I'd met inside the museum and then never saw again. A Guatemalan urban guerrilla *subcomandante* whom I met with in a seedy tiny hotel room in the center, who received me in his underpants and draped a towel over his lap as we spoke, and who passed me a large manila envelope thickly packed with U.S. bills that I was to smuggle in my luggage back to Guatemala City to hold for a stranger who would come to my door and speak a password. The *subcomandante* was going to cross back into the country on foot, with guerrillas, and he proudly showed me the multicolored cheap plastic barrettes arrayed on a piece of cardboard that he'd bought to hand out to the women and girls in the guerrilla camp. The *subcomandante*, as his cover, worked in Guatemala City as a photographer for a newspaper society page, while his clandestine role was to establish contacts with foreign journalists, human rights investigators, and the like, and we'd become friendly. In 1986, I think it was, he was forced to flee Guatemala, to Canada, which granted him political asylum, and I never heard from him, or anything about him, ever again.

A lot of memorable things happened during those first few visits to the DF, but it was a different city then. I traveled there again not long after the cataclysmic earthquake of 1985. There was rubble everywhere—collapsed buildings and lots filled with silent hills of concrete boulders and twisted iron amid the restored urban bustle—and dust was mixed like a thickening agent into the pollution and ubiquitous smell of sewage, with bright sunshine turning the air into a gleaming toxic haze, like a physical incarnation of the smelly, persistent aftermath of sudden death and trauma that ran out of your hair when you showered, and burned your eyes. Mexico City's south was mostly spared the earthquake's devastation because it rests atop a substratum of hardened lava flows, unlike the center and surrounding areas, which are constructed over what used to be Lake Texcoco, a vast mushy bed of volcanic clay, silt, and sand into which much of the city has been slowly sinking. Any visitor to the city's center notices the visibly awry tilting of many monumental sixteenth-century cathedrals and churches—a tour guide sets an empty soda can down on the floor of an old church and the can rolls away. Entire streets and blocks of old buildings, all drunkenly tilting, sinking unevenly into the soft earth. Aura grew up in the

DF, in the city's south, during the years of its pollution crisis, when nearly every winter day brought a thermal inversion emergency, and school was often canceled so that children wouldn't have to go outside. It was the probable cause of Aura's sinus problems. She remembered riding her bicycle in the parking lot of her housing complex and an asphyxiated bird dropping dead out of the sky, landing right in front of her wheel.

That first time I ever lived in Mexico City for any considerable length of time was in 1992, with my then girlfriend, Tina. It was her idea that we move there for a while, and she went down ahead of me from New York to find a place for us to live, which turned out to be in the more or less genteel colonial neighborhood of Coyoacán (square 186 in the *Guía Roji* grid, in the south). Tina found us an inexpensive room in the Casa Fortaleza de Emilio "El Indio" Fernández, the fortress-mansion constructed by Mexico's greatest Golden Age movie director, who was also an actor familiar to English-speaking audiences as Colonel Mapache in his friend Sam Peckinpah's *The Wild Bunch*. Perhaps not even Cortés had dreamed himself such a grandly triumphant and martial conqueror's palace as the one El Indio had built. Tina was initially charmed by the place because when she arrived there for the first time the massive wooden doors leading into the broad stone patio were open and a dead horse was being carried out in a wheelbarrow. When Fernández died there in 1986—on his deathbed he said, supposedly, "Heaven is a bar in the tropics full of whores and *machos*"—he was, or so his daughter Adela Fernández, a writer, has told interviewers, penniless, having depleted all his money to pay for and maintain his Xanadu. Adela had been estranged from her father after running away from home and the macho autocrat at fifteen; he wouldn't let her have boyfriends, and pressured her to be a "genius." She returned to live in the Casa Fortaleza with her two children only after his death, and began renting out rooms. The fortress-mansion has high walls built of ash-black-brown volcanic stone, the same stone cut into large bricks for the heavy, fortified-hacienda-style architecture inside, which included a massive watchtower with arched windows, topped by a crenellated mirador. To provide access during the fortress's construction, El Indio had to carve out a new side street, which he named Dulce Olivia after the actress Olivia de Havilland, whom he had some kind of thing for.

Three seemingly separate residences—did secret corridors or sliding bookcases connect them?—faced the main courtyard, which had a dry fountain in the middle. A broad stone staircase led back into the rest of the mansion, always permeated by the chill of cold stone, and filled with staircases and corridors and rooms and galleries and halls that had once held huge parties attended by Marilyn Monroe and other stars but that no longer seemed to serve any purpose. The whole place had the abandoned air of the ruined presidential palace where Gabriel García Márquez's ancient monstrous dictator lives out his last days in *Autumn of the Patriarch*, stray cows chewing on the velvet curtains. The mansion-fort was a mess. There was always dog shit in those long empty corridors, at least that's how I remember it. Our room was just off that main staircase. "Formerly a guest room," Adela told us when she showed us in. On its walls were colorful murals of wasp-waisted, long-legged nude woman bull-fighters with luscious, pointy breasts, painted by a friend of El Indio, Alberto Vargas, who was famous for his illustrations of pinup "Vargas girls" featured in *Esquire* magazine, back before

Playboy introduced its centerfold. Our horsehair-stuffed mattress was ancient, dingy, really disgusting-looking, but when I said that I would buy a new one, Adela declared that I certainly could not. "You don't know the great men who've left their semen in that mattress," she said. She then pointed to the big French windows and told us how as a girl she used to hide on the wide stone ledge outside and spy on her father's famous friends and their lovers. She had seen many immortals fucking on what was now my and Tina's bed. Anthony Quinn, André Breton, John Huston, Peckinpah, Agustín Lara—she rattled off a list of celebrities and artists, Mexican and foreign, who'd spent nights in that bed. That afternoon, Tina and I walked to the shopping center on the other side of Avenida Miguel Angel de Quevedo and bought a stiff plastic covering, the sort used for child bed-wetters, in which to enclose the sacred mattress.

The enormous windows in our room overlooked a deep-walled, now dry, stone pool in the back garden, which was both lush and desolate. We had a daily visitor on the same ledge from which Adela used to spy—a retired fighting rooster, a beautiful animal with lustrous brown-bronze feathers and scarlet comb and wattles and a furious, stupid stare, who not only crowed but always pecked manically and relentlessly at our window-panes in the dawn hours, waking us. One morning I opened the window and tried to nudge the rooster off the ledge with a broom, but instead of scooting away he just toppled off the ledge and plummeted, wings fluttering, to the distant bottom of the dry pool. The rooster, it turned out, was blind, his eyes pecked out years before in a fight. He wasn't injured by the fall, and Adela had him moved to some other part of the property. A tabby cat, with one clouded iris and a mottled nose, came in through the window one morning and adopted us for the rest of our stay. We named the cat Don Bernal, after the conquistador who wrote *The Conquest of New Spain*. Tina and I were allowed to use the huge Puebla-style kitchen, decorated with blue and white tiles, which in El Indio's time had produced the Mexican fare for countless lavish parties. It had an immense stove with deep ovens and seemingly as many gas burners as a golf course has holes; though this was also in ruins, and filthy, a few of its rusted burners still worked, and so we did cook there occasionally. Ceramic *ollas*, the traditional earthenware casserole-like big pots used for stovetop cooking, many probably not washed in decades, were stacked into such tall, crooked, swaying towers that we were afraid to touch them. The Puebla tiles were cracked or had fallen out of the walls. Tina and I spent one entire day futilely cleaning. Recently, on the Casa Fortaleza's Facebook page, I saw a photograph of the kitchen being restored, the Puebla tiles all in place and pristinely gleaming. It seems that the Casa Fortaleza is being transformed into a cultural center. Tours of the property are offered once a week, some given by Adela, who is now seventy, and, according to a newspaper article, reportedly suffering from cancer but still chain-smoking. I wonder if she shows visitors our old mattress and tells them about the great men and their semen.

When Tina and I were renting our room there, a gothic cast populated the house. I was never sure who did live there and who didn't, or where those who lived there slept. Adela told me that some of the men I saw, such as the one in late middle age who always looked hungover, sporting traces of blue eye shadow and lavishly long dirty fingernails, had been character actors in her father's films. There was an almost handsome, jug-eared young man who seemed to be a sort of houseboy. He was obviously mentally handicapped, his dramatic eyes perpetually fixed in a silent movie stare, his garbled speech almost unintelligible. Every now and then a man dressed in *charro* gear—tight seamed pants, short matching jacket, and sombrero—would call at the door and sit with Adela on the rim of the fountain in the patio, holding her hand as they conversed. She told me that he had been a stuntman for her father when El Indio acted in movies, and that now, during these visits, the stuntman was again standing in for her father, playing El Indio himself, conversing with her, repairing their sundered relationship. Adela was an alcoholic, a heavy *pulque* drinker. Sometimes women who said they'd been El Indio's lovers would show up at the enormous doors and pull on the rope to ring the bell that announced visitors. I remember a very pretty woman with long raven hair who came to that door and told Adela that El Indio was her father. Adela always invited the women in and gave them a tour. She lived in what had been her father's quarters, on the left side of the courtyard. She invited me in to see it only once, and I was surprised at how spacious, clean, and orderly it was, with everything supposedly just as he'd left it: a manly abode with an expensive feel; hues of rich wood, leather, and stone; filled with books, paintings, and other of the director's personal treasures, probably including some pre-Hispanic artifacts—a room suited to serve as the set of a Dos Equis "Most Interesting Man in the World" commercial. Adela's daughter, Atenea, a blond, ethereally beautiful girl, lived in the middle residence; she seemed rarely to leave her quarters, and it was rumored that she was ill. (Atenea died in 2002, at the age of thirty-seven.) The son, Emilio, wiry and always sneering, at least always sneering at me, lived on the right. He looked like what in high school we would have called a greaser. There was an old car up on blocks that he and his friends sometimes worked on. They gathered around it at night, drank, built fires, played loud music. Adela's son and I intensely disliked each other. Our few conversations, always gruff, were usually over household matters such as his having cut off the water supply to our room again. We faced off one morning in the middle of the courtyard, snarling insults and threats, and were moments from coming to blows. I felt committed to it, adrenaline surging, but the "houseboy" raced to our bedroom door to fetch Tina, frantically baying, "They're going to fight!" and she came running out and put a stop to it.

Adela frequently rented the Casa Fortaleza for private parties and for use as a setting in *telenovelas* and movies. Some mornings I'd come out of our bedroom and find the courtyard crowded with actors in period dress and film crews and equipment, and I'd help myself to breakfast at the craft services table. One evening when I was coming home women I didn't know refused to let me past the front doors. The house had been rented for a private lesbian lunar festival party, no men allowed. I furiously insisted that I lived there and had every right to enter, but the women allowed me past only after I promised to stay in my room. Another night there was a party for gay men, thrown, we were told, by the son of an important PRI politician, which was why police had blocked off the street. Back then, almost all the important politicians, even in the DF, were from the PRI, the Institutional Revolutionary Party. It had been governing Mexico since 1929, its candidates' victories in presidential elections every six years often abetted by widespread electoral fraud, until, in 2000, Vicente Fox Quesada of the rightist National Action Party (PAN) was elected president. Gay life in Mexico City was much more hidden in those days, back in the 1990s, than it is now. Gay marriage is legal in the DF, which has been governed since 1998 by a series of leftist governments affiliated with the Party of the

Democratic Revolution (PRD) and that have made progressive social policies a focus of their governance and campaigns. The only other place in Mexico where same-sex couples can marry, since 2011, is the state of Quintana Roo.

The party in the Casa Fortaleza that night was a bacchanal, an animated explosion of forbidden and repressed sexual energies. Men roamed the mansion-fort looking for private places to have sex—I would have thought the place offered multitudes of private hideaways, but our bedroom, maybe because of the legendary mattress, seemed to strike many as especially promising. The pulling, pounding, and even ramming against our bedroom door, while Tina and I huddled together in bed, having given up all hope of sleep, went on intermittently for hours. Not long after that night, Tina and I decided that it was time to move out of the Casa Fortaleza, and back to New York.*

During that year in the DF we had made a lot of friends, some who are now among the closest that I have. I don't remember how I met Paloma Díaz. She was a painter, a feline dirty-blonde from an eminent Mexican family who'd grown up in a large colonial house in Coyoacán with her parents and grandmother, a committed Communist who had a mural of Che Guevara over her bed. Paloma now also had a smaller home of her own several blocks away but seemed to divide her time between the two residences. We grew close, and she introduced us into her circle of friends. I remember long weekend afternoons, eight or so of us all gathered on a big bed in her house, smoking pot, drinking beer, slowly sipping tequila, talking, the hours drifting past, and then later going out to walk around the neighborhood.

---

* Adela Fernandez died on August 18, 2013. She was cremated and her ashes were deposited in a mausoleum alongside her father's in the Casa Fortaleza.

Most of those friends had known each other since adolescence and even earlier, had dated, eventually had even married each other. It was a relaxed, intimate, kind of sexy, and sophisticated way of being friends that was new to me, my experience of friendship being closer to a carousing, somewhat girl-shy antecedent of "bro" culture. In recent biographical works about Roberto Bolaño—the documentary by Richard House, *La batalla futura*, and Monica Maristain's book, a mixture of biography and oral history, *El hijo de Míster Playa*—Paloma Díaz has emerged as an important person in his youth. Born in Chile in 1953, Bolaño had moved with his parents to the DF in early adolescence. He met Paloma in 1976. Bolaño dedicated his poem *Olor a plástico quemado,* "The Smell of Burned Plastic," to her: "*Y las llamas escribirían tu nombre en el estómago del las nubes/ Palomita roja.*"* She told Monica Maristain, "He read it to me in his room and I almost died of embarrassment. I was eighteen or nineteen and nobody had ever dedicated a poem to me in my life. It made me nervous because I felt, frankly, that he was coming on to me, but I liked the poem." They shared a brother and sister love "that rarely exists between true siblings," Bolaño wrote in one of the long letters he mailed to her after he moved, in 1977, to Spain, where she visited him several times. Paloma never mentioned Bolaño to me, never said anything such as, "I have this other writer friend." That could have simply been discretion, but I suspect it also reveals how little even some of those who'd been closest to Bolaño in Mexico expected of him then, in the early 1990s, when he was living in obscurity though only a few years from becoming the most deservedly celebrated Spanish-language writer in generations. The book that established Bolaño's fame, of

---

* "And the flames would write your name in the belly of the clouds/ red Palomita."

course, was *The Savage Detectives,* published in 1997, at its core
a garrulous multivoiced channeling of his youth and friendships
in the DF. That year, 1992, when I met Paloma and her friends,
Bolaño was also only eleven years from his own premature death,
at age fifty. María Guerra, a brilliant and influential young independent art curator with a lashing wit; the shy and gentle artist
Marío Rangel; and Luis Lesur, a handsome, languid young man
who became a professional astrologer, were among the friends
who used to gather on that bed on those afternoons, and now
they are dead too—María and Marío of cancer, Luis a suicide.
Too many people die young in Mexico City. People were always
breaking off their friendships with María because they couldn't
withstand her often hilariously cutting and inevitably penetrating
remarks, and I, who received my share, and a few other friends
who also loved her, scorned those people as defensive wimps.
María had a freckled, impish face, wore her dark curls in a sort of
poodle hairdo, and had a raucous laugh. Her empathetic sense
of the painful human comedy, mixed with a disdain for self-pity
and for complacency, was expressed as a hectoring, teasing belief
in her friends' capacity to rally and do better. People were always
going to her for advice. I remember an afternoon in 1999, after
she had been diagnosed with pancreatic cancer, when I phoned
her at the hospital to arrange a visit and she answered weeping.
She said, her voice overwrought but also characteristically buoy-
ant, "Oh, Frank, I'm sorry, I can't really talk right now, I've just
been given terrible news," and only a few days later she died, in
her own bed in her apartment on Avenida Amsterdam, cared
for by her twin sister, Ana. Now, thirteen years later, around
the anniversary of her death, I've noticed how a few people still
leave flower bouquets on the sidewalk beneath what used to be
her window.

Through María I met Pia Elizondo, her husband, Gonzalo García, and Jaime Navarro, all still among my closest friends. Pia, a photographer, and Gonzalo—a painter, graphic designer, and editor and independent publisher—now live in Paris most of the year but come to Mexico every summer with their three children, in part to spend time with elderly parents and family. Both are the offspring of famous writers, Gonzalo of Gabriel García Márquez and Pia of the major Mexican avant-garde writer the late Salvador Elizondo. After that long night in the hospital when I wasn't allowed into the emergency ward to speak to Aura, within an hour after Aura died late the next morning, Pia was the first person to arrive at my side. In Mexico City, funerals occur within twenty-four hours of a person's death, the services usually held at a funeral home, often at one or another of the Gayosso establishments. The casket is usually on display, and people gather there, coming and going throughout the day, until finally, in late afternoon, the casket is taken to the cemetery, or the corpse is cremated. When I found Pia, now in her forties, in the summer of 2010, at the funeral of my good friend the artist Phil Kelly, an alcoholic Irishman who became a Mexican citizen, she said, "Well, here we are again. It seems like these are the only occasions where we get to see all our friends."

After Tina and I broke up in 1995, she stayed in our Brooklyn apartment, and I moved to Mexico City, and ever since, I've never been away for more than a few months at a time. I hadn't much liked Coyoacán—didn't like its beautiful but too quiet, melancholy, high-walled streets; its aura of hippie nostalgia; its complacent culture of millionaire Communists; the relative lack of raffish cantinas and bars; and its prominence on the tourist circuit—the museum-homes of Frida Kahlo and Trotsky are there. The Condesa, its exuberant transformation into a new kind of Mexico City neighborhood—a sort of Mexican version of early Soho, or Williamsburg—under way just as I was coming off of a broken seven-year relationship, was much more to my liking. My first apartment, on Juan Escutia, a streaming thoroughfare that channels traffic off the Circuito Interior across a flank of the Condesa, was on the rooftop and consisted of two unconnected rooms: the bedroom and the kitchen. There was no roof over the space between the rooms, so that when it rained I couldn't go from one to the other without getting wet, and when the rains were heavy, puddles spread inside from the doors, gradually swamping the floors. To reach my home, I came in through a gate off Juan Escutia, down an alley, through the kitchen of a ground-floor apartment rented by a scruffy Japanese couple and out its back door into a small courtyard where a narrow steel spiral stair-case, like one on an old freighter, led up past four or five stories to the roof. Mexico City, at an altitude of 7,940 feet, mostly a vast level basin until it climbs the distant valley slopes, always feels close to the sky. My rooftop, higher than most of those around me, looked out on a cubist reef of flat rooftops of varying heights, water tanks, gardens, weather-raked potted trees, hung laundry, complicated and tangled electrical riggings, wooden or cinder-block shacks at complete odds with the architecture of the buildings they're perched atop. (The beloved Mexico City writer Carlos Monsivais, in an essay listing the city's essential images, called the flat rooftops "the continuation of agrarian life by other means, the natural extension of the farm. . . . Evocations and needs are concentrated on the rooftops.") The wide sky overhead can seem like an element we're deeply submerged in, one that overflows the mountains rimming the horizon as if these were the walls of an extinct volcano's vast crater, inside of which has arisen a city. Mexico City's skies are always dramatic, sometimes soaring and azure, with long rows of choreographed white clouds, moving slowly or swiftly; sometimes the clouds seem almost as near and suggestively sculptured as they do from an airplane; or the sky feels leaden and suffocating, or low and churning, or densely black and menacing, billowing in from one horizon as if poured into water from a giant bottle of ink, as a storm approaches and the winds pick up. The city's pollution-abetted sunsets are spectacular conflagrations, blazing up over the western mountains, filling the sky with balloon dye colors, igniting the glassy modern office buildings that I can see out my rear windows into giant neon rectangles of scarlet. The night sky, sponging up light from the city below, is starless blackish phosphorescence, in which low clouds drift like mesoglea. When the moon is out in late afternoon it looms low over streets and buildings, enormous and pale yellow in the softer blue sky, like a ghostly school bus coming right at us.

I used to like to sit outside on my roof getting ready for the night with a few tequilas, music playing loudly on my boom box—no need to worry about disturbing the neighbors when you are up on a rooftop. Then I'd meet friends or head out alone, to my favorite cantina, or to a nightclub, or occasionally to an art scene party-performance or something like that in a gallery or in a rented space, an old cantina or club, often dragged there by María Guerra, and when everything else was closed maybe hitting an after-hours dive (El Bullpen, El Jacalito) or a *teibol* (as table-dance places, or strip clubs, are called), almost all of these places in the neighborhood, or in the Centro. I wasn't part of any 1995 equivalent of the decade-later hard-partying scenester Condesa evoked in Daniel Hernández's 2012 memoir of his life among the city's young "urban tribes," *Down and Delirious in Mexico City*. Still, I got around. Feeling newly liberated, at forty,

from a failed relationship and eager, if not desperate, to test myself, I set out every night in search of women. Those were happy,
free-spirited months. I brought a number of women, including
at least one *teibolera*, up to my rooftop before moving to a new
apartment and into what would turn out to be an obsessive, on-
and-off relationship with a young Mexican woman who lived
in the neighborhood. That relationship wouldn't completely
die out for another four years or so, and would finally leave me
depleted and fairly hopeless about love, which is how I would
mostly remain until I met Aura in the fall of 2002.

Since 1995 I've always lived within squares 168 and, only
this year, 169 of the *Guía Roji* grid, in six different apartments,
including the one on Avenida Amsterdam, in the Condesa, that I
moved into in 1998 and kept for five years. Amsterdam is a long
oval that follows the path of a horse racing track laid out in the
first years of the twentieth century for the Jockey Club of Mexico
on property belonging to the Countess of Miravalle, who owned
all the land for miles around; thus that neighborhood's formal
name, Colonia Hipódromo Condesa—Countess Racetrack. But
within a few decades—overlapping with the Mexican Revolution's 1911 overthrow of Porfirio Díaz, and the years of warfare
and political upheaval and reform that followed—all the countess's land had been subdivided. The racetrack quickly evolved
into what it is today, a tree-shaded, narrow boulevard without
beginning or end, lined mostly by single-family homes and apartment buildings of predominately art nouveau and art deco architecture, a Saul Steinberg–like conglomeration of curvy, sharp,
and jazzy shapes; austere and pastel-painted facades; wrought-
iron balconies, and others like ovoid bathtubs overhung with
tree limbs. In the 1920s and 1930s many Eastern European
Jewish immigrants and refugees settled in the Condesa. The ever

more numerous contemporary-design glass-concrete-and-steel apartment buildings now squeezed in with the older architecture reflect the neighborhood's swift transformation from what was then a low-rent, somewhat sleepy, insular neighborhood, where, in the early 1990s, you could still find dusty old Mittel-Europa cafés and bakeries, into Mexico City's epicenter of relatively affluent hipster-bohemianism. Over the last several years, much to the appalled annoyance of its now somewhat aging, family-raising, emblematic residents, its commercial blocks have also devolved into a party zone of raucous bars and nightclubs that draw young people and suburbanites from throughout the metropolitan area, and that raid the quieter side streets at night with a hit-and-run army of daredevil valet parkers.

But at night, walking on Avenida Amsterdam is like following a path through what can seem like a Pre-Raphaelite urban forest, the pinkish light of mercury-vapor street lamps suffusing and patterning the dark leafy effulgence overhead. Of course, you might get mugged walking down its cracked, root-humped sidewalks—two diminutive young thugs with punk-dyed hair and carrying razors suddenly emerging out of the darkness, crossing the street in perfectly angled pursuit to trap you on the sidewalk, which happened to me once, a few years ago, though a block away, by the park. On another night I was walking with Aura on Amsterdam when a gate opened in our path as a boy of about thirteen, moving quickly but glancing back over his shoulder, let himself out of a small, dark garden that softly flared with light as the front door of the house facing the garden opened and a girl of the same age slipped out, closed the door, and summoned the boy back for a hit of the joint she'd just lit and taken a pull from. The boy skipped back to her, took the joint, and after he'd exhaled she, a few inches taller than the boy, put her hands on his shoulders and gave him a deep kiss on the mouth, and then she went back into the house. It all happened very quickly. The boy darted back out onto the sidewalk, bringing a gust of marijuana scent, a scrawny, pretty cherub boy with messy curly hair, face beaming, and when he saw us he grinned hugely, his big black eyes skittering with excitement, as if exclaiming, Did you see that? Can you believe it?—and then he scampered away down the sidewalk, glancing back at us again, still grinning. We were sure that we'd just witnessed what must have been his first kiss, at least his first kiss with that girl. I don't remember if that incident occurred before or after Aura and I were married. She'd never liked my ramshackle Avenida Amsterdam apartment at all, but in December and January 2003—during her winter break from Columbia, where she was studying for her PhD—we'd loved each other there in the way couples do when a love that will happily endure is still new. That spied-on "first kiss" and those first Christmas vacation months with Aura, though they may have occurred as many as three or four years apart, now seem like part of the same moment in lost time, dispersed somehow into the leafy glowing nighttime darkness of Avenida Amsterdam.

Aura and I didn't have a car in New York but, as I've said, we took a lot of trips in rental cars, during which I almost always drove, and once, with her family, in Mexico, when we went to Taxco in two cars, I drove too, following behind her stepfather, becoming so dizzied by the incessantly curving mountain highway that I kept veering into the oncoming traffic lane and Aura became alarmed. Aura owned a car in Mexico, a small bright red Chevy hatchback, and I thought of her as a capable Mexico City driver, a nimble native of the ecosystem. Because she saw her mother,

Guadalupe, several times a week, she spent a lot of time in traffic, always driving back and forth from our part of the city to the south—when the traffic is especially heavy, which it usually is, bottlenecked to the horizon, it's a drive that can easily take an hour or more each way—to the UNAM, or to her mother's apartment nearby, or to meet her mother somewhere else in the south, for example in one of those shopping mall restaurants they liked. But not everyone remembers Aura as such a great driver. This summer the poet Nicolas José, her boyfriend when they were undergraduates at the UNAM, published a memory piece about Aura in his blog at the magazine *Letras Libres* that included this passage:

> It was truly dangerous to be in the car with Aura. Wrong way down one-way streets. For some reason we always ended up going the wrong way down one-way streets. Everything was just around the corner, according to her, and then we'd get lost. "Technicolor Butterfly" by Fito Páez—I hate Fito Páez—playing full blast and the two of us singing along like dwarfs.

Well, Aura did always get lost, even while, after four years of living there, walking around our neighborhood in Brooklyn. Whenever we had to meet up somewhere in lower Manhattan, especially, she almost always walked north when she had to walk south, or east instead of west, and arrived an hour or so late, and then she'd be miffed by even mild teasing, Yeahyeahyeah—she liked that Brooklynese yeahyeahyeah—I went the wrong way, hahaha, spacey Aura, so what.

* * *

On my first day of driving classes I was given a CD that on its title screen announced, "Defensive Driving. A theoretical course for the students of La Escuela Metropolitana de Manejo." On the next screen I read, "The fear of driving can influence the mood to such a degree that a person can endure suffering from the moment he gets behind the wheel," and a few paragraphs after that, "Does a red light mean nothing? Unfortunately this is a cultural problem of many people who live in Mexico."

My driving teacher from the Metropolitan Driving School was Ricardo Torres. He was in his forties, but looked older, his leathery face ravaged, and he had sagging, bleary eyes, sad-looking and a little mistrustful. I sensed in Ricardo, over the next week, a disposition of frayed gentleness, edgy nerves, wisdom earned by hard experience, constantly smoldering anger, and a sense of humor that is very Mexican, at once explosively sardonic and bemused. I explained my situation to him right away—fifth anniversary of my wife's death, wanting to mark it by learning to drive a stick shift in Mexico City. That seemed logical enough to him. He told me that two years earlier he'd gone through a divorce, after which he'd drunk hard and steadily for months, until he'd ruined his stomach. Now he could tolerate only a couple of beers, and those only with the help of two daily pills of *naproxeno sódico*. I told him that my loss had nearly turned me into an alcoholic as well, that I'd pretty much stayed drunk for the first five months. I didn't tell him, though, what had finally happened at the end of those months, when, after many hours of drinking, in the early morning hours after Halloween night, on Sixth Avenue in New York City, I was struck by a car. I remember thinking, Maybe there's a bar that's still open over there, and then eagerly striding out into the avenue, and waking up in the back of an ambulance, paramedics shearing my suit jacket and sweatshirt off me, and clasping monitors to my chest. A few hours later, in the hospital, I was told that I might die, CAT scans having revealed a spot of blood on my brain that could presage a hemorrhage. Those following two nights in St. Vincent's hospital were the first nights since shortly after Aura's death that I didn't get drunk. After I was released from the hospital, I tried to modify my behavior, telling myself that I had a duty to try to live in a way that wouldn't embarrass Aura, and I succeeded in certain ways, though regarding my drinking only somewhat, and not always. It seems, compared with Ricardo at least, that I have an iron stomach. None of my Mexico City friends were surprised when they heard I'd ended up in a hospital after being hit by a car. "Frank *anda al cuidado de Dios*" a friend said people had been saying about me during those months after Aura's death—"Frank is in God's hands," a Mexican way of saying that something bad was sure to happen to me.

In boyhood and adolescence, Ricardo was worshipfully attached to his father, a Mexico City police detective. When he was sixteen, his father was killed in a shoot-out with narcos in the upscale neighborhood of Polanco. Ricardo had to leave school and go to work to help support his family. Eventually he became a driving school instructor. The morning of my first lesson he picked me up in front of my apartment building in Colonia Roma Norte. I'd chosen the Escuela Metropolitana de Manejo at random in an Internet search, though it was also less expensive than other schools. The small black sedan in which I had my first lesson was older and shabbier-looking than most of the driving school cars I'd seen around. While I sat in the passenger seat, Ricardo drove to where I would have my first stick shift lesson, which turned out to be nearby in Roma Sur, on a long stretch of Calle Jalapa running alongside the walled park enclosing a public housing complex and an elementary school. The street didn't seem to draw a lot of traffic, and parking was prohibited, a rule that was more or less obeyed though a few garbage trucks were always parked there, and taxi drivers liked to stop there for a break. That no-parking lane was also popular with driving school cars. We parked and got out to switch seats. Ricardo had told me to bring a notebook. My first lesson was about the dashboard. He was giving me the beginning driver treatment. He insisted I write down everything he said, and then embarked on a methodically didactic tour of the dashboard. "That orange light indicates a mechanical problem," he said. "Whenever that light goes on, you must immediately bring your car to a garage to be inspected." These were memorized phrases he'd been speaking to his students for years, but he concentrated on getting them right, correcting himself whenever he fumbled a line. "Red light, that's the hand-brake light. This reminds us to release said brake. If we don't comply, we'll damage the entire brake system. *This* red light is the oil light. When this light is illuminated, it indicates that the motor has no oil. Procedure—park in a safe place, turn off the motor, and ask for help." Then he quizzed me, twice, pointing around the dashboard. Without glancing at my notes—my handwriting is usually illegible, but I haven't written so neatly in decades as I did in that notebook—I answered correctly every time. It was the first and perhaps the last time Ricardo would be so pleased with me. Though being unpleased, often vociferously, was what I suspect really gratified him.

We moved on to the clutch. "Basic procedures. How to initiate the advance from a full stop . . . Press down on the clutch, shift into first gear, accelerate by pressing your foot down on the gas pedal approximately a quarter of the way, at the same time slowly liberating the clutch until the point of advance. Maintain this position for the space of about two or three meters, afterward entirely releasing the clutch. Continue, gently accelerating." Ricardo spoke his memorized instructions in a reedy growling voice that could quickly turn cajoling and shrill.

Metallic crunch of gears, car jerked to a stop, both of us rocked forward and back. I feel victimized by my own ineptitude, by the baffling hostility of the machinery. "Fran, Frrra-a-a-an, why don't you listen to me? I said only a quarter of the way, but you press down too hard!" Or else I took my foot off the clutch too soon. But soon I, more or less, got the hang of it. We proceeded up that no-parking lane, me tentatively achieving the required balance between clutch and gas pedal to roll softly forward for those two or three meters, and then shooting forward a bit, and braking. After we reached the end of the block that first time, I received a lesson in how to back up. For a couple of hours, it seemed, we went up and down that block. Finally, maybe bored and tired of the repetition, of Ricardo's hectoring, of the ache in my neck from having to twist myself around to look straight out the rear window every time we backed up, I began to screw up again. The first day of driving classes ended with Ricardo driving me back to my building, both of us in a grumpy mood.

I started my driving lessons in August. I'd procrastinated nearly two months. In this chronicle I am taking a circuitous route through the summer of 2012, when it turned out that I didn't get to where I'd hoped to arrive quite by following the plan I'd laid out.

During the four years Aura and I lived together, because of her academic calendar, we always spent most of the year in New

York, coming down to Mexico for summer vacations and some but not all of the other school breaks and the occasional long weekend. In the DF, in the summer of 2003, we moved into a stylish one-bedroom loft-style apartment that Aura's mother had purchased for her, making a down payment before construction on the building was finished. We assumed the monthly mortgage payments, and paid for the work that still needed to be done on the apartment. The building was in a renovated factory or warehouse on a street in Colonia Escandón, adjacent to the Condesa, on a block between the major avenues Patriotismo and Revolución, in a far from gentrified neighborhood filled with garages and stores selling auto parts, hardware, tires, and paint. There were no nearby restaurants open at night. But across the street from our building there were two taco stands, both offering similar fare, including *suadero*, a thin-sliced brisket. One of the taco stands was thriving, and the other was a failure. Aura and I got our dinner at the thriving one a couple of nights a week, whenever we stayed in but didn't feel like cooking. Our treeless street was mostly deserted at night, except for the taxi drivers and other people from across the city who came, into the early morning hours, to the successful taco stand, where in front there was always a small crowd of waiting customers on the sidewalk, while the other stand was bypassed by all but the most impatiently hungry. When the owners of the successful stand arrived in the afternoons to set up for their long nights of work, they parked their expensive SUVs by the sidewalk. The owners or perhaps merely the employees of the other stand had no vehicles in evidence, though I imagine they had some method for delivery of their meat and supplies other than humping it themselves to the Tacubaya metro station and walking from there, or bringing it by *pesero* directly from a market. The owners of the successful stand were a pair of clean-cut, thick-necked young men who, somewhat atypically, rarely bantered with customers, so concentrated were they on the preparation of their tacos, and they took extremely good care of their impressive knives, and of their thick, gleaming cutting boards, on which they sliced and chopped with vehement speed. I had the impression they'd been at it for years already, earning good money and a reputation on this out-of-the-way, fairly desolate block, and that in another two decades or so they would still be there, with nothing changed besides the inevitable graying of their hair. The two skinny young men in the stand alongside—their cutting boards discolored pieces of thin plank, their knives cheap-looking, their little mounds of neglected meat unappetizing—mostly stood leaning with folded arms against the posts that supported their roof, looking diffident and bored, and sometimes as if they were asleep. Why didn't they leave or move their stand somewhere else? I'll never know. Maybe the logistics and expense of a move were beyond them. Sometimes you just get stuck.

Aura and I lived on the building's ground floor. At one end of our apartment a staircase climbed to the small sleeping loft and bathroom, and at the other end was a floor-to-ceiling window with a sliding glass door, essentially two stories high, that faced a little patio. That first summer I planted a row of bamboos in the patio against the back wall, along with some small *limón* trees. The bamboos looked like a row of young corn plants. Over the years they grew and grew, climbing like magical convolvulus, forming a soft solid mass of rich jungle green that completely hid the patio wall and rose well into the view of the apartment above us. Perhaps because the bamboos blocked sunlight, the *limón* trees never prospered, hiding in the darkened corners of the patio, looking stunted and crinkly. I hadn't seen the bamboos in over a year that summer afternoon of 2012 when I decided to take the half-hour walk I used to take once or twice daily when I lived there with Aura. During those first years without her I made myself take that walk regularly, like the drunken former British consul Geoffrey Firman in *Under the Volcano* as he perambulates the Mexican town of Quaunnahuac after his wife Yvonne has left him: "revisiting the landmarks, your soul dragged past them as at the tail of a runaway horse." I'd finally stopped seeking out that kind of pain, until this past summer when I took that walk again—one last time, I told myself—and found myself again standing out on our old street, looking at our old building, the glassy apartments visible above the high wall surrounding it. Inside, our patio was on the far side of our building's parking lot, separated from it by a concrete wall. I couldn't enter the building because I didn't know anyone living there now and had never met the uniformed doorman who was opening the front door to let people in or out. From where I stood in the street, looking over the wall, past the hidden parking lot, I could see our bamboos rising in the relatively narrow gap between the neighboring building and the windowed facades of our building. They'd grown so tall that whoever now lived in the apartment above ours must look out their own window and see little else but our bamboos, while the delicate shoots at the plants' pinnacles are probably visible through the windows of the two-story penthouse above. Those feathery trees certainly looked anomalous—like some green-plumed Mardi Gras or Tropicana nightclub gigantic hat stashed there—the only thing visibly growing, outrageously growing, in that narrow space between the two buildings.

For three of my first four years in the DF after Aura's death, I rented a room in the four-story art deco building owned by my friend Yoshua Okón, at the corner of Amsterdam and Ozualuma, a block away from the Glorieta Citlaltépetl. Yoshua lived on that top floor with his wife, Gabriela Jauregui, a friend of Aura's. My little room was on the floor below, where Yoshua had his art studio and offices. During the years when I had my own apartment on Calle Amsterdam, the ground floor of Yoshua's building housed an art gallery that he'd founded with friends, La Panadería, named in honor of an old Eastern European bakery that used to be there. The gallery opened in 1994, and before it closed in 2002 it had become one of the "new" Condesa's most emblematic places. Stark and punk, it was where a generation of now internationally prominent Mexican artists born in the 1970s—including Miguel Cabrera; Julieta Arranda; the artist known as Artemio; and, of course, Yoshua, among others—began their careers. There always seemed to be something going on at La Panadería. I remember walking past one night and looking in the window and seeing the place packed with nerdy-looking teenagers watching some kitschy B movie. Parties on the nights of openings, sometimes with live music, spilled out onto the sidewalks, and usually I'd spot someone I knew, and I'd stop by and have some beers. All this took place several years before I met Aura, but it's possible that we coincided at a few of those Panadería parties because for a while she briefly went out with an artist who belonged to a clique of *gueyes* (dudes) who hung out there. Like so many of the young Mexican women I've known, Aura was guarded about her private life and fairly secretive about her past. I'm often struck by how fearful many Mexican women are of the judgment of others, especially of being judged for behaving even somewhat as any Mexican male is allowed and even expected to behave; plenty of Chilangas cheat, lie, carelessly seduce, leave without any warning, and so on, but from the start their involvements often include an exaggerated element of secrecy, or at least a very high value placed on discretion. "Don't tell anybody about us. . . . Don't tell anybody . . . until . . ." Partly, I think, they instinctually protect themselves against a fundamental Mexican misogyny that they've known all their lives, that may not be as prevalent as it was in their mothers' time but is definitely still there. I mean less prevalent now in the DF, for in Ciudad Juárez, notorious for its hundreds of femicides in past decades, in México State, and elsewhere in the narco zones—which is to say in much of Mexico—that misogyny has grown more overt and deadlier than ever, and may be the most intractable, flammable, and depressing of Mexican pathologies. Social commentators and the like are always going on about how radically Mexican culture, especially in Mexico City, has changed over the last forty years; about a supposed breakdown of the Mexican family; and about how traditional mores have been replaced by the laxer, more tolerant freedoms of the developed West, the effects of feminism, and so on. While young women nowadays may seem to live a lot like even their wildest contemporaries in New York or Paris, beneath those apparently liberal surfaces, many women have told me, they can still feel caught between shifting paradigms, between modern freedoms and traditional expectations about how a woman is supposed to behave. "If a woman here says, 'Look at that guy over there, I want to fuck him,'" a friend, a twenty-nine-year-old newspaper editor, recently told me, "people still act shocked. There are exceptions, of course, but even with your girlfriends, they'll say things like, 'But you should wait until you're in a serious relationship.' More and more, I feel like I can't just say what I mean." I really didn't care who Aura had gone out with back whenever or what had happened, but sometimes she went to almost comical lengths to keep me from finding out. In the years we were together she was always a little paranoid about running into those particular Panadería guys. I had no idea which one she'd gone out with or if he was even around anymore, but she did occasionally indicate one or another of them to say that he'd been her friend in the Panadería days and that he now shunned her, wouldn't even say hello. It's a big deal in Mexico when someone who used to routinely say hello and exchange kisses on the cheek no longer does; it's called *quitando el saludo*, taking away the greeting, and it's meant to be cruel, in this case apparently *quitado* by manly art buddies banded together against the woman who'd dissed their boy years before. I could see that it was true, that this one and that one wouldn't say hello to Aura, including one flashy art world star who I wouldn't say hello to either, not just because he wasn't nice to Aura but because I detest his phony punk demeanor and conceited Rodent King smirk. But the hulking, extremely shaggy, extremely tattooed Artemio was always happy to scc Aura, and he did say something to me once about a friend of his having been hopelessly in love with her, or maybe he said totally fucked up by her. Artemio told me, after Aura was gone, that when he read *The Savage Detectives*, two of the young main characters, the Font sisters—both poets; both, in different ways, at least early in the novel, young heartbreakers and roamers of the city—had reminded him of the Aura he'd known in the Panadería days. Back then, when she was still a student at the UNAM, people knew Aura as a poet, Artemio told me, a girl who was always giving poetry readings and turning up at readings and founding and participating in ephemeral poetry magazines. That was how he would always remember her, he told me, as being like a Font sister.

Aura, the teenage and early-twenties poet, had barely figured in my sense of her. That's become a part of living in Mexico City too; every now and then someone tells me something about the Aura she or he knew before I met her. Or a message arrives from a stranger on Facebook, like the one sent by the young woman from Irapuato, in the state of Guanajuato, now living in Belgium, who shared some of her parents' memories of Aura's parents back when Aura's father was Irapuato's *presidente municipal*, its PRI-appointed mayor, during the first four years of Aura's life, before her parents split up and her mother brought her to the DF, where they lived, at first, in near poverty. Aura almost never heard from her father again after that and saw him only twice more in her life, when she was in her twenties, the last time by accident. A prime example of the "break-up of the Mexican family" that Aura tortured herself over, because she really never understood what had happened to her family, why her mother had essentially fled with her to Mexico City, or why her father wouldn't answer the yearning letters she wrote to him during those first years after or even phone on her birthday. Now, at least, thanks to that message, I knew that her father, when Aura was a baby, used to drive around Irapuato, Mexico's "Strawberry Capital," in a shiny white Mercedes Benz. Years later, by the time that her mother was established as a respected administrator and researcher at the UNAM, it was her father who'd fallen into relative poverty; that's something I'd found out on my own, when I went to visit him, in León, Guanajuato, weeks after Aura's death. Aura's father has since died too, in 2009. I didn't know that until I received another surprise message from a stranger—this a long, moving message from Aura's half sister, also an only child. Aura had not even been certain of her existence; in fact she'd told me that she thought she might have two half siblings, and didn't know whether they were male or female. But the sole half sibling *had* known that Aura existed and wrote that all her life she'd yearned to meet her, but that it was taboo in her house to even mention Aura, or her father's first wife. Undoubtedly Aura and Adriana, her half sibling, would finally have met, probably after their father's death. The mysteries of Aura's childhood and family history, which so preoccupied her, persist and go on being puzzled out in this phantom way, through me.

One late afternoon in the summer of 2008, during my first year living in Yoshua Okón's building, I was walking on Amsterdam, and had gone only about a block and a half when I came upon a commotion on the sidewalk, police cars and vans, yellow tape, a milling crowd, and a small cluster of women sobbing and wailing. Inside the tape, on the sidewalk, was a large pool of blood. A young man who'd come outside to walk his dog had been shot in the back of the head and killed by a man with a pistol, who'd run away. The corpse had already been taken to a morgue. The women, grouped outside the doors of a dingy-looking apartment building, one bypassed by the neighborhood's renaissance, were the victim's mother and sisters, an aunt perhaps, whom he had lived with. I felt waves of adrenaline surging through me, chilled ripples over my skin, and I began to cry too. When I went on walking, I was unable to stop crying. The next morning when I woke I heard newspaper vendors outside my window, down on the corners at the intersection of Ozualama and Amsterdam, baying in the same morose singsong voice as the evening bicycle tamale vendors:

Salio a caminar su perro y lo mataron. Salio a caminar su perro y lo mataron . . . He went out to walk his dog and he was killed . . .

The vendors were selling tabloid newspapers with the outside pages torn away so that the story of our slain neighbor would be the front page. They sold a lot of newspapers. I bought a copy, though it turned out not to provide any information that the neighborhood didn't already know. He'd stepped outside to walk his dog and was shot in the back of the head by a man who was probably waiting for him, and who ran away. Why? Over a woman? A debt? Maybe even his surviving family would never find out. Probably the shooter would never be arrested or brought to justice. Every morning, I realized, these morbid vendors must turn up in other neighborhoods in the city where tragedies have occurred the previous day, so long as they've been reported in the tabloid press. You never stop being surprised by the human ecology of improvisation, all the innovative, opportunistic, scamming, and desperate professions, some legal and many others not, that blossom endlessly in Mexico City's underground, or informal, economy.

For the next several days, I made myself walk by the spot where our neighbor had been murdered, always pausing to put my foot down on the fading bloodstain left on the sidewalk, mostly scrubbed away but still visible, and I'd feel those adrenaline waves and chills again, fainter now but still forcing me to take deep breaths, and my eyes stinging. I felt powerfully drawn to that stretch of sidewalk, and thought of the bloodstain as a secret door into my own world—a door to the *Pedro Páramo* world, where only the dead are alive—one now shared with the weeping women I'd seen on the afternoon of the murder.

In that year and every year since, there have been tens of thousands of murders in Mexico, 100,000 or so during the six-year presidency of Felipe Calderón, of the PAN party; tens of thousands have been abducted, many turning up in mass graves in desolate borderland deserts and ranchlands. Most are victims of the so-called narco war, including the violence, far from only directly narco-related, engendered by organized crime's grip on an estimated two-thirds of the country. In a 2012 report ranking the world's fifty most violent cities, nine were Mexican: Acapulco, with 143 homicides per 100,000 inhabitants, was ranked number two, second only to San Pedro Sula, Honduras, and was followed by Torreón (5), Nuevo Laredo (8), Culiacán (15), Cuernavaca (18), Ciudad Juárez (19), Chihuahua (32), Ciudad Victoria (36), and Monterrey (46). (The good news in the report was Ciudad Juárez, which had been ranked number two the previous year, and number one the three years before that.) The DF's 2010 murder rate, 7.36 per 100,000 people, was nearly the same as New York City's, 7.3; Mexico's national murder rate was 19.4. The impunity rate for crimes committed throughout Mexico has been estimated at an astounding 99 percent, though in the DF the police capture rate for homicides has improved over these last few years to, in 2012, 52 percent. In the many Mexican cities and municipalities where the cartels constitute the de facto local government and police, reporting on the narco war's violence and its victims is usually prohibited through censorship enforced with murder. In some places, news editors actually submit their copy before publication to the equivalent of cartel censorship offices. In one case I heard that the censor, in a city in Tamaulipas state, was a local journalist employed by a cartel who sat at a desk in a newspaper office making the final decisions about what that paper could publish and what it couldn't. Mexico is among the world's most dangerous countries to be a journalist in. At least forty-eight Mexican journalists were murdered during Calderón's recently ended *sexenio*, though some put the number of journalists— counting those who provide information anonymously via blogs and tweets—killed during the narco war at well over a hundred. Even obscure bloggers and *tuiteros* who've reported the violent incidents in their localities have been hunted down and murdered, their supposedly anonymous online identities deciphered by the cartels, often by sophisticated computer specialists and hackers kidnapped by the cartels for that purpose.

Scenes like the one on Avenida Amsterdam that afternoon, of women, of mothers, wives, sisters, daughters, weeping over the sudden and violent death or disappearance of a loved one, who perhaps only moments or hours before they'd seen alive and will never see alive again, are repeated all over Mexico, all over Latin America, all over so much of the world, of course, every day. Most family survivors weep alike whether the victim was a cartel assassin or an innocent. And most are entering, with those first sobs of shock and terror, the lonely realm of grief, of an absence for which nothing has prepared them, many into a shattering of all that had made their lives reliably routine, seemingly secure, and even much happier than that, and into an aftermath, often, of trauma, hallucinations, nightmares, and enduring depression, among other symptoms, and even psychosis. They're propelled through the portal of sudden loss into a world where the past is more vivid, more alive, than the present, which will seem to be an abyss that can swallow them if they allow it to. Most of these people, to say the least, don't have access to *tanatologas* like Nelly Glatt. The people going about their days and nights carrying the often silently riotous inner atmosphere of traumatic grief have by now filled much of Mexico, and Central America too, with an army of exhausted, lonely ghosts. They give pertinent new meaning to Bolaño's phrase about Latin America being a giant *manicomio*, a lunatic asylum. Little by little the ghosts may again be reconciled to life, in some cases they will even thrive, but many never will.

2

#YoSoy132

THE UNIVERSIDAD IBEROAMERICANA is an elite private Jesuit-sponsored university in Mexico City. It educates the children of the economically privileged, and has never had a reputation for political activism. "La Ibero" is a school where Enrique Peña Nieto, who looks like a Ken doll and was the PRI's candidate in the presidential election during the summer of 2012, might send his daughter. During his campaign, Peña Nieto never dared to visit the public UNAM, nor has he since becoming president. The UNAM, always a politicized campus even in an era like this when widespread political apathy and disillusionment were said to have taken hold even among its students, was considered a bastion of support for the left-leaning PRD's presidential candidate, a former Mexico City mayor, Andrés Manuel López Obrador. But Peña Nieto certainly would have believed, when he came to speak at La Ibero, on May 11, that he was in friendly territory. The PRI, having ruled Mexico for seventy-one years— "the perfect dictatorship," as Mario Vargas Llosa famously called it—had been out of power since 2000. But the transformation of Mexican politics and society that Vicente Fox's historic presidential victory seemed to presage never occurred. For two successive presidencies, first under Fox and then under his elected successor Felipe Calderón, the conservative PAN had governed Mexico, mostly ineffectually or worse, and the political establishment had remained essentially unshaken. For years many Mexicans had believed that the PRI—institutionally corrupt, murderously repressive—deserved to fade into irrelevancy. But according to polls published throughout 2012, Peña Nieto was going to win the elections easily. He promised a new PRI. What happened at La Ibero on what came to be called "Black Friday" opened people's eyes.

At La Ibero, the auditorium overflowed with students in noisy repudiation of the perfectly coiffed PRI candidate, who so resembles a Televisa *telenovela* star, and is in fact married to a Televisa *telenovela* actress. Furthermore, Televisa, Mexico's media monolith, was supporting Peña Nieto. Televisa controls 70 percent of the Mexican television viewing market, and TV Azteca controls nearly all the rest. Later that summer it was revealed in the non-Televisa media that Peña Nieto's campaign had been bribing the most influential Televisa news journalist for positive coverage. That seemed a superfluous expense. Televisa appeared to be as firmly behind the PRI as FOX News in the United States is behind the Republican Party. Many of the Ibero students that day were wearing Carlos Salinas face masks. The despised if brilliant Carlos Salinas de Gortari, considered among the most corrupt and influential PRI presidents of the latter twentieth century, was reputed to still be the power behind the PRI, and behind Peña Nieto. The call to greet Peña Nieto with a sea of Salinas masks had been posted on a student Facebook page just that morning, an Ibero professor told me later; rejecting the common perception that this generation of Mexican students was more apolitical than previous ones, she said that students now simply organized and communicated in ways that their elders didn't necessarily notice. At La Ibero that day, students chanted "Atenco," and that Atenco would not be forgotten. This municipality, in México State, was where one of the most squalid instances of government brutality in recent years occurred, in 2006, when Peña Nieto was governor of the state. During his term as governor, México State not only was beset by organized crime but saw a 106 percent rise in femicides. The notorious gang rapes, sexual torture, and murders of women in Ciudad Juárez were carried out as deeply depraved sport by members of drug cartels and other wealthy, powerful men whose total impunity for any crimes was institutionally protected by government and police authorities, locally and nationally, authorities long corrupted by money and intimidation. That is the conclusion of those who've studied the Ciudad Juárez femicides most thoroughly, such as the journalist and writer Sergio González Rodríguez; human rights groups; and international and national experts, including from the FBI and Mexican intelligence. "Why were they murdered?" wrote González Rodríguez in his searingly lucid book *The Femicide Machine*. "For the pleasure of killing women who were poor and defenseless."

In 2002, peasant farmers from Atenco had successfully organized to block PAN president Fox's plan to build Mexico City's new airport on illegally expropriated lands there; but the fight over those lands was not over. On May 3, 2006, in Texcoco, the town next to Atenco, 200 riot police evicted 40 flower vendors associated with a land-rights group from their market posts. When the flower vendors joined with residents of Atenco to protest the evictions, disturbances erupted, and dozens of protesters were beaten, many into unconsciousness, and arrested. The next day 3,500 state police invaded Atenco to subdue an estimated 300 resistors. Two young people were murdered: a policeman shot a fourteen-year-old boy, and a university student was clubbed to death with police batons. Protesters beat up a policeman, and other policemen were taken hostage and held for hours before being released to the International Red Cross. Police arrested over 200 people, including more than 45 women and even some children. Dozens of women were raped and sexually assaulted, in some cases repeatedly, by police; among those women were foreign human rights observers and foreign students who were swiftly deported from Mexico to prevent them from telling their stories. There is abundant video and witness testimony of what occurred in Atenco, including a video posted on YouTube, *Atenco: Breaking the Siege.** Viewers will see mobs of police encircling and frenziedly clubbing single unarmed protesters nearly to death; they will see a partially undressed young woman, dress hoisted around her waist, lying among the piled bodies of detainees in the back of a police pickup. Terrible crimes took place in Atenco that day, yet no police or officials have been convicted of wrongdoing. So too had Peña Nieto evaded culpability for Atenco, until that day at La Ibero when, flustered by the relentless questions of the students, he dropped his guard and defiantly said: "It was a decision that I made personally to reestablish order and peace, and I made it with the legitimate use of force that corresponds to the state."

So at La Ibero that day, Peña Nieto unrepentantly admitted responsibility for the crimes committed in Atenco, and flaunted his authoritarian character. The students responded with shouts of "Murderer!" and "Get out!" He returned a steely glare. Then he left, hurried by his security team, advisers, and hosts to the university radio station for a scheduled interview that never occurred; though he did reach the station, he then left it. The building's long corridors were filled with students still shouting

---

* youtube.com/watch?v=kh_RPDgBG5Y&sns=fb

"Murderer! . . . Get out! . . . Atenco . . . !" For approximately twenty minutes Peña Nieto and his entourage scurried along the building's hallways, looking for a way out. They hid for a while in a second-floor men's room. A video image shows a distressed-looking Peña Nieto standing in the corridor outside the restroom with his people pressed tightly around him, while his hand, clamped to the side of his brow, lifts a seemingly solid flap of gelled hair off his head.* Afterward, when that second-floor men's room became an instant landmark, students embellished the generic men's symbol on its door with a big toupee-like coif. Recently, students took me to see the men's room on the day I visited La Ibero for an interview—I had a book just out in Spanish—at the university radio station. The men's room, like everything at La Ibero, is sleekly modern, with smooth whitish marble-like walls, counters and toilet stall doors of burnished dark wood. I contemplated the possible emotions—humiliation, anger, even panic—that the future president and his aides may have felt as they huddled there while the corridors outside rang with riled shouts. No serious future biography of Enrique Peña Nieto or history of his presidency will be able to avoid mentioning that second-floor men's room.

That Peña Nieto seems to have a dark personal history— that is, there are many rumors—is not unusual for a Mexican politician, especially one who rose to power within the PRI. But even for a politician, he does seem unusually callow. He was especially mocked for his performance the previous November at the Guadalajara book fair: when asked which three books had most influenced him, he could name only the Bible and, after much stammering, the novel *The Eagle's Seat*, which

---

* videos.videopress.com/QO2HfJzb/capitancuevas_std.original.jpg

he misattributed to Enrique Krauze. He had probably never even read that, because the novel, by Carlos Fuentes, about the Machiavellian manipulations of a cynical Mexican PRI politician, suggests that Salinas, Peña Nieto's supposed mentor, may have been behind the 1994 assassination of the reformist PRI candidate Donaldo Colosio. While Peña Nieto was being widely ridiculed for his gaffe at the world's largest Spanish-language book fair, his daughter sent out a tweet describing her father's critics as *pendejos* (assholes), and *proles* (proletarians), whose derision was motivated by envy. When that tweet provoked a further media uproar, the candidate, trying to win an election in a country with tens of millions of *prole* voters largely indifferent to his reading habits, was forced to publicly apologize for his daughter. The horrific violence of Mexico's narco war is, of course, intimately tied to the political corruption that is the PRI's seemingly ineradicable institutional legacy. To fight endemic lawlessness, Mexico needs leaders committed to lawfulness. Now Mexico has a president who has publicly defended murder and rape as legitimate uses of force.

Peña Nieto's calamitous "Black Friday" visit to La Ibero made news all over Latin America, though on Televisa that night it wasn't even mentioned. Almost immediately following the incident, spokesmen for the PRI and other allies began putting out the claim, widely publicized by their supporters in the media, that the young people who had rowdily repudiated the president-in-waiting had in fact been not Ibero students but outsiders: *porros,* trained agitators infiltrated by his leftist electoral opponent, López Obrador, and by the PRD. Of course the ordinary Mexican media consumer would have no reason to doubt such claims. In response, during the next few days, an Ibero student requested over social media that other students make videos, and instructed them on what those videos should say. He received 131 videos that he edited into one and posted on YouTube. The video showed Ibero students, one after the other, avowing that they'd participated in the protest; saying, "Nobody trained us for anything" and speaking their names, displaying their university ID cards, and enunciating their ID numbers. Students at other universities, already intrigued by the reports of the incident at La Ibero—nobody had expected such an outbreak from a *fresa* school (a "rich kid" school) without any history of political organizing or agitation—took notice, and the video spread swiftly throughout the student and academic communities of Mexico and beyond, even becoming a YouTube "worldwide trending topic." Student bloggers pondered the meaning of what had occurred at La Ibero, and the opportunities it might offer. The July 1 elections were only a little more than two months away. Was there anything that students could do, with so little time left, to stop Peña Nieto from becoming president? And whom should the students prefer instead? Many of Mexico's leading activists, in the student community and outside it—including Javier Sicilia, an eminent poet whose son was slain by narcos in Morelos and who afterward launched a popular civic crusade against the violence of Calderón's war—had called on Mexicans to nullify their votes and turn in empty ballots, a position that made sense to many. The PRD's Andrés Manuel López Obrador, "AMLO," had barely lost the 2006 presidential election—he may actually have won it—and had stubbornly contested its outcome, vociferously alleging fraud, and then had finally had himself inaugurated as president in a ludicrous parallel ceremony that made him seem somewhat unhinged, or that at least made it easy for his enemies to portray him as unhinged. But heading into the summer elections of 2012, López Obrador remained the unchallenged leader of Mexico's left, with millions of ardent supporters. It couldn't be denied that his term as *jefe de gobierno* of the DF, from 2000 to 2006, had been a significant success. Nor could it be denied that for years he'd been the only major political figure articulating a political agenda on behalf of Mexico's poor, or that he is a tireless, grimly determined campaigner, endlessly visiting remote corners of the republic bypassed by other candidates. López Obrador had arisen from the PRI as a politician, and perhaps this was a source of his seemingly autocratic political personality. His speaking style is so ponderous that, after the first of the summer's televised presidential debates, people joked that the on-screen interpreter for the deaf looked like someone practicing tai chi. Among students there was a widespread feeling that none of the three major presidential candidates offered a solution to Mexico's problems and that all three represented only the continuation of an entrenched, corrupt, moribund political system. It was the political system, some students believed, and most immediately the electoral process, with its sinister and compliant relationship to the country's dominant media powers, that needed to be challenged. Now those media powers wanted the restoration of the PRI, auguring a demoralizing step backward for Mexico. Guillermo Osorno, my downstairs neighbor and editorial director of the influential magazine *Gatopardo,* wrote a closely observed piece for it on the birth and struggles of the student movement. Osorno reported that the day after students had driven Peña Nieto from La Ibero, a student from another elite private university, Antonio Attolini, who would soon emerge as the movement's most visible leader, had written a blog post, "Wake-Up Alarm: EPN [Peña Nieto] in LA IBERO." In it, Attolini criticized those establishment political institutions that had given Peña Nieto a free pass for what had occurred in Atenco, rather than calling him to account for those crimes and even bringing him to justice. "The criticism should be directed not at the candidate, but at the formalisms employed by the supreme court in the Atenco case." It was a student at the also private, elite Tec de Monterrey who posted a tweet reading, "#YoSoy132" (#IAm132). The still unorganized movement sparked by those 131 Ibero students, which came alive and spread with such extraordinary quickness, thus found a perfect name nearly as quickly, one that resonated and captured imaginations outside the student world. (Within weeks, wrote Osorno, marchers at Mexico City's annual gay parade would be sporting the #YoSoy132 insignia, on armbands and posters, writing it across their bared chests and bellies.) #YoSoy132 would become Mexico's first mass student movement since that of 1968, which came to a symbolic end on October 2 of that same year with the massacre by soldiers of peaceful protesters assembled in the plaza of the Tlatelolco housing complex, when a still unknown number of students and other citizens, including children, as many as four hundred, were murdered, though afterward the PRI went on murdering and repressing students for years. The PRI knows how to do what it knows how to do—twelve years out of power wouldn't have erased that. The Ibero students who'd bravely indentified themselves in the YouTube video soon began receiving phoned threats and reported ominous unknown persons watching their homes. Many of those students, most probably from Mexico's economic elite, were still adolescents, living with their families in the very sorts of neighborhoods populated by the likes of Peña Nieto, his political and business allies, and Televisa executives.

In the days after "Black Friday" students took their first steps toward organizing and defining their fledgling movement.

Small protest marches tellingly targeted various Televisa offices and studios around the city, as would many of the later mass protests. A coordinating committee was formed. The original core of the movement was in a few private universities—La Ibero, the ITAM, the Mexico City campus of Tec de Monterrey—but students from public universities and other schools began to reach out, seeking ways to become involved. Poor public education students from the DF and México State ventured by metro, buses, and *peseros* all the way across the city to attend coordinating meetings at La Ibero, whose immaculate landscaped campus looks like a high-tech college in Silicon Valley, with multiple parking garages and only one pedestrian entrance where security guards register the comings and goings of all visitors; SUVs carrying bodyguards pull up in front of that entrance to collect the fashionably dressed students—all girls, the day I was there—who hurry out through the gates to climb into held-open passenger doors.

Informal meetings were spontaneously organized around the city, often in parks or in Starbucks franchises, where students who ordinarily would never meet each other—"those with and without Internet in their homes, those with and without smartphones," wrote Osorno, incisively—came face-to-face. Looming over all these discussions was a single question: what degree of involvement could be expected, or should be desired, from the UNAM? With more than 200,000 undergraduate and graduate students, and a third as many more enrolled in its high schools, the UNAM has always assumed the protagonists' role in Mexican student political activism. The participation of UNAM students would certainly add muscle to the movement, but the great university was known for often recalcitrant and belligerent radical politics, and there was a fear that UNAM students could also seize the movement and make it their own. But the UNAM students who turned up at those first meetings, some of whom would soon hold leadership positions in the movement, turned out to be unaffiliated with their university's *ultra* groups, hard-line Communists, Trotskyites, anarchists, and the like. Over the next month those spontaneous meetings evolved into interuniversity assemblies, the first, in fact, held in University City, at the UNAM. Carlos Brito, a master's degree candidate at an elite research institute, was one of the leaders who presided over that first assembly, and he told Osorno that as he sat on the auditorium stage looking out at the students who had come from all over the country, from every economic class, from every kind of educational institution, he saw that many had tears in their eyes, or were outright crying, and he felt just as moved himself. That assembly session, like all of those that followed, lasted all day and well into the night and often grew chaotic; as might be expected students proposed wildly differing and sometimes incoherent, overlapping, or frivolous agendas. Countless committees and task forces were formed. Web sites, Facebook pages, and twitter accounts speaking for #YoSoy132 or claiming to speak for it soon proliferated.

What finally emerged from all those student assemblies and plenary sessions, in which professors also participated, was a charter that defined #YoSoy132 as a movement in which each university or school would have autonomy, sending its own elected leaders to future interuniversity assemblies, where decisions would be made. #YoSoy132 was to be nonviolent, and politically unaffiliated, despite the general and, of course, not inaccurate perception that abhorrence of Peña Nieto's candidacy had sparked the movement and quickly swelled its ranks. When #YoSoy132 sponsored its own presidential debate, with questions asked by students directly over the Internet, Peña Nieto was the only major candidate who refused to participate. The issue of how to vote in the elections was also debated at the assemblies, with students finally rejecting arguments to cast null votes in favor of "the useful and well-informed vote." A long declaration of principles submitted jointly at a plenary session debate by students from the ITAM and the UNAM Law School included a paragraph that expressed the movement's youthful defiance:

"We prefer ridiculous youth to the seriousness of old fogy youth; tweets and universities to universal news; count us at marches rather than counting us in other statistics. We prefer social networks to being tied in knots; we prefer to march than to be marched away. . . . We're not just one, or a hundred: sellout media, count us well: because united we're more than 131, that's how #YoSoy132 was born."

#YoSoy132 took off. Soon there were marches, especially in Mexico City, that stretched for three miles through the city streets, drawing as many as half a million people. In the city of Colima and elsewhere, the PRI, or mobs organized by the PRI, or the police in states and cities governed by the PRI, repressed some of those protests with violence, and arrested students. Following at least some of the Mexico City marches, as if to mark their difference from the ordinary citizens' perception of student protesters as insolent vandals, #YoSoy132 sent out squads to clean graffiti off buildings and monuments. Meanwhile Televisa, Television Azteca, and other pro-Peña media, which in much of Mexico, though not in the capital, are the only available news sources, continued to report that the movement was controlled, was funded by, and existed on behalf of López Obrador and his allies, airing one conspiracy theory and false allegation after another. In the middle of June the international rock star of student leaders, Camila Vallejo, until recently the president of the Confederation of Chilean Students, came to the DF, hosted by the Universidad Metropolitana Autonoma (UAM), the second most important of Mexico City's public universities. The now twenty-four-year-old Vallejo, brilliant, charismatic, and famously beautiful, a member of the Communist Youth of Chile, had led the Americas' and probably the world's most successful student movement through the so-called Chilean Winter of 2011. The Chilean student movement, originating in demands for an overhaul of the country's increasingly and unfairly privatized educational system, through a year and more of nearly weekly marches, occupations, strikes, and often cleverly staged events and flash mobs, had provoked and inspired many Chileans to question other aspects of their famously neoliberal society, leading to calls for other reforms as well, including reform of Chile's flawed electoral system; during that year, the rightist president Santiago Pinero's approval rating had dropped to 19 percent. During her visit to the UAM, Vallejo participated in panel discussions and gave a few interviews to the press, and throughout was careful to convey the impression that she was not interceding in the Mexican movement by advising it on how to proceed. "Education is the antechamber to democracy," she said, in one of her most quoted public statements. But Mexican student leaders, in whatever private conversations they had, must have listened closely whenever she shared her thoughts and experiences.

I'd covered the Chilean student movement as a journalist the previous fall and spring, and had spoken to Camila Vallejo a few times, and came to admire her, and the movement, with its numerous eloquent and courageous young student participants, representing all manner of sometime abstruse political tendencies. The example of Chile was with me during the #YoSoy132 marches and meetings I attended in the summer of 2012, when Mexican students were attempting, the eyes and hopes of much of the country now riveted to them, to invent in the space of two months a movement as potentially transformative and muscular as Chile's. But the Chilean student movement grew from a foundation of a university federation that was more than a century old and had weathered the repression of the Pinochet dictatorship, and now regularly endured the brutality of the Chilean army and police. The first #YoSoy132 march I attended, a night march, began to gather on a gloomy, rainy weekend afternoon in the Tlatelolco plaza of Las Tres Culturas, where more than forty years before, in 1968, the PRI massacre of students and others that still so haunted Mexico had occurred. The plaza, a gleaming slate gray in the rain, was overlooked by a shabby-looking public housing building, which, on that October 2, had sheltered infiltrated snipers, and where some apartments had taken a great number of aimed and stray bullets from soldiers outside. On the opposite side of the plaza were the ruins of the pyramids and ceremonial buildings of Tlatelolco, which on August 13, 1521, had been the setting of the decisive battle in the conquest of the Mexicas, or Aztecs, by Hernán Cortés and his Spanish conquistadores and their indigenous, namely Tlaxcalan, allies. Near one flank of the plaza stood the Church of Santiago, also built in 1521, one of the first churches in New Spain, with homely walls of muddy-red *tezontle* brick. On the day of the 1968 massacre, that church had locked its doors to panicked protesters fleeing for their lives, but had sheltered military murder squads inside (these were revealed, years later, to have been linked to the CIA). A monument at one end of the plaza listed the names of known victims of the massacre. Vendors circulated selling cheap rain

ponchos, candles, lanterns, food, T-shirts, and bandannas imprinted with the #YoSoy132 insignia.

I'd arrived early with América, a twenty-seven-year-old student at the UACM, a small public city university founded at the
initiative of López Obrador when he was mayor. We'd become
friendly over the several years that she'd worked at a bookstore
in the Condesa. At first I felt disappointed in the turnout. But
an hour or so later people began arriving, visible in streams
down the long sidewalks leading past the ancient ruin site to
the plaza, pouring in from metro stations or wherever they had
gathered to organize themselves, groups of students with their
institutional banners held aloft, some chanting school and other
slogans, banging on drums, and blowing horns, many wearing costumes and masks. I have to admit, I choked up a little,
watching all those young people arriving to join the march. But
there were people of all ages, mere civilians as it were. There
were no speeches, no visible leaders, no megaphoned marching
orders. América and I found the students from UACM, among
whom she had many friends. In the early evening, when the
rain had stopped, we began to file out of the plaza as if by mi-
gratory instinct. The march proceeded down avenues through
the working-class neighborhoods to the south of the plaza and
Colonia Guerrero, headed toward Paseo de la Reforma. People
lined the sidewalks, holding up signs; they cheered and pumped
their fists from windows. Student percussion bands carried us
along to a rousing beat; I wondered how much longer their arms
could keep swinging and pounding those sticks and mallets. Students marched in contingents behind banners announcing their
school or, in the case of the UNAM, the various departments in
which they studied. Many of the noisy call-and-response shout-
outs were school fight chants. The *Goooooooooya, goooooooooya,*

cachún, cachún, ra ra, cachún, cachún, ra ra, ¡Universidad! with
which UNAM students cheer the Pumas, the professional *fútbol*
team affiliated with the university, rumbled up and down the
length of the march. Most of the political chants and songs,
some of them raunchy, mocked Peña Nieto. My favorite was
the one, sung almost like a children's song, that went, *Hay que
estudiaaar, hay que estudiaaar, el que no estudie como Peña Nieto
va acabar.*—You have to study, you have to study, if you don't
study you'll end up like Peña Nieto.

At this march, and at the other I attended a few weeks
later, I broke away to walk its length, looking for blue-and-gold
UNAM banners and especially for one spelling out *Facultad de
Filosofía y Letras*, the department where Aura had studied and
even taught for a while, and whenever I found one, I tagged along.
I wondered what Aura would have thought about #YoSoy132.
You couldn't be much more UNAM than Aura was, though the
student strike of 1999, initially over a proposed tuition hike, that
had shut down and then paralyzed the university for nearly two
years after it was hijacked by *ultra* radical groups and government
infiltrators, had turned her into a political skeptic. She didn't like
López Obrador, or "El Peje" as he is also known, for *pejelagarto*, a
freshwater gar with an alligator-like snout common to his native
state of Tabasco. Once, after a 2006 presidential election debate,
when I said something favorable about El Peje's performance,
she scolded me, said that I had no idea what I was talking about,
and forbade me ever to opine on Mexican politics in her presence again. She didn't seriously mean it, but it's also true that
I didn't really know what I was talking about. I had never paid
much attention to Mexican politics. For years, I'd considered
the DF my place of escape from, or my neutral place between,
the two bordering countries where before I'd spent almost all

my adult life: the United States and Guatemala, countries whose politics are impossible to ignore if you live in either, and that can exhaust, sour, and depress anybody. "I fell in love with the girl next door," I liked to tell friends when they asked how I'd become so attached to Mexico. I'd thought of my old apartment on Avenida Amsterdam as a refuge where, as others went to writers' residences and colonies, I could hole up for months of long workdays and intense concentration. Often weeks could go by without my even opening a Mexican newspaper. I even used to boast about that. And in the years since Aura's death, my indifference to Mexican politics had only grown. So why was I so interested in #YoSoy132 and in the Mexican elections now, in the summer of 2012? It was an aspect of that summer's general awakening, I guess, but also of a specific awakening to what was happening in Mexico. Partly, too, it was a result of my encounter with the youthful energies of Chile after a magazine had unexpectedly sent me there to write about Camila Vallejo and the student movement. But it had something to do with my friendship with América too; we'd been meeting for evening drinks regularly throughout the summer. And it was also because of the UNAM and Aura, and my compulsion to try to imagine her participating in what she might have wanted nothing to do with. But, then again, she might have felt differently. In 2006, conveniently, Aura hadn't been able to vote, because she'd lost her voter's ID card. Who might she have voted for in 2012? Definitely not for Peña; nor for the PAN's candidate, Josefina Vazquez Mota; and probably not for El Peje either. But wasn't it because so many other young people felt the same way that #YoSoy132 had taken off? I knew that some of Aura's friends from the UNAM, including her best friend Naty Perez, now working toward her PhD at Princeton, were enthusiastic about the movement and that some, including Gaby Jauregui, were going to the marches.

I was also intrigued by the clusters of young people who marched behind banners identifying them as *los rechazados*, "the rejected," who, though they were not students, had been invited into the movement. The UNAM accepts only one out of ten applicants, and the much smaller UAM is selective as well, and so tens of thousands of students who couldn't afford private education, even many, according to the newspapers, with an A average in high school, found themselves without promising options to study for a career. Some of those young people had now organized themselves into *los rechazados*. The problem of the so-called ninnies in Mexico, unemployed young people with no place to study, is a national scandal. The demand for greater government spending on public higher education seemed one issue that #YoSoy132 could adopt, an education agenda like Chile's that might help it find another identity beyond its current focus on the looming election. But it was also hard to imagine a movement that could sustain itself on the indignation of students who were already on the inside over the plight of young people left out. In Chile, where everyone but the rich feels screwed by the cost of an education, there is nothing like the essentially free, massive UNAM. But the festive atmosphere of the Mexico City march did remind me of those I'd seen in Chile. It wasn't until long after nightfall, when, candles lit, we entered a long, narrow, alley-like street leading to the Televisa headquarters in Cuahtémoc, that I sensed another big difference between the two movements. People at the head of the march kept ordering us to stop. It seemed that there were *porros*, a PRI mob of thugs, waiting up ahead to attack us. An unidentified group of men in red T-shirts had been spotted. I was sure that it must be true, because the fear that spread so quickly among the marchers was contagious. Men were ordered to link hands to form cordons on both sides and women were told to gather in the middle. A number of the male students, laughing, playfully self-mocking, announced that they didn't want to fight anybody, that at the first sign of violence they were going to run, and kept themselves inside the cordons. We edged ahead, and were called to a halt again. Everyone was silent, straining to listen for a sign of what might be happening up ahead. Would there be screams, shouting, what? My candle had almost burned out but I managed to keep it lit and crooked inside my thumb even as I lightly clasped fingers with the man in front, telling myself, ridiculously, that the melting candle nub wasn't a bad weapon. I imagined a *porro* rushing me, and jamming the hot wax into his eye. But the nervousness all around me also brought home to me that difference between the inexperienced Mexicans and their battle-hardened counterparts in Chile, where in march after march the students steadfastly endure clubbings at the hands of militarized police, tear gas, pluming jets of burning chemically treated water shot from water guns mounted atop armored trucks, arrests, beatings, and sometimes torture in police vans and jail. Even Camila Vallejo had once been tear-gassed, at close range, severely enough to require medical treatment. The Chilean student marchers expected violence, and never backed down. These Mexico City students didn't seem at all ready for that, and most might never be. I wondered how many of them would come back again if this march or any subsequent one was met with violence. It turned out, though, that there were no *porros*; the men in red T-shirts were from a rural land-rights group that had traveled to the city to join the student march. The march went back to being a Mexico City march, yet another rather extreme form of fun, an almost all-night party. After some seven hours of marching, we, everyone who could, entered the Zócalo at a sprint.

The July 1 elections came too quickly. #YoSoy132 didn't save Mexico that summer, and could never have been expected to, even if it had the time. López Obrador did not ride the surging student movement to an unexpected victory, though the final results were closer than anyone had expected earlier that year, and closer than the polls had shown throughout the summer. Thanks to its being a multiparty election, in a flawed electoral process that doesn't require a runoff election between the top two candidates should neither reach 50 percent, Peña Nieto was elected president with only 38 percent of the national vote.

Though his claims had seemed more legitimate in 2006 because the margin in that election was razor-thin, López Obrador again refused to accept the results and demanded a recount, alleging fraud and media bias and manipulation. He was within his rights to do so. Although all of the parties engaged in some degree of vote buying, the PRI was reported to have committed 70 percent of it, mostly through mass giveaways of cards redeemable for purchases at a national superstore chain. That much was exposed largely owing to the pressures created by the successes of the student movement. #YoSoy132's own commissions of academic and graduate student experts, juridical scholars, statisticians, and so forth turned out almost daily arguments and evidence that the election had been essentially fraudulent and rife with illegalities, and that Peña Nieto should be prevented from taking power. Now the movement aimed to rally Mexico against the "imposition" of Peña Nieto as president. Even if it seemed unlikely, it really did not seem impossible that they might succeed. The election tribunal was to rule on the legitimacy of the election on September 6. What if enough irrefutable evidence could be presented to the tribunal and somehow enough pressure brought to bear on that establishment entity to sway a majority of its members before they ruled?

#YoSoy132 was now made up of more than 150 universities whose autonomous chapters did not always agree on what course to follow, but its popularity and influence had grown far beyond the boundaries of the student world. In Mexico City, at least, it seemed that nearly everybody wanted to be a part of #YoSoy132. Student leaders—it wasn't really clear, to those of us on the outside, who these even were—struggled to keep their movement at least tenuously under their own control. The question had arisen of what ties should be pursued with other civic opposition groups? To that end, #YoSoy132 agreed to participate in a national convention with the representatives of multiple civic groups called for the second weekend of July to coordinate strategies and actions over the coming months to stop the "imposition" before the December 1 inauguration. It was to be held in Atenco, the semirural town in México State where Peña Nieto had sent in his police to kill, beat, and rape civilians. América asked me if I wanted to go. We would have to sleep over, but she had a tent. I bought a sleeping bag, cans of sardines, and a bottle of *mezcal*. On Saturday morning I went to meet her on a corner so that we could catch a bus together. Waiting there also was a friend of hers, a young student from the UACM named Marcos.

When we arrived, I joined the long lines to register, and signed up as a member of the independent press, though I had no credentials and was not on assignment for anybody. We found a space for our tent crammed in amid hundreds of others on the concrete of the open market in the center of the plaza. It was the height of the rainy season, and almost the entire plaza had been covered with red-and-yellow striped tarpaulins. The convention opened with welcoming speeches. There was a stage backdropped by murals featuring, most prominently, Emiliano Zapata and his burning stare. The master of ceremonies was a woman from a group representing the victims of Atenco; the obviously intelligent, sophisticated, and pretty young woman from #YoSoy132 who gave one of the speeches seemed to come from another planet—but she did come from another planet, University Student from Planet Chilanga—than the handful of *compañeros y compañeras* who welcomed us on behalf of other groups and who mostly recycled the decades-old orthodox rhetoric of the Latin American left. Then we were split up into dozens of separate working groups. It took a while, but a #YoSoy132 student from Ciudad Juárez was elected leader of our group. Three or four others, all students as far as I could tell, were elected to sit with him at the white plastic table facing us. One—the only woman, of course—was charged with the useful task of taking notes, and I'm not sure what the others were supposed to do. The rest of us sat in folding chairs or on the grass, or stood. People were supposed to propose possible measures that students and civic groups and the society at large could take in the coming months to prevent the imposition: among others, strikes, marches on significant dates such as Zapata's birthday, seizing control of toll booths to allow traffic to flow freely into and out of Mexico City, a proposal to occupy Benito Juárez International Airport, and education squads to ride the Mexico City subways handing out information bulletins. Everyone wanted to talk; the meeting lasted—with a break for the simple lunch served by the convention organizers—into the evening. #YoSoy132 had adopted a sign language that it used at its assemblies to keep people from talking all at once, shouting over each other, or drowning out speakers with cheers or boos. To show agreement or approval, you wiggled your hands in the air, or else you wagged a finger in disapproval, and if a speaker was going on too long, you slid a hand up and down the other forearm as if playing the trombone.

By evening it was raining hard and the floor of our tent city was in danger of flooding. We had to pack up our stuff and carry it inside a building off the plaza, into what seemed to be a warehouse, almost like the sunken cargo hold of a freighter, where we pitched our tents. The space was so tightly packed with tents that wending our way back to the exit was like trying to find the only unobstructed path through a zigzagging maze. We bought bread and a plastic jar of a homemade powdery-gritty *chile* that locals were selling alongside the plaza, and made sandwiches with our sardines. Speakers from the stage continually warned that drugs and alcohol were prohibited. Despite the rain, we slipped off down a side street and into a small sheltered alley to drink *mezcal*. Back at the convention site, there was folkloric dancing onstage. Then the live music began, a few different groups of performers; finally a punk-thrasher band took the stage. The rain was falling even more heavily than earlier, creating a streaming muddy moat around the slightly higher floor of the central plaza. We stood underneath an edge of rain-drummed tarpaulin, water spilling over its edge, as we watched the band and the mosh pit that had formed in the open space before it, filled with hundreds of soaked #YoSoy132 kids, many with their shirts off, frenziedly slam-dancing.

At some point, Marcos, his inhibitions probably a little loosened by the *mezcal,* took me aside and confessed that he was in love with América. He was happy, and wanted someone to confide in, and encouragement. A few years younger than América, he was a really nice kid, handsome, cheerful, intelligent, formerly a math major at the UNAM but now studying history. I guess I'd seen it coming; all afternoon he and América had been puppyishly affectionate with each other. I felt no real jealousy toward Marcos. Mostly I had the familiar widower feeling of being in the way, of being where I didn't belong. Now the three of us were going to have to share a tiny tent together.

The next morning the convention took up the proposals decided on by all the separate working groups the previous day. Seated at the long table on the stage, essentially running the debate, were veteran members of various leftist groups and organizations; there may have been a #YoSoy132 representative seated up there but, if so, she or he was vastly outnumbered. People defended or criticized the proposals, and many launched into speeches. Campesino leaders waved their machetes in the air, and spoke of the hard, violent lessons of Atenco, Chiapas, Oaxaca, and other places. There was a pause to welcome a late-arriving delegation from Cherán, an indigenous Purepechan mountain town some three hundred miles away in the state of Michoacán, that had been battling illegal loggers protected by a narco cartel and local government authorities. The armed loggers had already consumed some 70 percent of the surrounding mountain forests from which residents of the town used to make their living; for years, Cherán had endured murders, rapes, kidnappings, and extortion at the hands of the loggers and their protectors. But then Cherán had fought back. Declaring themselves autonomous, townspeople expelled the local police and armed themselves with rifles expropriated from the police station. They blocked entrances to the town with bonfires that blazed all night. Cherán's combative autonomy was inspiring similarly embattled communities throughout Mexico to follow their example. People stood to applaud and shout as the delegates from Cherán marched along the muddy street leading into the plaza and onto the stage, where some gave rousing speeches. The atmosphere of the convention had grown more fervent and militant. One of the most debated proposals that day was a plan to storm Televisa's headquarters and take over the studios. Students silently wagged their fingers in the air, or wiggled their hands, or stood and raised an arm, waiting for the moderator to let them speak. Nonstudents spoke and shouted out as they pleased. One student argued that it would probably be impossible to occupy Televisa without resorting to some degree of violence, and would certainly be impossible without inviting a violent response, and that this would be a violation of the principles of #YoSoy132's charter—a declaration which prompted frantic hand wiggling in the audience, as well as taunting shouts. A peasant activist, a sturdy-looking man perhaps in his forties, spoke in support of the plan to occupy Televisa; he cited the example of the indigenous women who several years before had occupied a TV studio in Oaxaca during the often violent protests, sparked by striking teachers, against the government of that state's especially notorious and repressive PRI governor. "If we die, we die," the activist shouted at the crowd. "We need to be brave. If Peña Nieto gets in, lots of us are going to die anyway." That prediction seemed likely enough to come true, but did it include students? Were Mexico City students really going to die anyway? Now the students' hands were mostly still. You could sense their confusion. Was the student movement too soft? Was it out of step with the long, bloody history of heroic Mexican revolt, in which being prepared to die for your cause was not just a romantic fantasy?

But was theirs that kind of revolt? #YoSoy132 students, many originally inspired by arguments such as "Mexico's real problem is the formalisms employed by the supreme court in the Atenco case," now had to forge a common agenda with those who spoke a different language, a much older and entrenched one, the language of the organized political left in rural and proletarian Mexico. Those people had been struggling much longer—for their survival; for their lands; for basic human rights, jobs, and unions—and they also had a tradition of not backing down from violence, whether from the military, police, paramilitaries, or even cartel gunmen. Was there any way to form a future "progressive" majority for major political change in Mexico without those two groups—students and elites from the cities, and those from the rest of the country, from often violent and impoverished Mexico—finding a common language? López Obrador, in 2006, had succeeded, though not quite enough, and maybe now his time had passed, and many of the young people, at least, were speaking a new language, or trying to. Maybe the students were somewhat railroaded that day, maybe they gave in to guilt. América, Marcos, and I didn't stay around to hear the end of the debate—we went back to the city early in the afternoon—but over the next few days newspapers reported on the supposedly radical agenda finally approved at the national convention in Atenco, which the press tended to describe as a #YoSoy132 affair. The final accords had endorsed the plan to seize and occupy Televisa installations on July 27—so much for the element of surprise—as well as another proposal to surround Congress on the day of the inauguration and barricade the streets to prevent Peña Nieto and legislators from entering the building for the ceremony. Within days, #YoSoy132 leaders from various university committees were dissociating themselves from the

Atenco agreements. "It's absolutely false that the resolutions made this weekend . . . are #YoSoy132's," a student speaking for the private Anáhuac university chapter, Dante Mondragón, who'd attended the convention, told the press. "Regarding what we've set in motion, we need to be reasonable. We'll fraternize with and support our *compañeros* in the struggle, but from a more reserved perspective." Others pointed out that #YoSoy132 couldn't be correctly described as having agreed to any agenda at all until it had been set before the next interuniversity assembly, on July 28, and voted on there.

During part of the summer, well into August, I sat in on the weekly meetings between several #YoSoy132 students and a group of writers and artists they'd invited to collaborate with them in organizing a "popular tribunal," modeled on the one organized in 1967 in Paris by Sartre and Bertrand Russell to expose U.S. war crimes. Respected jurists, prosecutors, and investigators had already signed on. The students, easygoing and intelligent kids—one afternoon the UNAM architecture student sitting next to me mused out loud, "All three of the established political parties are corrupt, but they all have well-intentioned members"—argued that the tribunal should be a trial of the entire election process, not only of Peña Nieto. The tribunal never came to be—too little time, too many people heading out on late August vacations. But what especially began to dampen the enthusiasm of some members of the group, students and adults alike, was the perception that the popular tribunal was in danger of being usurped by MORENA, the National Regeneration Movement formed by López Obrador and his backers, who were, with good intentions, of course, offering to provide the infrastructure and support desperately needed to organize the event. Some of the adult advisers did believe that the movement should ally itself with MORENA, but others, and all of the students, thought #YoSoy132 should preserve its nonpartisanship.

Once Peña Nieto's presidency was a fait accompli, it became much harder for the student movement to get tens of thousands of people into the streets. During the summer months, millions of people across Mexico, and especially in Mexico City, had identified with and even felt inspired by #YoSoy132, though for most that signified only opposition to Peña Nieto and the PRI; by autumn, then, for so many, the movement no longer held much meaning. Antonio Attolini, #YoSoy132's most charismatic figure, and another prominent student leader even accepted jobs as political analysts on Televisa, bringing the student point of view on the news of the day, even on matters such as North Korea's nuclear belligerence, to the nation via the hated monolith, and seeding public derision of the movement.

More than half a year after the electoral summer ended, #YoSoy132 still exists, on social networks, in the universities, holding meetings and assemblies, putting out communiqués, but also still searching for what its role should be during the long wait until 2018 and the next presidential elections, when most current members will no longer be students. Whether or not #YoSoy132 ever evolves into a permanent and influential student organization like Chile's, or whether it turns out that the movement was like one of those exotic plants that wait years and years to blossom and then die, it left a legacy. #YoSoy132 brought Mexico's electoral process, and the manipulative power of its establishment media, under unprecedented scrutiny, and helped propel reforms to the nation's media laws to the top of the legislative agenda. The political sensibility of the students in

#YoSoy132 was shaped as much by life in contemporary Mexico City, I'll venture to say, as by classroom readings in political philosophy and beery student discussions of the Zapatistas or of the anarcha-feminist followers of the early-twentieth-century Mexico City anarchist writer Ricardo Flores Magon or of any others in the pantheon of Mexican rebels and martyrs. For all its idiosyncrasies and seemingly apocalyptic problems—pollution, crime, the ills of the water supply, traffic, crowding, buildings sinking into the soft unstable earth and so on—the DF is a great twenty-first-century city that in recent years has more or less been governed like one, which isn't to say perfectly governed by any means, but undoubtedly better governed than any other city or state in Mexico. In a way, all that many of those #YoSoy132 "student radicals" were demanding was for Mexico to be governed more in the way that the DF is. In the summer 2012 elections for *jefe de gobierno* of the Distrito Federal, the PRD's candidate, Miguel Ángel Mancera, running to succeed Marcelo Ebrard, was elected with 73 percent of the vote. In Ebrard's government Mancera had been chief prosecutor (like a district attorney) and could take some credit for a perceived drop in crime. But Mancera's landslide victory could also be seen as a referendum on how his predecessor, Marcelo Ebrard, had governed over the previous six years, and on the leftist city governments that preceded his. By contrast, in neighboring México State, governed until recently by Peña Nieto, the favorite son won the presidential contest by only 9 percentage points; in the DF's presidential vote, Peña Nieto received only 27 percent of the vote.

On the day of Peña Nieto's inauguration in December violence did break out in the DF. Young people, mostly, not all of them students, battled riot police in the streets outside Congress and elsewhere, smashed store windows, erected burning barricades.

There were no fatalities, but one student was severely beaten, and there were many arbitrary arrests, which fed surprised indignation over what some saw as the heavy-handed response, on that day of transition of power, of Mayor Ebrard's and Mancera's police. #YoSoy132 distanced itself from the disturbances, though undoubtedly, or probably, students who'd associated themselves with the movement took part. It wasn't hard to understand how frustrations had boiled over. The country's electoral institutions, resorting to the usual "formalisms," had chosen to overlook the illegalities of Peña Nieto and the PRI's campaign. The riots were also an expression of frustration with #YoSoy132's moderation. But then that was that; there was no more violence in the streets, of this sort anyway. The Distrito Federal went back to being the DF, a place apart. And Mexico went on being Mexico, as narco and military violence continued to grind down and traumatize so much of the country. However distanced they may feel from the bloody mayhem itself, it's not as if residents of the capital don't get depressed by the war as the death toll keeps climbing, or feel fear and a sense of impending doom that they try to push from their minds. *Vivimos adentro de una burbuja*—"We live inside a bubble," I'm always hearing people in the DF say. People sense the entire country collapsing, even vanishing, around them, becoming, as one friend put it, an "anti-country." The plague of terror, chaos, and murder is as close as the city's borders, already having consumed large parts of México State and its most populous municipalities.

Why has the DF so far been relatively immune from that violence? Is it only because the city isn't on a major drug trafficking route; or because of the near-ubiquity of its police forces and surveillance cameras; or because it is a big enough drug consumption market on its own that it's just good business to keep it relatively calm and prosperous, yet somehow not a big enough drug consumption market on its own for the cartels to go to war over? Those are all commonly heard hypotheses; but are there more conspiratorial reasons? I sometimes imagine that the cartels have been sent the message that if they don't want U.S. Navy SEALs and drone-fired missiles hunting down their capos and blowing up their mountain and desert ranch hideouts and *sicario* caravans—a nauseating solution, even if it were a solution, which it surely isn't—then they should stay out of the DF, the nation's economic vital organ and political and media capital. But I have no proof that there is any truth to this; it's just one of those paranoid hypotheses. What will happen now? Peña Nieto surrounded himself with what some regard as an experienced and capable cabinet, a mix of PRI "dinosaurs" and "new" technocrats just like those who have filled every Mexican presidential cabinet since the dawn of the technocrat vogue under Carlos Salinas. Will the PRI go back to dealing with the cartels as it is said to have done before, making pacts that benefit both sides, going in as partners as it were, tamping things down for the time being at least? It's widely assumed that the PRI is going to do something like that. But how will it or anyone else subdue the Zetas, "Mexico's most organized and dangerous group of assassins," as the DEA has understatedly described them? The Zetas are crime monopolists who seem to have lifted satanic self-interest and sadistic self-indulgence to a level hardly seen before in the world.* Let go of one thing, you let go of the ad-

---

* "The Zetas, where they dominate, dominate everything. They monopolize crime: kidnappings, extortions, assassinations for hire, narco-trafficking, the street trade, pirating, payments from the coyotes who move through their zones, it's all theirs." Oscar Martínez, of ElFaro.net, in his extraordinary book *The Beast*.

joining, and the adjoining. . . . Zetas are far from being the only ultraviolent organized crime group right now. There is a feeling that Mexico's lawlessness has spread too widely and too deeply now for anyone—even "El Chapo" Guzmán and the Sinaloa Cartel—to be able to reverse it. The U.S. drug consumption that fuels the war is not going to go away, even if marijuana is legalized in all fifty states, nor will U.S. weapons merchants stop supplying the cartels, nor are U.S. politicians likely to become less beholden to the gun lobby and do anything to limit those sales. Many people say that only years of implementing entirely new approaches; of major investments in many areas, not least public education; and of a patient transforming of the judicial and police cultures, and of government, by a kind of national government that Mexico has never seen before—probably few countries have seen it—could eventually bring about a change. Still, the Mexican economy is considered to be fairly robust; its national growth rate is twice that of the United States, with some 70 percent of the economy said to be tied up in one way or another with narco money; and in recent years forecasters have been predicting that the Mexican economy is about to take off, though this "Mexican moment" never arrives. Without a doubt, Mexico's so-called civic society, which manifests the conviction that change won't come unless the population forces it, has grown stronger and noisier—as exemplified by #YoSoy132; by influential civilian groups against violence, like the one led by Javier Sicilia; and by groups founded by the families of Mexico's disappeared. Church and civilian groups try to protect and aid the Central American migrants who in their grueling treks across the country to the northern border, fleeing the violence and economic devastation of their homelands, are preyed on by cartels, police, Mexican immigration authorities, *maras,* and random rural gangs—robbed, enslaved, forced into narco assassin squads, and raped. An estimated eight out of ten migrant women who attempt to cross Mexico suffer sexual abuse along the way, though sometimes at the hands of fellow migrants. Migrants are kidnapped en masse by Zetas, with the complicity of corrupted and terrorized local authorities, so that their families in their home countries or awaiting them in the United States can be subjected to extortion; while being held, the captives are tortured, raped, and sometimes massacred. Thousands of migrants have been killed or permanently maimed in falls from the notorious freight trains collectively known as "La Bestia," which they ride clinging to the tops of the cars. The corpses of tens of thousands of Central Americans lie buried along the so-called death corridor of the migrants' trail.

3

Mayor Ebrard Drives the Bus

THE LEFT, CITY MAYORS AND GOVERNMENTS associated with the Party of the Democratic Revolution, has governed the DF since 1998, following the first election in which residents of the capital were allowed to choose their *jefe de gobierno*—before that, the city government's leader was appointed by the PRI president. I was in Mexico City the night in 1997 when Cuauhtémoc Cárdenas was elected mayor and the streets filled with the celebrations usually reserved for important national team *fútbol* victories, people waving yellow PRD banners, honking car horns, a crowd gathering at the iconic monument El Ángel on Avenida Reforma. That night I was in a car, headed to an election party, with Cuban friends who'd left Communist Cuba to make their lives elsewhere and to whom the left's victory seemed ominous. "Change is bad," one of them kept repeating, though not without a touch of self-deprecating humor, which isn't to say he didn't mean it. "Don't these people know change is bad?" But change, at least for Mexico City, turned out to be good. The successive six-year terms, especially, from 2000 to 2012, of Andrés Manuel López Obrador and Marcelo Ebrard, transformed the city. In simplest terms, López Obrador laid a solid foundation of social reform, strengthening and widening the social safety net, in a way that helped to calm the city's air of perpetual desperation and emergency. López Obrador's government provided modest

monthly pensions to single mothers and the impoverished elderly that allowed them to live in at least austere dignity, and
to low-income adolescents to help them stay in school; gifted
children were identified and placed in suitable educational programs; unemployment payments were expanded and paired with
job search programs; and so on. Ebrard creatively built on that
foundation, practically urging a new personality on the city,
conceptualizing it as a dynamic modern world city that cannot
solve all its citizens' hardships but finds manifold ways to show
that it is not indifferent to them, alleviating hard lives at least a
little and providing outlets for diversion and expression, fostering
a sense of the city as a spectacle not only the well-off can enjoy.
"If you don't have people using the city's public spaces, if the
public spaces can't be enjoyed, then you don't have a city," Marcelo Ebrard told me when I spoke to him in the spring of 2013.
"You have to create conditions so that people feel that they're
part of a community. If you don't do that, the city doesn't work."

The winter skating rink in the Zócalo, with skates provided
free, may not sound like such a big deal, but you only have to
see the long lines of parents with children waiting their turn to
grasp what it could mean for a child from the city slums to ice-
skate for the first time, and for a parent to be able to provide that
experience. Mexico's paleontologists were invited to mount a
dinosaur exhibit in the Zócalo, and a temporary wooden gallery
was built to shelter the prehistoric skeletons and other displays.
Six public swimming pool beaches were installed around the
city with sand trucked in from Veracruz for poor children who
may have never seen the ocean. The exhibit of Rodins and Dalís
in the Faro del Oriente in the huge, poor *colonia* of Iztapalapa
broke city attendance records, defying, said Ebrard, "the idea
that beauty has become classist." More than three hundred new

children's playgrounds in the parks, and outdoor modular gyms. The free concerts that brought Paul McCartney, Justin Bieber, Britney Spears, and Shakira to the Zócalo. The musical and theater performances in poor neighborhoods. The city's museums open late and free one night a week. The popular and inexpensive (in pesos, less than twenty-five dollars a year) bike sharing program, sprouting up in one neighborhood after another, including the Centro, though not yet in neighborhoods like Itzapalapa; bike lanes all over the place; major avenues closed off for Sunday biking; late-night group rides—the DF, its traffic hardly hospitable to bicyclers, had nevertheless gone mad for bicycling. Abortion and gay marriage and gay adoption were legalized, over the predictable howls of the Catholic Church hierarchy—when the cardinal at Guadalajara publicly accused Ebrard of having bribed his own government's cabinet secretaries so that they'd support the reforms, Ebrard responded with a defamation lawsuit. "Our best program in terms of empowering women wasn't abortion," said Ebrard. "It was, in its massive societal impact, the 800,000 free mammograms. Why was that so important? Women didn't use to have their breasts checked; they didn't think it was in their power to go for an examination, because, let's say, of conservative cultural ways. We went door-to-door in the neighborhoods. Now they didn't have to ask their husbands for permission. Women got together with other women in their neighborhoods to go to the clinics. It was a great change."

None of this is to say that the DF's recent PRD governments have been entirely free of the ills of institutional Mexico. There is still a great deal of corruption, especially among authorities in the city's various delegations, manifest in the selling of illegal liquor licenses in exchange for kickbacks, or the frequently and futilely denounced selling of public lands to private interests, and so on. Iztapalapa, which alone packs in two million inhabitants, and other poor neighborhoods regularly endure cutoffs of their water supply, a hardship the city government would never impose on wealthier areas.

Marcelo Ebrard is a descendant of French immigrants, and pursued graduate studies at the École Nationale d'Administration of France. One of the reasons that Mexico City is so distinct from the rest of the country, he says, is the influence of immigrants who've settled there over the years, fifty-two separate ethnicities or nationalities from all over the world. Nearly 400,000 Amerindian Mexicans, migrants from the countryside, speaking various native languages, live in the city, and as mayor, Ebrard instituted in his municipal offices weekly early morning Nahuatl classes that he required his two adolescent children and the daily reporters covering him to attend. Ebrard, born in 1959, is a large and imposing man and his head seems especially large, with classic Gallic features, a big sharp nose, a high forehead, vivid brows low over his eyes, and a really Napoleonic chin, and his mouth is strict-looking but also lightly jaunty, just like his manner. When he received me in his private office in the Condesa, he was wearing Bermuda shorts. Mexican men almost never wear shorts, certainly not out into the streets. On a low shelf behind him was a framed photo of Rosalinda Bueso, the beautiful young woman he married in 2011, when she was thirty-three. Bueso is the former Honduran ambassador to Mexico. In 2009, when the president of Honduras, Manuel Zelaya, was overthrown in a rightist coup, Ebrard, married at the time to a tempestuous former *telenovela* star with a reputation for appearing drunk in public, provided police protection so that Bueso could enter her embassy, and apparently that was how she and the mayor met.

It's the third marriage for each. I've been left grinning dumbly the couple of times I've found myself in our building's elevator with Bueso, she so radiates warmth and gaiety. The couple live in an apartment that belongs to Ebrard's brother while their future house, on the other side of the plaza, is undergoing renovation and construction.

Ebrard saw the central focus of his government, he told me, as "human development," encompassing education, work, civic liberties, health, the environment—all those initiatives to help alleviate big-city alienation, to collectively form "a network that protects people." He said, "Mexican society is too unjust. Mexico's inequality is a scandal. The other day I was reading Alexander Humboldt, and I think about this the same way he did when he wrote, Mexico City is a beautiful city, I met many scientists while I was there, and if I hadn't had to return to Germany, I'd have stayed there. It would be my favorite city, but the only thing I didn't like and that preoccupied me is the poverty, which is overwhelming."

The ambitious restoration of downtown Mexico City, the old "Historic Center," to its architectural splendor of centuries past was begun under López Obrador; co-initiated and partly bankrolled by Carlos Slim, the Telmex magnate—Telmex, a privatized former state company, provides the world's most unreliable and costly cell phone and WiFi service—considered the world's richest man; and continued under Ebrard. I never thought the old downtown was so bad, but it wasn't a part of the city where tourists wanted to stay over. During the daytime every downtown street was choked with traffic, pedestrians, vendors, and beggars; the buildings, many dating from the seventeenth and even sixteenth centuries, were mostly in terrible shape, and universally begrimed. At night the center emptied, and its dark, deserted streets were considered dangerous, though urban pioneer types, especially artists, found gigantic apartments and studios to work in, and we all liked going to the old cantinas, and there was something of a club and rock scene. Now those same streets are vibrant and illuminated at night. Several streets have been turned into pedestrian malls. Resplendently restored buildings preen as if posing for their Condé Nast *Traveler* portraits. Tourist dollars matter greatly to Mexico's economy, and given the number of elegant new hotels and restaurants, it seems that the tourists are there and spending. On weekends the downtown streets fill with Mexicans, many from the surrounding working-class neighborhoods, families, young people, with their bags of Salsa Valentina–doused *chicharrón* and purple cotton candy, strolling and just hanging out like the residents of a European city, enjoying the Sunday calm of their beautiful ancient streets and plazas, which on weekdays are still centers of business, crowded and hectic. One tourist-friendly measure taken by Ebrard was to clear the arcades and streets around the Zócalo of the street vendors that had previously made them nearly impassable, famously shouting back at one vociferous protester, "*Aquí no vas a trabajar, cabrón!*" ("You're not going to work here, jerk!") The street vendors were mostly from the nearby market for stolen, pirated, or counterfeit goods in Tepito, a neighborhood notorious for crime. The vendors still come though, posting lookouts with mobile phones to warn of approaching police patrols; they pack up their merchandise in tarps and blankets, disappear in an instant, and return as soon as the police have moved on.

Ebrard has held posts in city government since 1989; a protégé of Manuel Camacho, who was then the PRI mayor, he left the PRI with Camacho to form a new, now defunct party, in 1995. Under López Obrador, Ebrard was chief of police, and then, after 2004, his secretary of development. While Ebrard was mayor, a new police academy was inaugurated, and police were now required to have a secondary school education. The city now has a police force of 90,000. As measured by statistics, crime did go down while Ebrard was mayor, but a better proof is how safe people actually feel in their daily lives. Throughout the 1990s, it was Mexico City rather than the country itself that was known for crime, especially for kidnappings and murders. But now people from violence-ravaged Mexico move to the DF in order to feel safe. In the late 1990s, not a week seemed to go by without my hearing about someone I knew being kidnapped in a taxicab and taken to an ATM for a maximum-amount withdrawal. Sometimes, after being pushed down onto the floor of the cab and driven to a garage, the victims were kept over two days, for two withdrawals, and usually the kidnappers beat them up, often badly. A friend of mine, forced to kneel facedown on the floor of a taxi, endured repeated knife jabs to his buttocks during the many hours he was being driven around while his sadist kidnappers were waiting for midnight to pass so that they could drain his ATM account's maximum daily amount again.

It happened to me one night, the driver, barely a block from where I'd gotten into his VW Beetle cab, pausing at a corner to fling the door open and let two men in. One sat next to me and the other crouched down on the floor where the front passenger seat had been removed—standard in those VW taxis—and pointed a pistol at me. But precisely because I'd known that I'd be hailing a street cab, I'd left my bank and credit cards at home, so, after driving me around awhile, they just took what cash I had and my purple rain parka, and let me go, ordering me to walk straight ahead and warning me that that if I looked back they'd shoot me. It was a long, chilly walk home. Another night, walking through Parque México on Avenida Michoacán, I saw a taxi idling by the curb with its *libre* light on, and two burly men hiding shoulder to shoulder behind the trunk of a nearby tree, apparently believing that it screened them from the view of whatever hapless, probably drunk, passenger might come along and think himself incredibly fortunate to have found an available taxi just waiting there. When the men behind the tree saw me looking at them they grinned hideously, like embarrassed criminals in a cartoon. I didn't call the police, because those two men probably were police. Now it's been a long time since I've heard of a friend being kidnapped in a taxicab; I've heard of only one, in fact, late at night when he was very drunk, over a year ago. Police patrol the Condesa and Roma and many other neighborhoods on foot and on bicycles, and police cars endlessly circle. It's also been a long time since I've heard of anyone I know being mugged in the street, though of course this still happens. Likewise, if not nearly so frequently as before, express taxi kidnappings still happen, and the kidnappers are still usually police or in league with them, their favorite targets being prosperous-looking women outside shopping centers and malls. Many people now phone taxis or go to taxi stands, especially at night, but the street cab fleet is more rigorously monitored than before. In 1998, 163 cars were stolen daily in Mexico City, but last year that number was down to 45, the lowest in thirty-five years. There are now some sixteen thousand security cameras posted around the city and in the subways, all monitored at a central police command center, the C-4. When I interviewed Marcelo Ebrard, he cited the security cameras as an important factor in the city's drop in crime, and added an interesting observation: the security cameras also watch over the police.

When I asked Ebrard why, in his opinion, Mexico City had so far been spared the carnage endured by so much of the rest of the country, he gave explanations I'd never heard before. When Calderón deployed the military to ostensibly fight the cartels, he said, the violence only increased. "But here there is no war," he said. "You don't have the army here. If we'd said to the *narcomenudeo*, the street trade in drugs, 'We're going to kill you,' there would be a worse war here than the ones now going on elsewhere." He also said, "We have a different culture here. This is a city where people's values have been changing more rapidly than in the rest of the country over the last forty years. Why? Because here you have the largest and the most universities, and that changes everything. It increases the number of people who think, criticize, discuss. They become more sensible and tolerant." In the DF, he told me, 61 percent of young people of standard eligible age are enrolled in one sort of university or another. Nationally the rate is 28 percent. To keep public high school students in school and relieve them from the humiliation of having to beg their strapped parents for pocket money, the city provides fifty-dollar monthly stipends in bank cards; as a reward for good grades, the amount can go up to ninety dollars. "And all that explains a lot of things," he said. Mexico City, he told me, has fifty universities, though it is also true, he acknowledged, that most of these are private and that poorer students don't have nearly enough options for a public university education. Expanding the public university system, he said, should be a national priority, and it requires massive investment. That is the federal government's responsibility, but, said Ebrard, "the city could do it, if they gave us more money. They take everything. We're the goose that lays the golden eggs, and they take the eggs." Mexico City provides 46 percent of all the country's federal tax revenue.

In terms of dollars, for every tax dollar the city contributes, it receives only seven cents in return. "That has to change," he said. "They should give us fourteen cents, which is still a good deal." Increasingly it's a challenge to the city to provide the services it does. "It isn't the city's growth," said Ebrard. "The city has grown hardly at all; it's the surrounding areas that have grown." Every weekday the city's population of nine million more than doubles because of all the people who come in from México State and elsewhere, mostly to work; the city government provides services, transportation, water, electricity, health care, and so on, for people who don't pay taxes to use those services. The DF, said Ebrard, is, of course, a very complicated city, and a complicated city to govern. "It's like the government of a country," he said. "It has twenty-three different secretariats, and you can't give the same detailed attention to all of them. You need to apply logic, and decide what things are most important, what needs to be looked at every week, every month, every six months. The water situation is a grave challenge. Public security is always a delicate matter. Human development. Sustainability. The renewing of the economy. But the first thing a city needs in order to function well is transportation. If transportation is good and is inexpensive for people to use, that's the basis of a city."

Distrito Federal mayors leave their mark on the city by doing something about the maddening traffic congestion. For López Obrador, it was the touch-the-sky elevated traffic lanes, known as the *segundo piso* ("second floor"), erected over eight kilometers within the DF of the Anillo Periférico, the fifty-eight-kilometer expressway that rings Mexico City, circling through parts of México State—the Circuito Interior is the inner-ring expressway—packed with dense traffic at almost any hour and freewheeling nevertheless, unless bottlenecked to a complete stop. Instead of using public funds to extend the *segundo piso*, Ebrard raised private investment for the construction and turned those new stretches into private toll highways. That public money went into public transportation. Ebrard's government contributed the Metrobús, a rapid transit bus system whose four lines run both ways down the inner lanes of major DF thorough-fares. The smooth-running, sleek buses, linked by accordion-like bends, arrive within minutes and often within seconds of each other, packed with riders, at long, covered station stops every several blocks. The Metrobús makes life easier for the innumer-able people who need to cross the city to get to and from work or school. I take it all the time. Ebrard's government also built the new Number 12 subway line, which runs from Tláhuac to Mixcoac, transporting passengers from some of the DF's south-ernmost and poorest areas in swift ultramodern new cars with a police guard in every car. One regular rider, a working mother who before had depended on buses and *peseros,* told me that the new subway line had cut her daily commute from two and a half hours each way to forty-five minutes. Ebrard is especially proud of the bicycle-sharing program, which he describes as an "ideo-logical initiative." Cars are isolating, he said; cars are competitive, because people want the biggest, the newest, the most expensive; cars are the enemies of pedestrians—but bicycles are "ideological." Bicycles look alike. "You can't have a two-story bicycle, though someone will probably build one. They don't run over people. On a bicycle you feel vulnerable, along with the people walking. Bicycle riders tend to relate to other bicycle riders."

On July 11, 2012, Ebrard inaugurated a new fleet of mod-ern buses, each equipped with air-conditioning and security cameras. The mayor drove the first bus himself, transporting some thirty passengers, mostly press and security people, for 3.8 kilometers, down Viaducto Río de la Piedad, until he mis-timed a turn without braking onto the Eje 4 East, causing his rear tire to jump a curb and ride half a meter onto the sidewalk. Then, headed back to the Autodromo bus base from which they'd started out, Ebrard missed a turn and went the wrong way, "leaving his security detail disconcerted," according to the report in the newspaper *Reforma*. Ebrard pulled over, parked, and ceded the driving to the "transport impresario and leader Fernando Ruano, who recalled his beginnings as a microbus driver, and with one maneuver corrected the error, though he invaded the lane of the Eje 4 Metrobús, made an illegal turn, and went through a red light."

4

Driving Lessons

IF RICARDO TORRES HAD GRADED me for my class in learning
to drive with a standard transmission in Mexico City, maybe I
could have pulled a D. Maybe I would have passed by just that
much, because I did manage to complete the route around the
long, anvil-shaped housing project several times, Calle Huatab-
ampo to Orizaba, a left onto Coahuila, through an intersection
of five converging streets and whizzing traffic for another left
onto Tonalá, and back onto Jalapa. But I stalled a couple of
times, jamming the gears, bringing time itself to an explosively
jolted and humiliating halt, and putting an incredulous snarl on
the wearied face of my driving teacher. The diagram of the gears
on the shift's knob had completely worn off, so that sometimes,
when I meant to slide the shift into fourth, I dropped it into
reverse. Maybe if I practiced just about forever, I'd one day be
ready to head out into Mexico City traffic. But how could I do
that now, if I'd be constantly looking down at the stick shift, not
even trusting myself to divine fourth from reverse, and stalling?
How might I do, driving stick shift, nervous in aggressive and
impatient traffic, never knowing where to go? Ricardo didn't
want to find out. If my intention was still to learn and practice
driving in the city under his tutelage, he suggested we do that
with an automatic transmission. With so much stop and go, said
Ricardo, automatic was more practical for city driving anyway.

With a secret sigh of relief I let go of my dream of dexterous road mastery, car synced to hand, engine purring at my touch, darting in and out of traffic as I traversed the complex arteries of the *Guía Roji*. Sometimes it really is just too late for some things. How would I do now if I tried to learn Mandarin? That's been a daydream ambition of mine ever since, maybe a decade ago, I'd read a piece in the *New York Times* about a woman who for years met with her Mandarin teacher in a teahouse-restaurant in Chinatown, sitting with her tutor for hours, sipping tea and slurping delicious dumplings, pronouncing and drawing Mandarin characters, until she finally became fairly fluent. But where would I ever find the time to do that, and, supposing my brain was even up to the task, how many years would it take me to learn? For now I would have to settle, hopefully, for being an adequate automatic transmission driver in Mexico City traffic.

The next morning, Ricardo collected me in front of my apartment in a different driving school car, just as dumpy and grime-coated as the previous one. I drove from the start, around the plaza in front of my building, and out, after a few turns, onto busy Avenida Cuauhtémoc. You see? I know how to drive. Still, Ricardo had his hectoring criticisms. He kept lifting his hand to my steering wheel and pulling, trying to make me take corners more closely; and if I resisted by pulling almost unconsciously against him, taking my turns more widely, at a sharper angle, as I even recalled having been taught as a teenage student driver in suburban Massachusetts, Ricardo would bleat, "Frannn, Frannn, *qué haces*? Why do you resist when I turn the wheel?" What did we call that teacher in high school, a large, fat, very pale, laconic man with the air of a washed-up Vegas gangster who never removed his dark glasses? Mr. Dick, something like that. I specifically remember Mr. Dick praising a crisp ninety-degree turn I'd made off Highland Avenue. But in Mexico City, I deduced, it's smart to take turns more tightly, it leaves you less exposed out there in the middle of an intersection, less likely to be swarmed inside by traffic, cut off from making your turn. I could see how it fitted into the Metropolitan Driving School's theory of defensive driving. Traffic comes at you from the most unexpected angles, the dreaded *peseros* pulling into or out of quick stops at almost ninety degrees too, nearly shearing off your fender, every driver seizing any possible opening. "Mexico City drivers are really *decisive*," a friend visiting from Guadalajara had observed that summer as we'd sat at a bar table on Alvaro Obregón watching the traffic, and the friend from Oaxaca had concurred; and they'd both agreed that the drivers in their cities are anything but, and what amazed them both, and also me, is that in Mexico City you never seem to see a traffic accident. You have to be especially careful whenever you nudge your car to the left or to the right, with so many motorcycles zipping through the tight spaces between cars on both sides. I remember what a friend, the first in her family to attend a university, told me about that first morning when she took a *pesero* to the UAM for the start of classes: just as she stepped off the *pesero* a passing motorcyclist, without slowing, reached out and grabbed off her shoulder the backpack that held her new laptop and sped away with it; also, about the time, again on her way to class, she got off a crowded *pesero* and discovered that the back of her jacket was splattered with semen. Everywhere, you have to watch out for people wheeling their laden vendors' or delivery carts out from in front of an idling bus, or coming sharply around a blind corner on a bicycle with a large tray in front filled with wrapped *tortas,* cigarettes, candy, bottled water, and trinkets; or old women carrying groceries stepping out into traffic from between parked cars; or office workers in a hurry to reach the taco or *comida corrida* stand across the street. Mexico City drivers are *decisive.* I began to get the hang of it, charging forward, seizing any brief opening, breaking into the next lane. Ricardo didn't criticize me too much, mostly ordering me not to accelerate so heavily, to break more gently.

Of course there were things that other drivers did that I wouldn't do. Ahead of us, cars taking advantage of a brief lull in traffic coming from the left, spurted ahead through a red light, one after the other, and Ricardo crowed, "Everybody wants to go through the Arc de Triomphe!" Later we were on one of the six-lane *eje viales*, and Ricardo told me to get into the fourth lane, the second from the left. Why, specifically, the fourth lane? I wondered. "How do you know which lane to get into?" I asked, and Ricardo matter-of-factly answered, "Well, you have to know where you're going." He was anticipating an exit on the left still some way ahead. You have to know where you're going. I could see how that was going to be a problem. The lanes themselves, on this *vial*, were problematic, as Ricardo delighted in pointing out. They looked as if a squad of drunkards or abstract expressionists had painted them, the faded lane lines in the pavement wobbling, swerving, and merging into each other, more recent sets of lines painted in indiscernible relation to older but still visible ones. The summer's heavy rains, along with the daily pounding of traffic, had left the pavement badly cratered. The guard line of bright yellow knobs warning drivers away from the perimeters of the *vial* were missing in many spots, including a stretch where rains had collapsed a big chunk of the road's shoulder, opening a gaping drop into a steep abyss. Only the most alert and quick-to-react driver, hewing to the left side of that lane at night or in a heavy rain, it seemed to me, would be able to evade it.

Ricardo treated me like a beginning driver most especially when he hadn't slept well the night before—he suffered from insomnia—and was in a testy or sullen mood. We left a major thoroughfare and entered a neighborhood whose name I don't recall, and it was like dropping into a peaceful small town, or even a village. The point of this exercise was to drive around the tree-shaded blocks, practicing stop signs, and how to proceed through street crossings where there are no stop signs, and taking speed bumps. I snuck glances out the window at the sidewalks, trying to catch an impression of life there. The neighborhood seemed lower middle class, or solidly working class, probably a mix. A smattering of the usual food and juice stands and carts. A little music school. Recently, whether I was in a driving class or not, I'd noticed in every neighborhood I passed through signs, often affixed to telephone poles, guaranteeing one-minute mole and wart removal. An announcement for Friday night dances for singles over forty, painted in black on a white wall. The most heavily trafficked street in this particular *colonia* led past a high school, and a man was walking up and down holding a cardboard sign offering his services as a math tutor.

Later, headed toward the south, we cut through a much poorer neighborhood, where some of the streets were unpaved. Cracked, heavy-looking concrete and adobe walls, painted in primary colors, or else in smog-and-rain-dirtied white. Here there were few trees, and few people out on the streets. Ricardo had me pull over and park next to a two-story house, painted white and blue, and he got out of the car and went into the house. After he'd returned and I asked, he said that it wasn't his house, but didn't tell me why we'd stopped there. Then Ricardo reached impulsively into the side pocket of the passenger door and brought out two little plastic bottles of shampoo and conditioner, of the kind supplied in hotels. He stared down at them, chortled, and spoke the name of another man, another driving instructor, it turned out, who also used this car. It was obvious, said Ricardo. His colleague had seduced one of his students, or had been seduced by her, and they'd gone to a hotel. That happened all the time, he explained; it came with being a driving instructor. I asked if it had happened to him and he said of course, but after I'd listened to him awhile, I thought that if it actually had, it hadn't been recently. Ricardo grew animated. Women who take driving classes, he told me, are *muy aventada*, meaning, in Mexico at least, daring, or eager to air their problems, or both. Women students often told him about their bad marriages, he said, their loneliness, and their cheating husbands. The women wanted to be listened to, he said; they craved attention, and I could see what that often led to, couldn't I? He went into a long story about an adolescent girl he'd had as a student. I steeled myself, listening nearly in disbelief. She came from a rich family, he told me, and her boyfriend was the son of a TV Azteca magnate. During her driving lessons, they were trailed by an SUV filled with bodyguards supplied by her boyfriend's family. Ricardo had a picture of the girl in his wallet. We were stopped at a red light. He took the picture out and showed it to me. It was tiny, and looked like a school portrait. She was fair-skinned, dark blond, with a pretty smile. He put the picture back into his wallet. That was the story.

He told me about another wealthy family who'd hired him to teach their teenage son to drive. When Ricardo arrived for the first class, the boy's mother rudely interrogated him, demanding that he produce identification papers and driving instructor credentials. She was worried that he could be part of a kidnapping gang, impersonating a driving teacher. Insulted by

her disrespectful manner even more than by her words, Ricardo
had refused to teach her son to drive. He'd just turned and left
the house. As he told me about the incident now, his anger and
indignation, his injured pride, were reignited; he spoke as if it
had happened only a few hours ago.

Today Ricardo was tired; he hadn't slept. We were in the
city's south, near University City and the Olympic stadium. It
was a Saturday, and the Pumas were playing, the streets crowded
with people walking to the stadium and souvenir and food vendors, and whatever route Ricardo had intended to take, through
the UNAM perhaps, had been blocked off. It was my last day
of classes. We ended up on a long tree-lined avenue with a median, in the sparsely populated outskirts of upper-class Pedregal,
practicing, over and over, speed bumps, U-turns, and how to
drive through the wide, deep puddles left by the previous day's
heavy rain without damaging the brakes. The only other cars
on that avenue also belonged to driving schools, and clearly all
the drivers were beginners. I was kind of annoyed. I wanted
Ricardo to show me how to drive on the Circuito Interior. It
was a beautiful sunny day, though, and the avenue reminded me
of one of those poplar-lined roads through the French countryside. Up and down we went, practicing U-turns every time we
reached the end of that stretch of avenue. Ricardo found plenty
to criticize, I don't even remember what anymore, by then I'd
pretty much stopped listening. Then I drove us all the way back
to Colonia Roma and my apartment. We took Avenida Insurgentes Sur, the same avenue I'd charged down so confidently,
though drunkenly, more than a decade before in my Cuban
friend's commandeered car. Who was the person who'd driven
that night? He seemed remote from me now. Would I ever drive
like that again? I couldn't imagine even trying to.

But I'd stuck to my plan. I'd taken a week of classes in preparation for my "driving project," including the lost days of learning to drive with a stick shift. Ricardo thought I still needed a few more days of practice. We hadn't gone onto the Anillo Periférico or the Circuito Interior, or taken on the challenge of a major rotary, but I didn't want more classes. Was I really ready to venture out on my own into the city's traffic, trying to reach whatever street and neighborhood my finger had landed on in a randomly opened page of the *Guía Roji*? Now or never—it was already mid-August, and I had to be back in New York for the start of a new teaching semester at the beginning of September. My life had taken a surprising turn in the three weeks since the fifth anniversary of Aura's death. The "new start" that I'd originally hoped my driving project would somehow instigate had, most unexpectedly, even absurdly, already come to me. I'd done nothing to earn it other than enduring, not always admirably, what I'd endured. If I was in a better place in my own *circuito interior* than I'd expected to be earlier that summer, this was no time to take a dishonorable early exit from the route I'd planned through it. It all might even become undone, I felt, if I failed to complete that route, and didn't honor what I'd initially meant to honor.

That evening I sat down with my *Guía Roji,* prepared to reveal my first destination. I had a witness. My apartment mate, Jon Lee, was there on one of his rare visits. I closed my eyes, opened the *Guía Roji* on my lap, and put my finger down on the page. My finger landed directly on Calle Begonias, inside map-page 113. I turned to the index. Mexico City has ten Calle Begonias (and almost twice as many named Calle Begonia). Mine was in a neighborhood called Fraccionamiento Las Margaritas. Margaritas, Spanish for daisies; a *fraccionamiento* is a housing subdivision. It was outside the DF, in Tlalnepantla, a municipality that a friend later described to me as an industrial wasteland, with the only slaughterhouse in the Mexico City metropolitan area. He'd gone there once because there was nowhere else where he could purchase and drink a glass of bull's blood, prescribed by a Mexico City shaman who was trying to cure him of his allergies to cat and dog hair (it didn't work). After about a fifteen-minute search, I found Calle Begonias and Fraccionamiento Las Margaritas on my giant wall map, a bit north of its center. Not all that far away, but it still looked pretty hard to get to.

Flowers—daisies and begonias. Mexico City neighborhoods often have thematically named streets. Polanco has streets named for writers and philosophers, Homer, Schiller, Tolstoy, Lope de Vega, and so on. Monte Everest; Mont Blanc; Cerrada de Monte Libano, where Nelly Glatt has her office, in Las Lomas. Colonia Napoles' streets are named for cities and states in the United States: Chicago; Vermont, which Mexicans pronounce *vearrr-mont*, accent on the first syllable. Neighborhoods with streets named for rivers, famous bays, pre-Hispanic nations and tribes, European painters, the metalworking occupations, of course, and so on. Colonia Doctores evokes a melancholy roll call of long-forgotten medical eminences, or a neighborhood of Pessoa homonyms: Calle Dr. Velez, Calle Dr. Jimenez, Calle Dr. Miguel Selva, Avenida Dr. José María Vertiz, Cerrada Dr. Norma, Calle Dr. Ricardo Reis. Aura and I had invented a neighborhood of our own, in which all the streets were named for Mexican food. In what was like a children's nonsense game for passing the time on long car rides, we were forever adding new streets to our Colonia Culinária Mexicana: Calle Torta (I want to live there!),

Calle Pozole. Calle Pozole Estilo Jalisco. Avenida Enchiladas Verdes. Callejón Enchiladas Mineras. Calle Chiles en Nogada, Calle Salsa de Jumiles . . . *Jumiles* are a pale-green beetle. Eating protein-rich insects has been a locavore custom in Mexico since pre-Hispanic times, and the menus of even the trendiest DF restaurants often feature maguey worms, usually *comal*-roasted; *chapulines,* fried grasshoppers; and *escamoles,* ant eggs, called "Aztec caviar." In Taxco, *jumiles* are traditionally eaten alive. "Eat one," Aura whispered in my ear, so that I wouldn't seem like a squeamish gringo in front of her Taxco relatives. *Jumiles* are not quite M&M crunchy, and their insides are like a pine resin jelly, owing to their mountain forest habitat. You buy a small plastic bag filled with live *jumiles* clinging to a pine sprig and each other, and pop the insects into your mouth one at a time. They can also be mashed into a paste in a *molcajete* with tomatoes, onions, and *chiles* to make a salsa. Because Aura had fond girlhood memories of having *salsa de jumiles* with her *que-sadillas* at her grandmother's home in Taxco, when we returned to my Avenida Amsterdam apartment with our bag of *jumiles,* she asked me to make it for her. Our *jumiles* seemed moribund after their long drive from Taxco, so I just poured them into the volcanic stone bowl of the *molcajete* and brought the stone pestle down, not very lustily, maybe crushing one or two pale green bugs while the others came to frenetic insect-zombie life, climbing over the rim, dropping onto the counter, scurrying, and dropping to the floor. Aura screamed and ran out of the kitchen, and I screamed too.

I always tell people that Aura was the funniest person I've ever known. It's the truth that I've never laughed so much, or so constantly, with anybody else, and she was committed to humor itself like a great comedian who thoroughly enjoys and

develops her gift. Eventually Aura formed the conviction that
we'd evolved (or devolved) our own sense of humor, one that no
one else would find funny or understand, that was roll-on-the-
floor hilarious only to us. This could be another way of saying
that because only I got her quirkiest jokes, I was the only one she
shared them with. One quiet spring evening soon before we left
New York for that last summer in Mexico, when we had nothing
else to do and were just sitting at our long dining table, Aura,
really just like that, came up with a game of inventing anonymous messages that we could mail to people, and it consumed us
for the next half hour or so. A cardboard fish in an envelope, with
the message, "Hello, this fish is your cousin. Take good care of
him." An envelope mailed to a friend who was always borrowing
money, containing a pair of dollar bills and the message, "Hello,
here is two dollars for your cigarettes in jail." I guess you had to
hear the way she pronounced "Hello" in English, lowering her
already chesty voice, "Hell*ooo*," and that adorable grammatical
slip, "is," and see her wide-eyed deadpan expression. Giggles
igniting into laughter, practically quaking, as we imagined our
friend's nervous bewilderment when he opened the envelope,
it just grew and grew, hahaha, two dollars for your cigarettes in
jail! Well, it really was only supposed to be funny to us. Aura
said it was my turn. I said that I thought it would be funny to
mail somebody an envelope with only some toothpicks inside.

Together we'd look at that final page of *The New Yorker*,
which always shows a cartoon without a caption and challenges
contestants to come up with one. We'd always invent captions
that seemed pretty clever to me, though we never submitted any
of them. After Aura was gone, whenever I looked at that page,
no funny caption ever came to me.

*   *   *

The Colonia Roma apartment that I rented at the start of the summer is on the sixth floor, overlooking the Plaza Río de Janeiro, its living room window offering a big view of sky over the tree-filled plaza and buildings on the other side. I love to watch the summer afternoon rains from that perch at the front window, especially when they are torrential, heavy and dense or lashing, with diffuse lightning flashes startling the purplish-gray chilly gloom, followed by shattering thunder, and then rattling hail, otherworldly like a storm on Mars; you hear sirens wailing all over the city. But often the rains are peaceful and luscious. The rains clean the air, bringing, when they wane, the fresh scent of trees, churned earth, and wet stone. Concentration and hours to write come more easily to me in the DF than anywhere else, but especially when it rains. Time in Mexico City, at least to me, seems somehow slowed down, so that days feel twice as long there as they do in New York. A mysterious energy seems to silently thrum from the ground, from restless volcanic earth, but it is also produced, I like to think, by the pavement-pounding footsteps of the millions upon millions who labor every day in the city, by their collective breathing and all that mental scheming, life here for most being a steadfastly confronted and often brutal daily challenge, mined with potential treachery but also, in the best cases, opportunity, one sometimes hiding inside the other as in a shell game; also by love, desire, and not so secret sexual secretiveness, the air seems to silently jangle with all that, it's like you breathe it in and feel suddenly enamored or just horny; so much energy that in the late afternoons I don't even need coffee. The writer Juan Villoro says that all Chilangos carry a seismograph inside. Like everyone else who lives here, I have experienced earthquake tremors that have turned my knees to jelly, and maybe it is partly that too which helps me to focus here, my senses alert, both inwardly and outwardly. That inner seismograph senses more than just literal earthquakes.

The Colonia Roma apartment was a luxury I couldn't really afford, but I wanted to live there and decided what the hell. Something good is going to happen here, so it's worth the money, that's what I felt. The place is huge, three bedrooms and a maid's quarters, the living room large enough to toss a football around in, which is what I often ended up doing with my friends and sometimes people I barely knew, during this summer when the apartment became a late-night-into-dawn and sleepless morning hangout and crash pad, the football zinging through the air, rarely careening off the ceiling, pretended drunken circus catches in the far corners, bodies banging against walls or dropping to the parquet floor. It was funny how quickly Mexicans who'd hardly ever or maybe never tossed a football in their lives picked it up. The football had been in storage for nearly five years, but it still had air. After Aura died, her mother, nearly crazed by a grief that sought an outlet in blame, expelled me from our Escandón apartment, and I'd hurriedly packed up and taken nearly everything into the cramped storage space in the basement of the building where Fabiola's parents lived. Later those possessions were moved into a spare bedroom into the apartment she now shared with her boyfriend Juanca (Juan Carlos) in Colonia Juárez, cramping their living space, though with their characteristic generosity, they hadn't said anything about it. Then last May we hired a moving truck and brought it all to my new place in Colonia Roma. The movers piled what they could into the elevator, and hauled the furniture up the six flights of stairs. Boxes of Aura's books, papers, and other such stuff, some of it dating to her childhood, went into the putative maid's quarters behind the kitchen. Will I be carrying all of that from place to place the rest of my life? I threw out some things: clothing and obvious junk. Here were the industrial black rubber boots that Aura had bought only a day or two before we'd left for our long-awaited beach vacation in Mazunte. What happened that day came back to me with the clarity of hallucination: Aura, in her discreetly mortified way, tersely telling me only not to use that bathroom and that she'd be right back, leaving the apartment and then returning soon after with that pair of black rubber boots, which she must have purchased at the cavernous hardware store down the block. She got a mop from the kitchen and carried it upstairs with the boots. Minutes later she spoke to me, I don't remember what she said, only that I looked up and saw her at the top of the stairs. To mop the overflowed toilet mess in the bathroom, she'd donned the boots and a pair of red gym shorts, and I was suddenly dazzled by the beauty of her legs, that symmetry of gliding toned thighs and ballerina calves perched just over the boots' gaping tops. That was far from the first time I'd been struck by the beauty of Aura's legs, but in that instant I was especially struck; that contrast between utilitarian plumber's boots and feminine shapeliness, so young and vigorous. She'd worn the boots only that once, to mop the bathroom, though I imagine she would have used them again, to walk in rain-flooded streets. There was no way I was throwing those boots out. We—Fabis, Juanca, and I—unpacked boxes of kitchenware, pots and pans, cutlery, dining sets, glasses and cups, appliances, much of it wedding gifts. The yellowing, dusty newspapers all those kitchen objects had been wrapped in nearly five years before were printed with the dates of some of the most vibrantly happy and promising days of my life, because there was so much that we were looking forward to, not least our imminent beach vacation, dates that also marked the last days and weeks of Aura's life. They caused a surge of sadness, as if I'd just understood—*as if,* because I guess at that moment I didn't understand anything other than that the familiar sadness had just overtaken me—that time itself, for me, wasn't the challenging drama I thought it was but just something made of dust, paper, and old forgotten, irrelevant news. It was like a rebuke of my current conception of those nearly five years since Aura's death, their relation to ongoing time itself, as being like an invisible but weighty hibernating animal inside me, sides always rising and falling, that I somehow had to get moving again before it would all be too late, that I had to expel from inside myself and follow out into the world. Cleaning out our apartment after Aura's death, I'd decided that any of my clothing that was not solemnly colored had to be packed away. Now I stuffed most of it into garbage bags to be thrown out, knowing that it would all be scavenged and put to use, but I kept a couple of old favorites, a linen shirt-jacket with a zippered front, a pair of pants I'd bought in Hong Kong with Aura. It felt strange, but also kind of hopeful, to be wearing clothing I'd last worn back when I was married to Aura. But it was strange, too, the way that this clothing practically fell to shreds over the coming months, ripping not just in the expected places, such as knees and elbows, as if it were made of the same substance as those old newspapers. Our several pieces of furniture looked miniature, like toy theater props, in the enormous front room. The writing desk I'd bought for Aura would now be my desk. The beautiful, large, and very heavy set of wooden bookshelves that we'd hired a carpenter to build just before leaving for the beach in Oaxaca and that Aura never got to see was carried up the building's back staircase. Every landing was a slow, awkward, grunting battle for the movers, trying to turn the corner with their massive burden and hoist it up another floor, until, on the fourth-floor landing, the space and the turn inexplicably narrowed, and so, after a futile struggle, they had to carry the bookshelves back down. One of the movers, sweat drenched and out of breath, said to me, "My father warned me but I never listened. Now this is what I get for not having studied in school."

The Plaza Río de Janeiro, directly in front of my ten-story building, built in the 1960s, probably the only architecturally ugly building facing the plaza, has a fountain in the middle, and in its center, mounted on a pedestal, is a black cast-iron replica of Michelangelo's *David* encircled by rising plumes and jets of water. The statue is not a very good copy: in fact it seems subtly misshapen or misconceived in some way that makes it monstrously bad; partly it's the way the plumed water often falls continuously only on the statue's lower part, making its muscular horse buttocks gleam wetly and black in the sun, while leaving the upper torso and head a salt-stained-looking gray. Only a few days ago, when I was briefly in another country, I heard a Mexican remark, as if it were settled fact, as if he'd read it in a book by an unimpeachable authority, that the statue in the Plaza Río de Janeiro is the ugliest reproduction of *David* in the world, and I felt pleased with myself for having come to the same conclusion on my own without ever having particularly noticed or maybe even seen another replica anywhere else. Though for most people, including myself, the statue isn't ugly enough to ruin the plaza because the plaza, really a park, is beautiful. It's like a tropical suburb of the Jardin des Plantes, a compact jungle of enormous trees, palm plants, and shrubbery traversed by curving stone paths lined with short, barred iron fencing. A concrete esplanade surrounds the fountain. Children swim in the fountain's wide basin and play in the spray and so do dogs, and I've seen homeless men wading in it too. On weekends, Boy Scouts engage in sumo-like wrestling matches in the water while their scoutmasters look on. During the hot, dry, gritty days of April, when the rainy season is still a month or so away, the water plumes are turned up higher so that anyone walking anywhere near the fountain passes through a cooling misty cloud of spray. Rainbows sometimes hover in the air alongside the statue. There are musical dance-step aerobics classes for elderly people who in their youth may have mamboed to the likes of Peréz Prado in Mexico City's legendary old dance salons, and who still shuffle their feet and move their hips, if not so limberly, with impressive rhythm and grace. Every weekend, a pair of grizzled, sinewy old Mexican men turn up to practice what appears to be a strenuous, ancient form of Chinese swordplay, synchronizing their movements, holding their kicks in the air, two-handedly thrusting and whirling their huge swords, letting out ferocious shouts. Bicyclists coming down Calle Durango's bike lane, which stops at one edge of the plaza and continues on the other side, meanderingly circle the fountain and move on. A flash mob of teenage hula hoopers invaded the park one weekend afternoon and stayed for hours, blasting music from speakers, a hundred kids or so twirling and tossing their neon-colored hoops and dancing inside them, one, two, three hoops at once, up and down their lithe torsos and limbs, and I wandered among them for about an hour, entranced by the sweet joy of that unexpected circus and wishing that I were a father raising a teenager in this neighborhood. At dusk, when the fountain's water jets have been turned off, the plaza fills with neighborly dog walkers who stand chatting or sitting on the fountain's rim while their dogs race around; parents bring their children to the little playground and stay past dark.

In the daytime, especially, there are always lovers making out on the plaza's park benches, splayed out in each other's arms or otherwise closely entangled. Most are teenagers—there are a few secondary and middle schools in the surrounding blocks—but there are also older young and not-so-young couples, students, office and shop workers, from busy, ramshackle Calle Puebla, lined with food and juice stands and the burned-out shell of an old mansion that now shelters indigents and junkies, one block away, just off the Glorieta Insurgentes metro station, one of the city's busiest hubs, or from the nearby office building blocks just beyond the Circuito Interior and Avenida Chapultepec. In the Plaza Río de Janeiro, the partly fenced-in, solid concrete benches along the shaded paths are the most coveted by lovers; whenever I head out hoping to be able to sit on one and read for a while, they're always all taken. Recently I asked David, the younger of my building's two doormen, who spends hours standing in the door or on the steps watching the plaza, what was the most memorable thing he'd ever seen there, and he answered without hesitation in his soft-spoken, working-class singsong, "*Gente cogiiiiendo*," people fucking. People fucking in broad daylight, when the plaza is always so full of people, he'd really seen that? Where? "*Esa es la buenaaaa,* that's the good one," he said, gesturing at the park bench closest to us, across the street, just inside the plaza. He described a couple, in their early twenties, he guessed, the guy sitting on the bench and the girl straddling him. But how did he know they were fucking? David explained that they'd draped a sweatshirt over their laps, but when the girl stood up, the sweatshirt fell away, briefly exposing panties down around her thighs. He said that he saw female couples too, teenagers mostly, kissing and *manoseando,* fondling. I said that I'd never seen any of that going on in the plaza, and David said that if I stood there and watched long enough, I would.

From my front window, trees hide most of my view of the plaza, though on those rare days when the sky is pure azure, that famous "transparent region" of the pre-megalopolis, I can see the distant, snow-covered white slopes of the dormant volcano Iztaccíhautl on the horizon. Iztaccíhautl, "white woman" in Nahuatl, is said, because of the pre-Hispanic legend of tragic lovers that gave the volcano its name, to resemble a woman sleeping on her back, though what I can see from my window more resembles a very distant, floating, crumpled origami of white tissue. A mountain pass connects Iztaccíhautl to the live volcano Popocatépetl, 17,800 feet high, though it seems to be outside my window's viewing range. In the legend, Popocatépetl was the name of the Tlaxcalan warrior lover who kneels in eternal vigilance before the snow-covered body of his dead princess, a chief's daughter, both of them turned into mountain volcanoes by pitying gods, Popocatépetl spewing ash and lava in rage and grief over the loss of his beloved, as that volcano still does all these centuries later. In one variation of the legend, Popocatépetl carries his princess's body to the top of the mountain and lays her down in the snow, hoping that its icy cold will wake her.

Mexicans are often thought, especially outside the country, to have a special relationship to death, even to be in possession of a unique understanding of death. This is mostly because of the worldwide renown of Mexico's carnivalesque Day of the Dead and its popular iconography of festive skeletons and skulls. But the idea that these express a nearly "occult" national relationship to death, or an intrinsic or buried ancient knowledge of death passed down from the Aztecs, is no truer of Mexico than it is true that in the United States, because of Thanksgiving, we are a nation of turkey whisperers. Still, as Claudio Lomnitz demonstrates in his *Death and the Idea of Mexico,* actual death and its many representations were explicitly present in the formation of the Mexican nation and its identity in a way that certainly isn't true of the United States, say, or even of other Latin American countries. (Perhaps only Haiti is somewhat comparable.) It seems that no one can say with absolute certainty when or where what became known as the Day of the Dead began; its origins seem buried. Did the Day of the Dead emerge from Aztec death culture, its ritual sacrifices, its cannibalism and skull racks, and its concept of circular time if not necessarily of anything like the soul's afterlife? The Zapotecs and Mayans and other native Mexicans, especially in the Yucatán and southern Mexico, did practice ancestor worship. In the holocaust that befell native Mexico during and shortly after the conquest, some 90 percent of its population was lost, mainly to European-borne disease but also to violence, slavery, overwork, and despair. The Spanish Catholic missionary priests brought a new culture of mortuary beliefs and imagery, the moral hierarchies of the afterlife and the death pageantry of medieval Europe, which were laid over or absorbed into whatever was left of what native survivors of that nearly inconceivable and swift dispeopling had understood about death before, such as the Mayan belief that it was the manner in which you'd died, naturally or violently and so on, rather than how virtuously or not you'd lived, that decided where your soul or spirit went in the afterlife. Mexico, understandably, had a death obsession from the moment it entered the history of the West as New Spain, and nothing happened over the next nearly half-millennium to lessen it.

Throughout its long premodernity, widespread violence and the harshness of daily life for the poor, that is to say for nearly everybody, made Mexico notorious as a land of ubiquitous and cruel death—"Barbarous Mexico." Regular outbreaks of war and foreign invasions spawned a new martyrology of slain revolutionary and patriotic heroes and leaders: the birth of a nation steeped in necrology. At some moment, somewhere, probably in the south, some Indian villages more or less began to appropriate Catholic All Saints Day and All Souls Day on November 1 and 2 for the expression of their own furtively maintained beliefs. To lure the souls or spirits of their dead relatives, villagers brought food and other offerings to family grave sites, built altars to house those souls or spirits, and stayed to honor and accompany them with drink and song throughout the day and sometimes through the night. What became known as the Day of the Dead evolved and spread. Once a year, throughout much of Mexico, people enduring harsh and often violent lives converted their cemeteries into places of family and community festivity. The Mexican Revolution seized on the Day of the Dead as a new icon of national identity. Fearless revolutionaries "laughed" in the face of death. Skeletons, *muertos*, represented the fundamental equality of man through the universality of death. Life and society remaining so unequal, the skeleton was also a perfect medium for satiric commentary on matters large and intimate. When the late-nineteenth-century penny-press engraver and genius José Guadalupe Posada's cartoons and images of animated, dressed-up skeletons—a skeleton priest hanging himself, for example— were rediscovered by artists decades later, they inspired André Breton to coin the term "black humor," and were celebrated by the hugely influential Diego Rivera and Frida Kahlo as totemic of autochthonous Mexico. The Day of the Dead and *muertos* "provide a space," writes Lomnitz, "for the expressions of a whole array of political desires and anxieties." But by the mid-twentieth century *muertos* culture had been folklorized and pushed outside the margins of modern urban and consumer society as a primitive remnant of death-obsessed Old Mexico, as something to be sold to tourists. Foreign writers such as Malcolm Lowry and Cormac McCarthy incorporated the Day of the Dead into novels set in Mexico, but the Chilean Roberto Bolaño, who grew up in the 1970s in Mexico City, never even alludes to it. But whenever "Mexican death" suddenly became politically useful again, it was reclaimed: skeleton imagery was deployed to protest against the massacre of students in Tlateloclo in 1968, for example, and to counter the influence of U.S. consumer culture as manifested by the upper classes' enthusiasm for Halloween. The Mexican middle and upper classes generally like to mimic U.S. lifestyles, but the sight of costumed children in wealthy neighborhoods going door-to-door with their trick-or-treat bags was more than many, on both the left and the right, could stomach. A Mexican writer, María Luisa "La China" Mendoza, quoted by Lomnitz, wrote, "In other words, while we decry the hunger and needs of so many disinherited children who ask for pennies, sell chewing gum or clean windshields, our bourgeoisie mimic the Texans and allow their children to go into others' houses dressed ridiculously and to ask for alms, which they WILL receive." In response to the "threat" symbolized by Halloween, national and local governments began to encourage a secularized revival of Day of the Dead festivities and their adoption in places that had never celebrated the day before, such as the country's northern regions. The festivities took hold, and why not? It's a nice holiday, after all, and it is authentically Méxican, and it's undeniably healthy to set aside a day for the memory of the dead in a way that isn't lachrymose or morbid. Día de los Muertos is now a two-day national holiday in Mexico, though in Mexico City far more people are likely to take it as an excuse to escape to the beach than to visit their family graves. Still, in urbane Colonia Roma, as throughout Mexico, there is a public altar competition; the extravagant and often comical and politically pointed constructions line Avenida Alvaro Obregón's median.

There is a Catholic middle school behind the building I live in. From my window I could see the huge altar students had made in the playground. During the week of the Day of the Dead I stopped into the school for a closer look. In the foyer, a big bulletin board was entirely filled with small orange cardboard skeletons lined up in rows, and every skeleton was imprinted with the name of a student or teacher. It was a charming sight, but also a bit unsettling. It returned you, however cheerfully, to those original ideas of skeletons representing the universality of death and of our fundamental equality. I tried to imagine what it would mean to me, as a twelve-year-old, to have my own personalized skeleton hanging on the wall of my school along with all the other exactly alike skeletons of my classmates and teachers. During my Massachusetts boyhood I was not often inspired, especially in school, to ponder the meanings of my own skeleton, except now and then in biology class—though I did grow up next to a cemetery, where in winter we slalom-sledded through the gravestones.

What does death in Mexico mean now? Whenever I read cultural commentary, often by U.S. academics, that gushingly recycles such phrases as "Mexicans revere death," or Octavio Paz's assertions that death is Mexico's "most enduring love" and that Mexicans play with, caress, and entertain death—just Google

"Day of the Dead" and you'll see what I mean—I feel a surge of revulsion, and I wonder about the persistence of these kinds of romantic clichés affixed to entire nations, so similar to rah-rah politician rhetoric ("The American people are————"). Are the femicides of Ciudad Juárez or the barbarities of the narco war and the migrants' trail in any way manifestations, or do they ever at all evoke, that reverent and playful love of death? "If any of that were true," the journalist Diego Osorno, author of *La guerra de las Zetas,* told me, "with so much death all around them, Mexicans should be in some kind of perpetual ecstasy now." There sure is no ecstasy in Marcela Turati's disconsolate piece "The National Decay," in which she visits the Matamoros morgue after the news gets out that yet another mass grave has been discovered in the area. "Hundreds of people from across Mexico," Turati explains, "came to see if their vanished loved ones—whom they were too terrified to report as missing—were here, among the executed." On the lonely highways and winding roads between cities and towns in the state of Tamaulipas, buses and cars are routinely stopped by gunmen of one of the two cartels waging war against each other in the state—the Zetas and the Cartel del Golfo—and the passengers are ordered out of the vehicles and are often murdered right there, or kidnapped and murdered in whatever place they're taken to, usually an isolated ranch. One of several possible reasons cited by Turati is that the cartels murder passengers in order to prevent young men from traveling into an area under a rival cartel's control and becoming its forced or willing recruits. "About this, little is known for certain," writes Turati, "because the local press cannot report on it, and correspondents from the national and foreign press would be in grave danger if they even tried to set foot there to investigate." Yet neither the federal government nor state governments warn people about the danger of traveling by bus on those roads. In "The National Decay," people outside the morgue tell Turati about their missing family members.

> "They motioned to my sister (Luz Elena Ramírez, a thirty-year-old mother) to come over to a gray car. She walked up; they grabbed her by the shoulders, and that was the last we saw of her."
>
> "I'm looking for Édgar Silquero Vera, manager of a gas station in San Fernando. We just found his Expedition truck. Soldiers were driving around in it, but they said they don't know anything about what happened."
>
> "My son would be about twenty years old now. They took him in a mass roundup in San Fernando, because they take everyone there and force them to work. But it would be better if you erased his name."

The morgue workers take another break and come out to smoke.

It is Thursday, June 14, 2011. They have been working all week and have just heard that another truck with a dozen bodies is set to arrive.

The daily newscast reports that the Tamaulipas state government will promote the state as a tourist destination during Holy Week.

"Those bastards are so full of shit!" says a furious prosecutor from the district attorney's office.

A local reporter, noting the general fatigue, comments: "And to think, they still have to excavate the grave sites in Camargo, Alemán, Guardado de Ariba y de Abajo, the towns of Los Guerra y Comales, Ciudad Mier, Valle Hermoso, Anáhuac, Cruillas, González Villareal, Nuevo

Padilla, Nuevo Guerrero . . . The whole state is full of hidden graves."

Everything around here reeks.

The people Turati speaks to and observes at the Matamoros morgue express and project sorrow, anguish, heartbreak, fear, and rage. Nothing marks them as responding any differently from how people anywhere else in the world would respond to such a grotesque tragedy as that faced by the families of Mexico's disappeared and murdered. When I observe the spectacle of Mexican death from inside the Mexico City "bubble," it seems all too contemporary, both all too horribly familiar and unfathomable.

Maybe I'm getting Octavio Paz wrong. Maybe when he wrote that Mexicans have a love affair with death he didn't mean that they have a love affair with actual death—certainly not in the way that some sects, in other cultures, have seemed to. What did he mean then? Paz obviously meant something deeper than that Mexicans, many of them anyway, love their harmless Day of the Dead festivities and trimmings, sugar skulls, *pan de muertos,* and Catrinas. These do have their origins in the deep feelings and convictions of hard rural lives that are now buried in time and that may no longer speak to us. Was there a time when Paz was right, and has the contemporary world flushed that Mexico away? Does some residue remain?

For whatever reasons, enduring a complicated grief was a vastly different experience in Mexico City from what it was in New York. Maybe I've never really fitted in in New York, have never felt truly at home there, and the loneliness of grief starkly exposed that. Maybe it was only because New York doesn't have cantinas.

Are Mexicans at least more "comfortable with death" in a way that most people are not if they haven't grown up in societies where they see themselves depicted as skeletons in school? Few people are comfortable with the looming specter of their own death or that of loved ones or neighbors, no matter how prevalent death might be around them, as anyone who has ever spent time in a war zone knows. Under the most sustained horrific circumstances, as in many parts of Mexico now, people may become resigned to the possibility of violent death, a melancholy experience, however tinged with dogged disbelief or defiance. But Mexicans are comfortable with death in the sense that they're neither squeamish nor willfully anodyne about it, not freaked out by it—by dying friends or family, or in the company of the bereaved—in contrast to the "denial of death" cultures in the United States and Western Europe that have so often been criticized. Of course, in recent decades, there has been something of an informal movement in the United States to correct this, variously expressed—as in many high-profile books that directly or indirectly address the subject (though in Hollywood movies the beloved dead still return as loving ghosts, young and beautiful forever). That's one reason—the presence of huge numbers of Mexican migrants in the country is another—that the Day of the Dead and its imagery became so popular there. From what I've observed, people in the United States usually overcome whatever aversions or fears they may have and do come through for their dying family members and friends, often heroically. But as many of those people discover after their loved ones have died, a bewildering and lonely bereavement often follows. In the way that such corrective societal lessons tend to be absorbed into practice in the United States, what overcoming the "denial of death" often translates into is highly self-conscious, awkward behavior. Many people seem to feel now that they are obligated to be "supportive" of the bereaved, which means making an effort to sincerely converse with a bereaved person about what they believe he or she may be suffering. They are even ready to offer, as it were, an instant therapy session, often involving the stumbling enunciation of practically memorized phrases, including, with now notorious frequency, the seemingly encouraging but actually rebuking advice about "moving on," about how now may be the time to "move on," or about how— soon or someday—the time to "move on" will inevitably arrive like rain after a long drought, bringing the blessing of renewed life and release and relief from the suffering that so wearies and bores us all. Of course because even the possibility of having to endure such a conversation would discomfort almost any sane person, people can't help avoiding the bereaved. Or else they stand their honest ground and say bizarrely self-revealing things, like the friend, a writer of course, who told me that he envied me because now I had a tragic but beautiful love story attached to my life, one that I'd be able to write about. Who wants a bereaved person and the accompanying obligation to be supportive at a festive dinner party? Is festivity even allowed in the presence of the bereaved? One New York friend stopped inviting me to his home because he and his wife couldn't bear to tell their daughter that Aura had died, and while this did not end our friendship, I suppose it did loosen the bond between us.

When I did, *very* occasionally, get invitations to dinner parties in New York, I was sometimes the only single person at the table, and often found myself sitting among people whom I'd never met before and who didn't know why I was single, and I would sit there wondering if politeness obligated me to pretend that Aura had never existed so as not to cast a pall over the dinner party, or if anyone was going to mention her, or if I should go ahead and blurt it out, or should I just swill more

than my share of the wine and try to take part in the dinner
conversation—I always embarked on the last, getting smashed
behind my Noh mask, but usually got around to blurting too,
and then sometimes the host would jump in to gallantly fill out
the narrative, usually with an air of embarrassment but also of
relief, as if he or she too had been tied in knots about whether
or not to mention Aura. It was never a comfortable moment.
Why do these moments have to happen? What, if anything, are
these well-intentioned people doing wrong?

I did have wonderful friends in New York who never shunned
me during the worst of those grief years, and around whom I never
felt even the subtlest pressure to submit to an amputation of myself
so as not to discomfort others. Most though not all of them were
women, some good friends of Aura's too. They somehow did know
just how to be with me, and understood that mostly I wanted
to drink and hang out and talk about whatever or just be silly,
and they would talk about Aura in a genuine manner whenever
I or they wanted to talk about Aura, and, anyway, they were still
grieving for her too. They understood not only that it is perfectly
OK to be "festive"—funny, I mainly mean—in the presence of
the bereaved but that this is often just what the bereaved person
craves, along with the simple nourishment of listening to people
being themselves, unembarrassed to talk about their own problems
even though these might not be as tragic as yours.

Of course, as in Mexico, I preferred to talk as honestly as I
could about what I was going through with my therapist. Kim
helped lead me where I knew I was going anyway, on my own,
deeper and deeper into the inevitable solipsism of the thing, for
traumatic grief—such was the diagnosis—discharges an apparently narcotic-addictive adrenaline throughout your body and
you live in its dark atmosphere like a hooked lab rat; of course

she also wanted me to take psychotropic pharmaceuticals to help "take the rough edges off," but I didn't want to take those edges off, and refused, my stubborn conviction being that to go all in was the only way out, to exhaust and deplete the thing until I'd finally be left with a hard-won alchemical residue I'd be able to live with forever. "*La muerte no se reparte como si fuera un bien. Nadie anda en busca de tristezas*," says Susana San Juan, in *Pedro Páramo*. "Death is not divided up as if were a property. Nobody goes around looking for sadness." No, you own it pretty much all by yourself, and you'd be able to give out only empty handfuls. I think this is something that all of my Mexican friends just simply understood: that I wasn't trying to share it out.

In Mexico, I never sensed that anyone felt obligated to say or display anything in particular in the presence of a "bereaved person," and nobody stopped inviting me anywhere. Nobody, once, ever, said anything about "moving on"—does this slogan even exist in Mexican Spanish? Aura never felt like someone I had to hide, even among strangers, because they simply weren't discomforted, and certainly never looked as if they'd just been electrocuted when they learned that my young wife had died in the summer of 2007. When I spoke about all this at a Mexico City dinner party one recent night a guy there shrugged and only said, "*La ligereza*," and maybe that's all it is, an easygoing quality that certainly feels prevalent in the DF. That good-natured *ligereza* is an often remarked-on Mexican cultural trait, a complicated one, in combination with Mexican formality, that also conceals. Outside commentators frequently describe Mexicans as a people who mask their "true" thoughts and feelings. I usually feel that I don't need people to express their "true" thoughts and feelings. It was always a good way to pass the time, with my friends in a cantina, where there was little possibility that my bereavement or inner gloom would cast a pall over a table and its alcohol-buzzed *ligereza*.

"Being now arrived at middle-life, he resolves never to quit the soil that holds the only beings ever connected to him by love in the family tie," Herman Melville wrote of his fictional John Marr, the retired sailor who relocates to a Midwestern prairie town where his young wife and infant child are carried off by fever, and buried there in a coffin built with his own hands. "While the acuter sense of his bereavement becomes mollified by time, the void at heart abides. Fain, if possible, would he fill that void by cultivating social relations yet nearer than before with a people whose lot he proposes sharing to the end."

It's Mexico City that feels like home how. Many of my closest friends in Mexico City are a lot younger than me, in their thirties and forties. Some were among Aura's circle of friends, and they became and remain my friends, and through them the circle widened. People my age, in their fifties, tend not to go out so much at night; they stay home with their families or else, especially in New York, socialize at dinner parties with friends more or less their own age. Of course, when I was married to Aura what I'd planned to be doing in the near future was staying home with my family too. But if I've always liked to go out at night, widowerhood turned it into an obsessive need. That summer of 2012, I put in long hours of work every day, but I also drove myself hard at night, too hard, in a self-destructive but often euphoric fury, toward a finish line that I no longer believed was even going to be a finish line.

The Covadonga, just around the corner on Calle Puebla, is where I mostly went last summer, and throughout this past year. The

Covadonga is actually a Spanish place; it doesn't provide free food with drinks, as the best traditional Mexican cantinas do. It used to be a center for the Spanish community that settled in Mexico City especially during the years of the Civil War and the establishing of what would be General Franco's long dictatorship. There's a restaurant and sort of ballroom upstairs, but I've rarely been upstairs. I always go straight into the cantina, a sprawling, brightly lit room with marble columns, a wood-paneled bar, television sets all around, fans twirling from the ceiling, and long rows of square tables that can be pushed together for large parties—for the huge parties of revelers of which, especially on Thursday and Friday nights, there are always several. The waiters wear white shirts, black bow ties, and vests. They greet regulars by name, *"Buenas noches señor Frank,"* and always remember what you like to order first; even the washroom attendant and resident shoeshine man always comes by to shake your hand. On the wall is a trio of large, framed, somewhat crude copies, painted on tiles, of Velázquez's *The Triumph of Bacchus,* two close-up sections and one of the whole work. The original hangs in the Prado and is popularly known as "The Drunks." The painting depicts Bacchus outdoors with a rowdy cluster of men getting smashed at his side, two of those ruffian drinkers staring straight out from the canvas with the haggard four a.m. expressions—one with an arrogant drunken grin and the other with ribald hilarity—of *gueyes* who've been drinking *mezcal* all night and slipping off to the washroom to snort coke. The Cova closes relatively early, at two, though I doubt that this has anything to do with why in the copies of the paintings the drunkard's malicious grin, probably the most memorable and iconic detail of the original, is a muddied grimace, and the puffy-cheeked man at his side looks as if he's trying not to throw up instead of sharing some lewd joke. When I mentioned the missing famous grin to the waiter he went away to ask some veteran about it, and when he came back—by then I'd pretty much forgotten all about it—he recited the name of the painter who'd done the Cova version, as if that explained everything, and he repeated, almost apologetically, that it was only "a replica."

In the afternoons in the Cova there are always elderly men from the neighborhood sitting at the tables playing dominoes. They are there at night too, whether it's a slow night and they are almost the only customers, the big room nearly silent but for the clacks of dominoes falling like tripped circuit breakers, or whether it's one of those nights when the place is mobbed and the elderly domino players sit at their scattered tables surrounded by a noisy sea of hipsters, young and not so young art world and literary types, rock 'n rollers, journalists, newspaper reporters and editors, and so on. On those nights I can go there alone and I will always find someone I know at one of the tables. Up until a few years ago, when I went to the Covadonga at night, occasionally a waiter used to stand in front of the bar and shout out a name, and people in the cantina would respond with cheerfully roared shouts of "*Culero!*" or "Assfucker!" Initially, I'm not sure why, I thought the waiter was calling out the names of people whose credit cards had been declined, but then I found out anybody could pay the waiter to call out a name and make everyone shout *culero*. I don't recall how much it cost, but it wasn't much. That waiter had a strong, almost operatically resonant voice that cut through the cantina roar on a busy night and silenced it. Later I found out that the other waiters referred to that voice, and to the waiter himself, as "the Bell." A few summers ago when Colm Tóibín was visiting, that ritual delighted him, and he decided that he just had to have a name shouted out. So we both paid to have the names of writers we disliked shouted out and, twice, in short succession, the Bell's voice rang out, badly if loudly garbling each of those Anglo surnames that probably nobody there would have recognized even if they'd been coherently articulated, and twice the room roared back, "*Culero!*" In New York and Dublin, perhaps, moments apart, two pairs of ears went red, and two literary minds thought the same thought: Someone somewhere is talking about me, with admiration and love, of course! The drunken *pícaro* grin in the Velázquez painting was suddenly restored, and appreciatively widened. Last summer, when I moved to the neighborhood and became a Cova regular, I noticed that this call-and-response wasn't being performed anymore and asked about it. I was told that decades before, when The Bell was a newly hired waiter, he'd introduced the ritual. The waiter had retired a year or two before, and had taken his bell home with him.

On July 25, I went to evening Mass at Sagrada Familia, a Jesuit church just around the corner from my building and the plaza. Out the left-side window by the desk where I work I can see the church, its Gothic spire and silvery glittering dome, and the tolling of its bell often wakes me during predawn hours when it's easy to fall back asleep. As I've done every summer for the last five years, I went to a church office several weeks before July 25 and signed up and paid to have Aura's name read out during the part of that day's Mass when a prayer is said for the souls of the departed. Aura wasn't a churchgoer, but insisted that she wasn't an atheist, and, like most Mexicans, she had an at least folkloric or inherited devotion to the Virgin of Guadalupe, so it has felt like the correct thing to do, to have a prayer said at Mass for Aura on the anniversary of her death. For the first four years, I always invited our friends and some of Aura's relatives to Mass at Santa Rosa de Lima, a church in the Condesa. This year, I wanted to be alone, so I didn't actually tell anybody. However, at the end of a Facebook post asking people to remember Aura on that day, which included a paragraph quoted from her writing, I dutifully included the information about the Mass. I arrived a bit early at Sagrada Familia, and sat in a pew in the middle of the congregation, on the side of the church facing a portrait of La Guadalupana. I wanted to be alone to be able to especially concentrate on this being the fifth anniversary, to find within myself, and be able to mark this date with, a comprehensible and even sacred significance. Why is this day different from all other days? To me it symbolized the arrival of the once dreaded day when I had now been apart from Aura longer than I'd been with her, but did that really signify a tangible before and after, or augur a change? Perhaps it really wasn't different from any other day, and didn't and wouldn't. A British composer and musician, more an acquaintance than a friend, came into the church accompanied by a pretty, chic-looking blond woman—she turned out to be a Slovak photographer who was collaborating with him on a project—and sat down alongside me. He'd seen the Facebook post. It was kind of him to have come with his friend, of course, but there went my yearned-for solitude. Aura's stepfather, Arturo, came into the church, and sat in the back. Sagrada Familia is a pleasant church, with high vaulted ceilings in the nave, chandeliers, long stained-glass windows, lots of paintings, and a statue of the Holy Family behind the altar, and it is permeated with a rich smell of old wood. The Mass began, and I knew it would be a long wait until the priest would read the names of that day's departed, including Aura's. The priest was old, perhaps ninety or so, roly-poly and bald, his perpetually smiling bronze face reminiscent of one of those ancient Chinese figurines of laughing old men. The deacon had to help him up the stairs to the altar, and throughout the Mass, as he slowly shuffled from one spot to the other, altar boys guided him by the arm. The British composer is Jewish and whenever something about the Mass or the church itself struck him as remarkable, beautiful, confusing, or odd, he spoke to his companion about it. My mother is a practicing Catholic and I've long been accustomed to being in church. Later we all agreed that the old priest was adorable and funny. The priest's sermon included a riddle that had been either posed or solved by Santiago, St. James, and that the priest now put to the congregation and, receiving no answer, completed himself, nearly doubling over with chortled laughter—that Santiago, what a card—his hands clasped to his ample belly. The acoustics of the church and the priest's own softly croaking speech made it hard to understand what he was saying, but I understood for sure that he dedicated some of his sermon to a protest against Mexican social injustice and impunity, and against the "imposition" of Enrique Peña Nieto as president of Mexico. When at last it was time for the prayer for the departed, the priest mispronounced Aura's name, calling her Aurora Estrada.

After the Mass, we, including Aura's stepdad, went to a little bar across the street for a round of beer and *mezcal.* I excused myself just before the next round was ordered, and went back to my apartment.

Every summer, Aura and I used to throw a big barbecue. Mostly I made hamburgers, using a classic 21 Club recipe, but also ribs,

sausages, and some grilled portobello mushrooms for the veg-
etarians. Fabiola always contributed *fideo seco,* a Mexican pasta
dish that she'd learned to make from her grandmother Mamá
Loti. We held it in the bamboo-shaded patio of our Colonia
Escandón apartment. After Aura's death, Fabiola and I decided
that we should continue the tradition, holding it on the same
day as the Mass or within a few days, on the weekend. We used
the patio of Fabiola's apartment, just across the hall from where
Aura and I had lived. I do not much enjoy parties but I love
to barbecue, so standing over a grill for hours, drinking, lost
in my own thoughts or talking to whoever has come to stand
around the grill with me, has always been my preferred way to
get through a party if I have to be at one. Because it was July, it
always rained at some point, usually late in the afternoon, and
though somebody always stood by me holding up a shaky beach
umbrella, I inevitably ended up covered in a wet smoky grime,
which I also liked. We always set aside a moment to toast Aura
and share memories, and one summer we held a group reading
of her writings. But by the fourth summer, it had really just
become a party. Juan Carlos Reyna, from Tijuana, the Nortec
Collective guitarist and writer, a handsome, irrepressible fellow
in his early thirties, never knew Aura, though he'd become one
of my closest friends. He brought along to the barbecue a girl
he was fucking—there's no other way to put it, with him there
always seem to be one or two or more a week who never stay in
his life very long—who got very drunk and asked me if I was
gay. It wasn't her question that offended me. I said no, and asked,
"Don't you even know why we're holding this barbecue?" Reyna
told her, and she broke out in embarrassed tears, sobbing really
loudly, and I wished he would just take her away, and wondered
if it was time to put our annual "Aura" barbecue to rest. Still,

this summer, it being the fifth anniversary, we decided to do it again, but as Fabiola had sublet her apartment in our old building to move in with Juanca, we held it in her parents' condo in Las Aguilas. Fabiola's parents' patio was much larger than ours in Escandón, with a view overlooking the city. It turned out to be a good party, mostly good friends in good humor, plenty to eat and drink, though there were people there I'd never met before. Reyna's close friend, the young rock musician Juan Cirerol—often described as a kind of Mexican punk Johnny Cash/Bob Dylan—showed up, and played a few songs. Gonzalo and Pia's fourteen-year-old son, Jerónimo, is a guitar prodigy who was fronting a band, in Paris where they live during the school year, with other musicians a few years older than him. In Paris, he'd downloaded Cirerol's recordings, and had taught himself those songs, so it was a thrill for Jerónimo to play in duet with Cirerol, and pick up some advice. Afterward, though, Fabiola and I decided that this did seem like the right time to end our summer "Aura" barbecues.

5

The Driving Project

BY NEARLY MIDNIGHT on August 23, a Thursday, it had been raining so heavily since the late afternoon that many streets flooded, especially in the city's south. On a section of Avenida Insurgentes Sur, the water rose so swiftly that it reached the door handles of stalled automobiles. A fifty-three-year-old man named Gerardo Ortiz Gutiérrez apparently panicked and sought to save himself from being drowned inside his car. Carrying some papers or documents high in one hand, Ortiz Gutiérrez got out of his car and, up to his waist in water, waded toward the Marcela de Joya Metrobús stop, clearly intending to haul himself up onto its platform. A few steps from reaching it, he vanished beneath the water's dark surface. It turned out that he'd been sucked down a deep drain that was missing its sewer lid. For days, deploying robot cameras and scuba divers, firemen and workers from the Mexico City water system searched the network of possible underground routes down which the storm-propelled water could have carried Ortiz Gutiérrez, but they were unable to find his body. The newspaper *Reforma* published a story about the frequency with which the heavy cast-iron sewer lids were being stolen in the city, apparently to be sold for scrap. Scuba divers finally found Ortiz Gutiérrez's corpse six days later in a sewage drain in the center of Tlalplan, 1.5 kilometers away from where he'd disappeared. Family members came to the morgue and were able to identify him only by the clothes he was wearing.

I didn't want to drive to Calle Begonia in México State. I decided that I should confine the *Guía Roji* project to the DF. The driving project had been conceived as a way to make or find something new in my relationship to the DF, to Aura's DF and mine, not to Peña Nieto's México State. I put the big map book on my lap and went through the routine again, and on the second or third try my finger landed inside the DF, on Calle Tonacatecuatl, in Adolfo Ruíz Cortines, on map-page 205 of the *Guía Roji*, a neighborhood where the surrounding streets had similarly unfamiliar pre-Hispanic, probably Nahuatl, names (Omecihuatl, Calmécac). I wrote to a professor acquaintance at CIESAS (an institute for advanced studies in anthropology) to ask about the etymology of Tonacatecuatl. A Nahuatl expert at the institute, after talking it over with a colleague, informed her that it was a historically nonexistent word and hypothesized that it must be a Hispanicized version of Tonakatekwani, which means "our meat of the jaguar." Did that mean something like "this jaguar meat that we're going to eat" or "jaguar meat that is corporeally or spiritually a part of who we are"? I don't know.

During the last week of August, the day after Ortiz Gutiérrez was sucked down the drain at the Marcela de Joya Metrobús stop, I finally rented a car at an Alamo outlet on Paseo de la Reforma. It was the cheapest one available, a red Chevrolet compact, and I drove it back to my building in Colonia Roma and parked, alongside my bicycle, in the apartment's reserved space in the garage. My first solo drive in Mexico was complete. But before setting out for Our Meat of the Jaguar Street, I wanted to practice. The route I'd mapped out would begin with a long drive up Avenida Insurgentes Sur, which I'd be able to get onto via La Glorieta Insurgentes, a traffic circle only a few blocks down Calle Puebla from the Plaza Río de Janeiro. The taxi drivers I'd polled regarded that multi-spoked dervish roundabout, along with Glorieta Camarones, in Colonia Sindicato de Electricistas, in the city's north, to be the city's most challenging. This is how, in *On the Road*, when late in the novel the characters take their ridiculously goofy trip to Mexico, Jack Kerouac describes legendary driver-supreme Dean Moriarty's encounter with a Mexico City roundabout: "He got on a circular glorietta drive on Reforma Boulevard and rolled around it with its eight spokes shooting cars at us from all directions, left, right, *izquierda,* dead ahead, and yelled and jumped with joy. 'This is traffic I've always dreamed of. Everybody *goes*!'" I'm not sure which *glorieta* Kerouac was describing, or whether those eight spokes were an exaggeration of memory or perhaps an amalgamation of two roundabouts, the four-spoked one circling the Ángel de la Independencia on Reforma and the nearby five-spoked Glorieta Insurgentes. Kerouac visited William Burroughs in Mexico in the late 1940s, long before the city mushroomed into a megalopolis, and though I don't doubt that drivers did *go*—Kerouac describes a bus driver as if writing about a contemporary *pesero* road warrior—nobody ever recalls traffic having been a problem back then. I thought that I'd better practice roundabouts. There was another one in Colonia Roma, the also five-spoked Plaza de Cibeles. But the high-speed roller derby of Glorieta Insurgentes feeds into and out of major avenues, while Plaza de Cibeles channels traffic off relatively quiet streets.

I backed the car out of the garage, and drove to Plaza de Cibeles, whose central fountain, with a bronze statue of the

Roman fertility goddess in a chariot pulled by lions, is a replica
of the marble original in Madrid. I whizzed around the rotary,
accelerating ahead of a car trying to angle across me from the
inside, and shot, homeward, into Durango. But I took another
left, got back onto Oaxaca, and circled the rotary again. *Woohoo!*
If not quite yelling and jumping with joy, I felt impatient to
take on the Glorieta Insurgentes. Calle Puebla, as usual, was
choked with traffic. But even advancing at a crawl, I bafflingly
missed the turn onto the *glorieta*. From the Zona Rosa, I made
a few turns, found Chapultepec, and then, only a few blocks
from home, got lost and somehow ended up on multilane Niños
Héroes. I had no idea where I was going but I drove fast because nothing makes Mexico City drivers pounce on their horns
and furiously shout obscenities out their windows like another
driver's hesitation. Impulsively exiting down a side street, and
following my not always keen sense of direction, I came upon
the very street where I'd had my stick shift lessons with Ricardo
Torres. A driving school car was wanly rolling in reverse down
its long no-parking lane. In the lobby of my building I ran into
Guillermo Osorno, who told me that construction or repairs
were being done on the Glorieta Insurgentes—that that was why
I hadn't been able enter it off Puebla—and he suggested an easy
alternative route onto Insurgentes Sur.

I tried that route the next morning. I followed Alvaro Obregón into the wide Insurgentes intersection and, so as not to
drive across a row of raised safety reflectors in the pavement that
also confused me, turned sharply left, directly into a northbound
Metrobús lane. A Metrobús was bearing down on me and in
panic I swung a heedless U-turn back onto Alvaro Obregón.
My hands were shaking. What, I couldn't find my way onto
Insurgentes Sur on my own, not even that, *caray*? Humiliated

and discouraged, I drove home and parked. I didn't take the car out again that day. I brooded over the *Guía Roji*. There was another way to get onto Insurgentes Sur off Puebla that would skirt the *glorieta*.

The next morning I drove up Puebla again, and followed a sign indicating a right turn onto Insurgentes Sur. In fact, it led directly into the Glorieta Insurgentes, which was open again, and I was shot into the dreaded circle of fast dense crisscrossing traffic—it felt at first like a bout of madness—streaming off or angling toward a series of exits, Avenida Chapultepec, Insurgentes on the north side, Chapultepec again, Oaxaca, all two-way multilane avenues . . . I would have to go almost all the way around the *glorieta* to exit, headed south, onto Insurgentes Sur. But quickly, instinctually, you understand that the only option, the only way around, is to keep faith in the sanity and competence of other drivers, and that the worst thing to do is not stay up to speed; just aim for your exit no matter how perilously squeezed by the other cars or trucks closing in around you, ease up on the accelerator just enough when it is obvious that you have to, and trust that others will do the same for you.

The drive down Insurgentes Sur was long and uneventful. I mostly stayed in the inside lane next to the one now occupied by the Metrobús. Many drivers initially were upset, or they are still, about having lost a driving lane to the Metrobús on such a crucial thoroughfare—Insurgentes is one of the world's longest avenues, traversing the city from north to south—though they were at least partly compensated by the elimination of *peseros* and other buses from the route. I only needed to guard against being edged by traffic into the long yellow slabs that border the Metrobús lane; the Metrobuses often swooshed by close enough to touch, wafting hot wind through my window. Whenever one of the buses idled alongside at a red light, it was as if an oven door had opened. There's really nothing especially fun about a long slow hot drive down Avenida Insurgentes. I played rock loud on the radio; listened to a lengthy and interesting interview, on the same station, with a group of teenage working-class transsexuals; inhaled traffic fumes; watched out for motorcyclists in the side mirrors. I passed Parque Hundido, where in *The Savage Detectives* Ulysses Lima stalks Octavio Paz. Stopped at red lights, you have to be ready to aggressively wave your finger no or shout at the ragged kids who close around the car to clean the windshield, or have coins ready for when you haven't reacted quickly enough. You want to be supportive of the effort, but don't need your windshield cleaned six times on a single ride either. At red lights vendors stroll between cars while performers rush out into the intersections: fire-eaters; jugglers; grown men with little girls, apparently though not necessarily their daughters, standing on their shoulders, shaking their grotesquely or farcically padded big butts. They end their acts in time to be able to pass down the rows of cars asking for change before the light turns green. The DF's vital principle, the hard everyday hustle all around you. Live here long enough, and you might stop really noticing and hand out your coins almost automatically, unless you're not the coin-giving type. Taxi drivers, something like the mounted infantry of the daily struggle, often hand out coins through their windows too, and that always impresses and chastens me. Insurgentes, headed south, is lined for most of its length by office and apartment buildings of gleaming glass, concrete, and steel, including the fifty-two-story World Trade Center; restaurants and fast-food places, the usual American crap purveyors and local franchises, like Hamburguesas Memorables, whose name entices me, though I doubt I'll ever get around to trying a *hamburguesa*

memorable. Many of these restaurants, mall-style steakhouse franchises from the north, Sonora and the like, are the kinds of places
where Aura used to go with her family on Sunday afternoons,
and to which I accompanied them many times. I keep my eye
out for a restaurant whose name I don't even remember but that
was the last one we all went to together, on an Easter Sunday
afternoon, and there, just past the Eje 6 intersection, I see and
recognize it, Palominos: *arrachera* served with pasty enchiladas
and a goopy puddle of beans and guacamole; *micheladas* and
tequilas; the family comedy or drama of undisguised personalities, facial expressions as emblematic and seemingly permanent
as those of Benito Juárez or Sor Juana on Mexican peso bills;
the stupor of dessert, coffee, and anise; the substratum of love
and nerve-eating passions and enervation of family. On my drive
to Our Meat of the Jaguar, I pass two Hooters, the one in Del
Valle where I sometimes go with friends to watch NFL football
games, and the one in San Ángel where I sometimes watched
games with Aura's stepdad, who was a star running back for the
UNAM "American football" team during one of the rare seasons
when it unseated Tec de Monterrey for the Mexican university
championship. The avenue seems endlessly lined with nightclubs,
discos, mall-type bars, casinos, and strip clubs with awnings and
valet parking out front. These always fill me with curiosity. Who
goes there? Office workers, I'm always told. And what is their
nightlife like? How is it different from ours?

Insurgentes finally brought me to the edge of the UNAM,
and Copilco, where Aura grew up. I needed, via Avenida Copilco,
to get onto Avenida Pedro Henriquez Ureña. And there, on my
left, was the housing complex where Aura grew up, in the two-
bedroom apartment where she shared a room with her stepsister,
the setting of so many of the short stories she started and only

sometimes finished during the last two years of her life. It was also where we'd spent our first night together, in August 2003, days before she left for New York to begin her studies at Columbia. Aura was living alone there because her mother had bought a new apartment in Las Aguilas, alongside the Periférico. I hadn't seen the Copilco housing complex in years, maybe in almost a decade. I pulled over, parked against the curb, and looked across the avenue at the long row of matching buildings, their stucco facades with alternating horizontal rectangles painted Picasso harlequin colors, carmine and cream-yellow. I couldn't identify which building had been Aura's. A low whitewashed wall running the length of the complex hid from view the parking lot where Aura used to ride her bicycle and roller-skate, the grassy parts and benches where barely adolescent Aura liked to hang with older teenage neighbors, furtively smoking and drinking; some of them, I remembered now, were the children of exiles from the Argentine Dirty War settled in the complex by a government agency. Painted in red on the wall outside was a long "♥ MORENA"—Andrés Manuel López Obrador's new political organization.

Just past the housing complex, Avenida Copilco bends sharply to the left, but the *Guía Roji* map in my head failed me and I went straight and found myself on Paseo de los Facultades, a narrow street running along the outskirts of the UNAM. To get back onto Copilco, I turned onto an even narrower street called Facultad de Filosofía y Letras, and had the sensation of having driven directly into Aura's past, for Filosofía y Letras was the department Aura had studied in. The street was nearly impassable with students; it was like driving into the middle of a rural village on market day. Kids in their late teens and early twenties, almost all of them raven-haired like Aura, in denim and T-shirts, skirts and loose blouses, sweatshirts and hoodies, a backpack over everyone's shoulder. Nobody parted to let my car pass, I rolled along at their walking pace, in a state of near hallucination, not sad, a mix of happiness to have suddenly found her, for Aura was surely somewhere in this crowd, and of *saudade*, for surely she wasn't there, the presence of an absence. If I had been able to choose where to scatter Aura's ashes—the truth is, I don't know what Aura's mother did with her ashes, because she took the box holding them home with her after the funeral and I haven't seen her again since—it would have been somewhere in the UNAM, in the sculpture garden that was her spot for solitude, or maybe in the stretch of shaded lawn near Filosofía y Letras known as *el aeropuerto*, a favorite place for students to lie back and get high. I think that as I drove along Avenida Copilco again, I already understood that unexpected diversion onto Calle Facultad de Filosofía y Letras as a long-postponed leave-taking, something that finally had to be, a first ceremonial good-bye, though there will never be a final good-bye. So now there is a place in this city that marks that good-bye as surely as, maybe even more surely than, spreading her ashes there would have been meant to do. Wasn't this what I'd hoped the *Guía Roji* driving project would bring me to in the first place? The combination of will and chance, of getting lost in order to unexpectedly find, had brought me close to Aura in this new way, one in which she was both present and absent, both asserting a permanence and letting go.

The rest was anticlimax. Avenida Pedro Henriquez Ureña to Candelaria to Avenida División del Norte, actually an expressway, busy avenues that wall in a maze of quiet working-class neighborhoods and streets, amid which Our Meat of the Jaguar is like one strand of a particularly dense cobweb of streets hung between two parks. Almost at random I chose a street, Árbol de Fuego, off División del Norte, and entered the walled maze. I drove around inside it for a long time. I am dyslexic enough to confound my sense of left and right and complicate my map reading. Over and over, I pulled to a curb to study my *Guía Roji*. One problem was that all the streets were one-way but the map in the *Guía* didn't indicate which way, as it does, with minuscule arrows, for avenues. I'd get very close, Calle Omecihuatl-or-Temoc-close, but was unable to get closer, pulled away by a street going in another direction, and then farther and farther away, as if by a malevolent spell, all the way to Popocatépetl, and then I'd chart a path back. On that *Guía Roji* map-page the streets were crowded together so closely that their names were in especially tiny print, which I was unable to read even with my eyeglasses on, and so I resorted to the magnifying glass I'd bought at the *Guía Roji* store. Some of the streets leading directly into Our Meat of the Jaguar were left blank because there was no space to squeeze a name in. And then, while I was pulled over, studying the map, the magnifying glass slipped from my fingers and disappeared under the seat and I was never, for the rest of the week that I had the car, able to find it.

I finally found Tonacatecuatl—Our Meat of the Jaguar— where it crossed Calle Xoloc. The streets in all four directions had hardly any traffic, and there were even fewer pedestrians. One- and two-story cement houses, painted in Mexican primary colors, in cobalt blue, or in two shades of pink or yellow. A few scraggly trees throwing stark afternoon shadows onto the concrete sidewalks. I'd parked by a little *tienda* on the corner, and went in and bought a bottle of water, and went back outside. An old man sat on a stool alongside the front door, next to a small table displaying raw roughly plucked chickens covered in flies. I tried to start up a conversation. The neighborhood was *tranquilo*, he said. At night too? I asked. At night you had to be careful, he responded indifferently. He was in no mood to talk, this old Aztec merchant with his festering clumps of jaguar meat. I leaned against the car, drinking water, smoking a cigarette, my back sweaty and prickly with car seat itch, surveying this small bleak territory as if I were its discoverer.

I took another route home, blundering my way back to Avenida Insurgentes Sur. With poor Gerardo Ortiz Gutiérrez in mind, I'd set out in the morning in order to be sure to avoid the afternoon rains. But it was five hours later and the sky was dark when I pulled into my building's parking space, feeling drained, with stinging eyes and a headache and nauseated from traffic fumes. It's a terrible way to spend your day, or even a couple of hours of it, in Mexico City traffic. People who commute by car endure that daily, to say nothing of taxi drivers.

"You know what I learned," former mayor Marcelo Ebrard told me. "You can beat the traffic thing by planning your day intelligently. Try not to leave your zone. It's when you leave your zone that you have problems. Half of the problems people have when driving come from not planning their day. Eighty percent of people do the same thing every day."

Of course, most of those people have little choice in the matter, when it's a matter of driving to and from work. In my case, if I had to cross the city to get to work every day, I'd definitely prefer to go by Metrobús or subway and maybe even by *pesero.* I couldn't have agreed more, though, about staying in your zone. I always try to stay within my neighborhoods, at least in the daytime. And I always prefer to walk.

The poet Efraín Huerta (1914–1982) was known to work on his poems even when stopped at red lights in his car. There is now a street named after him in Colonia Chiconaulta 3000, map-page

66 in the *Guía Roji*, near the top of the grid, in Tecamac, a municipality in México State. Huerta was considered a sort of Mexico
City bard, his poetry an aesthetic expression of the city itself and
of the splendors and miseries of an ardently lived life there, somewhat in the manner that near contemporaries in the New York
School, Frank O'Hara for example, expressed New York City. In
1977 Huerta published a long poem, "Circuito Interior," that is,
juxtaposed with other metaphorically interrelated aspects, an ode
and also a dirge, about love, loss, and walking in the city. It begins:

> One inconsolable day I said, I'll call you tomorrow,
> and tomorrow, that morning, I say, never
> came to us—nor the clear mirror in which you see yourself,
> whole and nude as joy. . . .

And it continues:

> Because to be in love, fall in love always
> With an idler city is to walk around blank;
> Conjugate and suffer an icy verb
> Walk the light, trample it and remake it
> And go in circles and circles and start again. . . .

And it ends:

> City in love, well, a city
> in which to be hopelessly in love,
> and to live inside her and suck on her—immense udder—
> from feet
> to head,
> her.

During my first years of living in the DF, I was under the sway of the commonplace that the city was uniquely surreal and that this surrealism was the key to grasping the city's personality, its "truth." I used to set out on long walks determined to not turn back until I'd witnessed or discovered something that expressed that surrealism, a living moment or image of the sort that the famous photographer Manuel Alvarez Bravo, the maestro of Mexico City surrealism, might have captured with his camera. Alvarez Bravo found his surrealism in intimate and static moments and images that were quietly strange, lonely, off-kilter, fantastic in the most ordinary, easy to overlook way, and that were also somehow very Mexican, amid the hurried chaos of the city. The elderly student driver circling the *glorieta* near my apartment counted, for me, as one of those found images—it was a very short walking expedition that day. One night I had to walk a very long time until, at about two in the morning, maybe even later, I came upon, on Calle Durango, a small beauty salon with its venetian blinds down and the sound of *ranchera* music and voices coming from inside. I peered through the blinds and saw three middle-aged women, still in their beautician uniforms, sitting on folding chairs, a boom box and a nearly finished bottle of tequila at their feet.

Maybe the most surreal moment I witnessed was in a taxi one night: at every dog we passed in the street, the driver slowed his taxi and barked loudly out the window.

Eventually I stopped exoticizing the city like that, less like a photographer following an aesthetic compulsion than like a pretentious tourist. I no longer wanted or needed to frame the city in that way, by distinguishing certain moments or images from all other moments and images as being uniquely characteristic of the city, which they're not, no more than what I saw while walking down Alvaro Obregón the other day is: two lovely-looking long-haired teenagers, a boy and a girl, standing in the doorway of an apartment building, each lifting a handful of the other's hair to his or her nose. They kissed, and the girl went inside. Why were they sniffing each other's hair? To test whether the scent of marijuana in their hair would be discernible to their parents, or at least to the girl's?

You don't usually catch scenes like that from a car. It's the kind of scene you might see in any big city, but, as I walk on down the sidewalk, it makes me feel bouyant with memories of teenage stealth and sexy intimacy. Even if I experienced very few moments, if any, of such intimacy when I was a teenager, it was all that I wanted back then, and as I walk I remember the lonely, insecure kid I was and share his desperate daydreams and yearning for a moment just like that, sniffing my pretty girlfriend's hair before she goes inside to her parents.

The other day the Colombian writer Santiago Gamboa, who was visiting the DF, said that every time he walks down the sidewalks of Colonia Roma he wishes he were at least ten years younger, so that he'd be able to enjoy the life here. I felt a little defensive, since I'm older than he is. Even though I do enjoy the life here, I knew what he meant. Roma and Condesa too, maybe like no other part of Mexico, are magnets for beautiful young people. The island of luscious-skinned tattooed youth, endlessly cycling by on their *ecobicis*, strolling down the sidewalks, hurrying across the Plaza Río de Janeiro with their artwork tubes or rolled yoga mats slung over their shoulders, sitting at the outdoor tables outside *mezcal* bars and cafés, smoking on the sidewalk outside the Cova. Their music and voices pouring from their apartment windows high above the street at night. Over the past several years those lives had come to seem more mysterious and distant from me than when I was with Aura, of course, though during the summer of 2012, they became a little less mysterious, and sometimes, in the predawn hours, came right into my apartment.

The walk we took, David Lida, Jovi Montes, and I, late in the fall of 2012, on a Sunday afternoon, our bellies full, from Ka Wong Seng, a Chinese restaurant in Colonia Viaducto Piedad, back to la Roma. Ka Wong Seng is the best Chinese restaurant in the city—Lida discovered it—certainly New York Chinatown quality, and I've never had a better wonton soup anywhere outside Hong Kong. It's a family-run place, with generic old-fashioned Cantonese decorations, in a remote, nothing-much-goes-on-around-here, lightly industrial, somewhat shabby and melancholy neighborhood. The reason Ka Wong Seng is located here is that the family's real business is the importation of Chinese food ingredients, which they sell and deliver to restaurants throughout the city and beyond. Their warehouse is here and their delivery trucks are parked on side streets. The owners' pretty daughters sometimes work as waitresses, and at least one seems to have a Mexican husband who sits with their infant at the family table on Sundays. A little Chinatown has taken root in the surrounding streets, mostly unappetizing hole-in-the-wall restaurants, clothing shops, and trinket and toy shops. The walk home took us through three *colonias*: Vista Alegre, Obrera (female worker), and Doctores. Quiet, shaded streets, small homes, sooty pastel hues, livelier than the neighborhood around Our Meat of the Jaguar; in the city's sometimes hard to decipher economic ladder, these *colonias* seemed more prosperous. As I walked, I daydreamed about buying a little house and disappearing into this neighborhood: life, work, maybe a wife, living there as if inside one tiny panel depicting one not-much-goes-on-here street in the infinite comic book that depicts every street in the world. But I will particularly remember this walk because I felt so happy, and was chattering away, I realized, as I hadn't done in years, and that was because of Jovi—I am getting closer to that part of this chronicle, how I met Jovi and the night that redeemed the summer of 2012. We walked down a street where all the Sunday-shuttered businesses offered *suajeados*. What was that? Not even Jovi knew. And why here, on this street? Later I found out that a *suajeado* is a cylindrical metal machine that cuts patterns into cardboard, fabric, paper, or other materials, to make jigsaw puzzles, for example, or those polyurethane maps with detachable countries. If you need that done in Mexico City, this is the street you must come to.

Another time I walked with Susana Iglesias—winner of the first Premio Aura Estrada—from the center to the Merced, the old market quarter, near Tepito. Susana grew up in those neighborhoods, near Tepito. She was soon to publish her first novel, *Señorita Vodka*. She's a rowdy hard-partying girl who makes vodka in her bathtub, used to blog as "Miss Masturbation," works with street dogs, and sometimes on her days off brings street dogs back to her apartment and gives them haircuts and shampoos. Colm was with us too. We went into an old-fashioned department store because Colm wanted to buy a portable CD player and it seemed like the kind of place that might still sell them, though it didn't. The bakery in the store's basement reminded me of the bakeries of my childhood, the lurid thick frostings and glazes, the fat sugar cookies, the rich buttery smell. We walked from Isabel la Católica all the way to the *eje de circunvalación* at the far edge of the Merced, leaving behind the restored Historic Center and passing through progressively rougher neighborhoods, stopping in a little clandestine bar situated beneath a tenement stairwell where people, mostly students, sat on chairs sipping from the thirty-two-ounce *caguamas* of beer that were handed out through a narrow door. It was night by the time we were on the *eje*, looking for a taxi. Everywhere people were packing up market stalls, wheeling stacked cartons, products, and mannequins on dollies. The *eje* route out of the Merced was lined with vendors and their makeshift outdoor stalls, which they have to set up every morning and take down again at night, packing up their wares and bringing them home or to some other place of storage. The nearly futile-seeming massive endeavor of it all, of so many people selling by the side of the *eje*—it seemed impossible that they could all earn enough to feed themselves and their families. We were in a taxi, stalled in traffic, when I noticed a woman on the corner, in her late twenties or thirties, packing up her wares, pulling down cheap plastic toys—superhero figurines, masks, and such—that were hanging from her aluminum racks, putting them away into a large cloth sack. She was wearing a red clown nose. How many more toys did she sell, how much more food was she able to provide for her children, thanks to that nose? That modest innovation, a toy seller wearing a clown nose, did it give her at least a small edge over her competition? I hope so.

6

The Party Bus

ON SUNDAY, APRIL 21, 2013, I was standing in the bathroom when I said to myself in the mirror, probably in a whisper, "There's going to be an earthquake today." And all day I felt uneasy and sometimes frightened. There's going to be an earthquake, all day and into the evening that thought and the fear it stirred up kept coming back. At about eight-thirty that night, it hit. I was at my desk. The long unfastened window to my right was clanging in its metal frame, as were all the other unfastened windows; throughout the apartment, doors were opening and slamming shut. Everything was moving. I opened the apartment door and saw the heavy, long mirror hanging in front of the elevator swinging wildly back and forth like a thing supernaturally possessed. The building was groaning, seemingly from deep within, a sound of straining wooden beams as on an old wooden sailing ship caught in a storm at sea.

I didn't know what to do. Should I run down the six flights of stairs? Or should I just stay inside the doorframe? Stay inside the doorframe. That's the advice usually given to people residing on upper floors, on the theory that in earthquakes doorframes hold up better than stairwells. In my mind's eye I watched the ceiling and walls slowly giving way and crumbling, the floor splitting open and collapsing around me, and myself surviving within a rectangle of beams in a still-standing grid with doorframes. I trusted the building to hold up, and stayed calm enough, but also understood that in minutes or seconds I might be dead. The shaking wouldn't stop. Later people said the quake—5.8 on the Richter scale—went on for about two minutes. Then silence and stillness returned, to the walls, at least. Outside sirens were wailing, all over the city, it seemed. Though my knees felt wobbly-weak, I ran down the stairs as fast as I could. In the dark stairwell, on two different landings, elderly neighbors were standing flattened against the service elevator doors, inside their sturdy steel frames, and they smiled as I passed. When I reached the lobby, Marcelo Ebrard and his wife, Rosalinda Bueso, were just coming back inside from the sidewalk. They wore matching short white bathrobes, initials monogrammed on the lapels, their long legs bare. He grinned sheepishly, and we shook hands, and I shook hands with his wife too. She was holding their schnauzer under her arm and grinning like an embarrassed schoolgirl. The Ebrards live on the fourth floor. So it must be the right thing to do, to run down the stairs and out of the building, because if anyone should know what to do, it would be the former mayor. Incredibly, the quake caused little damage in the city. Last year, when I was in New York, the DF endured an even stronger one and people still talk about how terrified they were, but those were the most prolonged strong tremors I'd ever felt.

The next week, when I was back in New York, I told my therapist how I'd sensed a quake coming all that day and that then it had come, and she said she wasn't surprised. What I'd been through in my own life, she said, had heightened my sensitivity to disaster. Could that possibly be at all true, that I'd developed something like my own extrasensory early warning system? Then how come I hadn't at all sensed the violent incident of the night of August 2 in Mexico City that ended up so altering my life, after assailants left me lying nearly unconscious on the pavement? Because it turned out not to be a disaster at all?

But there's been plenty of violence in my life. I used to fear that once I'd reached the proverbial nine lives of a cat in incidents involving guns and knives that in some way menaced me, then it would all be over. Some of those incidents were minor, others perhaps not, but I kept count of them and then I passed that number. Serious fistfights and beatings, of which there have also been too many, were not included in that countdown, though I've had too many concussions, and have a few nasty scars on my scalp.

There was, in about 1979, the time in Livingston, Guatemala, on the Atlantic coast, when a drunken German hotel owner held a pistol to my head at about five in the morning because he'd caught me trying to leap the hotel wall and thought I was a thief. The reason I was going over his wall was that I'd slept over in the hotel with an Austrian girl I'd met in the town and it was nearly time for both of us to catch the dawn ferry to Puerto Barrios and the hotel's front gate was locked. Maybe just in the nick of time, she heard his uproar and came out onto her balcony and saw what was happening and started to scream.

There was, in the early 1980s, the bodega holdup on the Upper West Side that my then fiancée Bex and I walked in on, she bolting out the door just as the robber was aiming his sawed-off shotgun at my chest, but he kept his cool and ordered me to lie down on the floor in back with the other terrified customers, then bashed the bodega owner in the face with the butt of his weapon and left with his stolen cash. That same year, I walked in from the sidewalk into the armed holdup of an elderly neighbor in the vestibule of our apartment building. After I reflexively hurled a bottle of grapefruit juice at the mugger's head that missed and shattered against the wall, he fled out the door with his pistol. There was the kid who robbed me of my wallet with a blade held to my heart on Avenue C.

In Nicaragua, at the battle of Teotecacinte, I climbed out of a Sandinista trench to stretch my limbs even though I'd been told not to and a line of Contra machine-gun fire from the surrounding Honduran hills tore a line in the dirt about ten feet in front of me.

There was that late afternoon in Guatemala City in 1984 when Jean-Marie Simon, the photographer and human rights reporter, and I were walking from the apartment we shared—it was where my late great-aunt had lived, over my late grandparents' house—to the corner store when four men got out of a black Cherokee that had been tailing us and drew weapons out through the open doors, but we "escaped" by throwing ourselves down behind the row of parked ambulances in front of a small private hospital, and then we got up and sprinted alongside a bus that suddenly drove between them and us and jumped onto it, and the Cherokee rocketed away down the long straight avenue, running red lights. The next morning when I went to the U.S. embassy to report the incident the consul somehow already knew about our encounter with a death squad and said, "They could have splattered you all over the sidewalk like tomato sauce if they'd wanted to," and that it had been "a heavy-handed tail, meant to send a message."

There was the time Jon Lee and I had to stay over in a fleabag pension in Sayapulas, a grim military garrison town in Quiché, and a drunk lieutenant carrying an automatic rifle tried to break down the latched double doors to our room, hurling his weight against them and kicking, shouting that he was going to kill us, while we crouched on either side of the doorway in our underwear, each of us brandishing a jaggedly broken beer bottle.

When I was living in Crown Heights, Brooklyn, at the height of the so-called crack era, I came out of my building and obliviously stepped into the middle of an imminent gun battle, kids crouched behind parked cars in front of me aiming at the also armed kids directly behind me on the sidewalk, but I don't know if that one should really count, since they weren't threatening me and no shots were fired.

A pistol was trained on me the night I was kidnapped in a Mexico City taxi. And there was the other night that I've already mentioned, in the Condesa in the summer of 2008: the two punks on Avenida Mexico brandishing frightening-looking razor blades in my face while I handed over a considerable amount of cash, having just collected it from the half dozen people Mariana and I had dined with in a nearby restaurant where I'd paid the bill with my credit card. When they demanded Mariana's bag too I told them they couldn't have it, because I knew she'd spent the day at the French embassy getting the papers she needed for her move to Paris, where she was soon to begin graduate school at the Sorbonne. Now she was crouched behind me against a building wall. The muggers seemed jumpy and nervous, one of them, punk haircut dyed blue, dancing his razor close to my face as he demanded Mariana's bag. I practically shouted that I'd already given them enough. If they slash me, I thought, I'll tell her to hand the bag over, but I knew they didn't have much time, because probably people in the apartments behind us could hear our "argument," and we were near the house that Mayor Marcelo Ebrard was then living in with his second wife, on Parque México, so I knew there must be police around, and sure enough, the punk robbers turned and bounded away like startled hares. Later Mariana wrote a blog post listing all the objects that she'd been carrying in her deep bag, which did not include her papers for France after all—she'd forgotten to tell me that she had to go back to pick them up the next day.

There was an earlier incident that I considered the most furiously violent and dangerous of my life, in 1996, when I was subletting a ground-floor apartment in the Edificios Condesa. At lunch I'd outlined in my notebook the last chapter of the novel I was close to finishing, and then hurried home abstracted and excited to get back to work. Standing in the hall outside my apartment door were two adolescents collecting money for a home for orphans. Kids from that home came by fairly frequently, and I usually gave them money or spare clothing. I vaguely noticed that these two were a little older than those other kids usually were, but otherwise didn't give it a thought. I told them I didn't have anything for them today and when I unlocked my door they shoved their way inside behind me, pulling the door shut, and began beating my head with their fists while simultaneously trying to tackle me. But I kept my legs churning as if seized by the muscle memory of an old high school football drill, and I knew that I had to reach the door before they got me down onto the floor. Falling forward, I extended my arm and managed to strike the latch and the door popped open, and on hands and knees, their blows and kicks striking my head and ribs, I crawled out into the corridor and toward the courtyard shouting for help. Now those boys had no choice but to flee. It was lunch hour, and there were going to be people coming and going in the long apartment-lined courtyard. I managed to get up and stagger after them, shouting for the security guards, while they, walking fast instead of running, looked back at me over their shoulders, snarling threats. They fled out the gates onto Avenida Mazatlán before any security guard reached me. When I went back to my apartment, bloodied, my jaw feeling broken—it wasn't, but it would be weeks before I could yawn without pain—I found two nylon laundry bags that they'd discarded on the floor just inside the door, and a long knife. What were they planning to do to me, at that hour, when there were always people going about in the courtyard, if they'd been able to plunder the little of value that was in that apartment?

Thirteen incidents in all—I left a couple out of this list—thirteen cat's lives used up. The one I count as fourteen—though no guns or knives were involved—was about thirty-six hours away when, on the night of August 1, 2012, I went to a party at Yoshua Okón's. The plan was to stay up until the Olympic gold medal *fútbol* match between Mexico and Brazil was televised from England at about six in the morning, but as the night wore into the morning hours, people began to leave, and others, like Yoshua, whose idea the marathon party had been, fell asleep on couches. Near dawn, only Reyna, an American female friend of his, and I were awake. We walked back to the Roma and found a restaurant on Alvaro Obregón that was open early and showing the game. There's much to say about this game and this team and about Mexican *fút*, but I'll keep it brief. In the Olympics, national teams consist of players twenty-three and younger, plus seven more players who can be older. This team consisted mostly of players from Mexico's Golden Generation, who had been triumphing in international youth tournaments—seventeen and under, nineteen and under, twenty-three and under—and were now on the verge of the greatest victory in the disappointing history of Mexican *fútbol*. Decades of TRI teams—so called for the *tricolor* of the national flag—had been good but never quite good enough, or seemingly excellent teams had always fallen

short of expectations: when what should have been a historic
Word Cup victory against Germany ended in last-minute defeat,
and in those fierce matches and rallies against Argentina that
always ended up breaking their fans' hearts. This new generation was said to have overcome the defeatist characteristics of
earlier ones; the players liked to win, knew how to win. The TRI
squad had a thrilling run through the Olympic tournament and
now was facing a Brazilian team that was said to be the same
team, under the same coach, that was likely to take the field at
the 2014 World Cup in Brazil. Mexico won the gold, defeating
Brazil 2–1. On that morning, August 2, people poured out onto
Avenida Alvaro Obregón, and into streets and plazas all over the
DF, all over Mexico, to celebrate the victory. (The national joy
would somewhat dissipate a few days later when the "grown-up"
National Team did something it had never done before: it lost
to the United States in the Estadio Azteca.)

But we went back to my apartment to sleep, and after we
woke up in the afternoon, Reyna's woman friend went home.
Much later that night—by then we were in the morning hours
of August 3—Reyna and I were back in the trendy after-hours
club on San Luis Potosí where we'd ended up so many nights
that summer. I was having a good enough time flirting with
a pretty bartender. She'd asked me for my telephone number,
telling me that because she had a boyfriend I shouldn't call her,
but they were breaking up soon, she said, and we could meet
one afternoon later that week in a cantina in the Centro. Reyna
was talking to a pair of wealthy fortysomething American guys
in another part of the club; they were corporate types from the
Northeast, New York City probably, in the city on business. Then
Reyna was pulling me away from the bar, saying that we were
leaving. Why? I was having a good time, I protested, I didn't

want to leave. Reyna said that the Americans were inviting us to a party. I followed them out of the club, out onto the sidewalk.

There was a two-decker bus waiting in the street in front of the club, thumping electronic music pouring from it, and a young woman was leaning out one of the windows, calling to one of our new American friends. He'd apparently arranged for this "party bus" to pass by there to collect him and his friend. The woman, I learned later, was the daughter of one of his Mexican business partners or clients. Party buses are one more dreadful thing that rich young Mexicans have decided to "import" from the United States, one more ostentatious way for them to display their separateness and status; such displays are apparently considered, in their very particular culture, the ultra of cool. I didn't want to go on a party bus, and if I'd had the time and lucidity to think about it, or if it had been any other summer but that one, I would have decided to just go home. Instead I followed Reyna and the Americans up onto the party bus. I hated it instantly. How the hell does anyone find it fun to drink and party on a crowded, moving bus? I climbed the stairs to the open second deck, and decided to just wait out the night there. A light drizzle was falling, and a few times I just barely managed to duck overhanging tree limbs, but otherwise it was all right being up there atop the bus, watching the streets go by and considering what silly or mystifying assholes we must seem like to the people observing us from the sidewalks. Even when it started to pour, I endured it as long as I could, but finally retreated back down the stairs.

The party-busers were very young, in their early to midtwenties I suppose, and dressed, many of those *muchachos*, in the Brooklyn hipster style that has become fashionable in certain *fresa* circles: plaid shirts, jeans, goatees. I'd been seeing such kids around all summer because they often came to the neighborhood's bars and clubs at night from their homes in Las Lomas, Polanco, and Pedregal—they live with their parents until they marry, I'd been told. Others among these party-busers were dressed more Ralph Lauren preppily. They belonged to the same demographic and were from or close to the same age group as the La Ibero students who'd sparked #YoSoy132, but I seriously doubt there were any even secret student activists on that bus. There were some American girls on the bus too, recent graduates of Stanford business school, who were visiting a Mexican classmate. It turned out that the party was to celebrate the birthday of the son of a well-known and politically connected businessman, the owner of a chain of pharmacies, who is close to Peña Nieto. During his presidential campaign Peña Nieto had promised a government program to benefit the poor by providing pharmaceuticals produced by this businessman and sold in his pharmacies; according to Peña Nieto, the PRI government was going to purchase these from him at a really good price.

So there I was, on a party bus with, basically, the children of the PRI elite. The hours—it seemed like hours—went by. When were we going to be let off? I stood alone near the back, keeping to myself, spacing out, tired, still at least a little drunk, just waiting. I didn't even notice when the bus stopped to let off the Americans who'd invited us; they left without saying goodbye, at least not to me. I spoke to one of the Stanford business school grads for just a little bit—she was working for an Internet start-up in San Francisco—and to not one other person. Then Reyna, from the front of the bus, was urgently waving, summoning me. I pushed my way forward, and noticed, as I got closer to the front, that the atmosphere was very heavy. There were hard stares. A fair-haired, leanly muscular kid snatched the cigarette I'd tucked behind an ear to smoke later, and he lit it. His steady ice-blue narrowed stare was one I'd learned to recognize when I was growing up around Boston as an invite to a fistfight that I might not be able to get out of, a stare that ordinarily might have sent fear coiling through me, and then he told me to give a cigarette to his girlfriend. But now that stare, which I returned, brought something out of me, perhaps from very long ago when I didn't always back down from fights I knew I was going to lose, and I answered, Fuck you. Which was a stupid thing to do. He moved toward me as if he was about to punch me but his girlfriend grabbed his biceps with both her hands and held him back, speaking into his ear. I pushed on, to the front, where good news awaited: the bus was stopping to let us off. We were on a bleak avenue—División del Norte, I think—on the outskirts of Polanco. As we were getting off the bus, someone shoved Reyna from the back, sending him in a scrambling tumble down the stairs, though he managed to stay on his feet. *Ay, mi querido pinche* Reyna, you're usually out of control by this hour anyway. I didn't know that he'd hit on the birthday boy's little sister, though it certainly isn't surprising that he had. Why should he have known that she was, apparently, still a teenager? The birthday boy, Reyna told me later, had gathered his friends around him, as if Reyna's having flirted with his little sister was something that demanded a response that could only be decided by committee or mob. I knew none of this, as I stepped off the bus. But then someone shoved me too, hard, from behind, and I almost fell down the stairs, and fury rose inside me. It wasn't as if I didn't already hate these people, as if I didn't already feel ashamed, at my age, to be among them, which doesn't necessarily justify how I responded but does make it seem to have been, in the moment, inevitable if also foolish. I shouted up at the bus, at its still open door, at whoever had shoved me, "Coward! *Ven!*" and gestured, Come here, with my hand, and stood there planted, fists ready, steely scowl, like a character in *Blood Meridian.* Would I really have fought the *fresa* asshole who'd shoved me? That would have been another mistake, of course, but yes, at that moment, had he dared come down the stairs after me, I would have. But he, whoever he was, wasn't going to come alone. All the boys on the bus, like paratroopers in a World War II movie leaping one at a time from the fuselage of a plane, were clambering down the steps. I turned to Reyna and shouted, "Run!" And I tried to run too, but I have a bad knee. Later I learned that two of them reached Reyna farther down the avenue, and that he held them off with kicks of his cowboy boots. The rest swarmed over me. I was down on the pavement, my arms folded over my head. There were about a dozen of them, maybe more. All of them seemed to be kicking me in the head, or trying to, and battering my ribs and back, kick kick kick kick. I believe this kind of mob attack, in the United States at least, would be considered assault, or maybe even aggravated assault; but that is, I admit, given the circumstances and place, a ludicrous consideration. While the boys did their business, the party bus driver patiently waited. I wonder if later they gave him an extra large tip. I am not sure if it was then, while they were taking turns kicking my head, or a little later, that the video I'd seen of a mob of Peña Nieto's police in Atenco clubbing a single protester nearly to death, which had truly horrified me, flashed into my memory.

Finally it was over. They filed like tired, heroic firemen back onto the party bus and it drove away, trailing bad electronic music like an ice cream truck from the Moronic Inferno. I lay motionless on the pavement in the rain. It was as if, in that

1:1 Borges-like *Guía Roji* map of the city, my body, instead of just my finger, had been plunked down on this wet, deserted stretch of avenue, as if on every edition and copy of the *Guía Roji*, on that map-page, on that avenue, a tiny red splotch now appeared, cipher of a transformative humiliation. When I stood up, the world seesawed one way, and then back the other, and I smelled ammonia in my breathing and thought I was going to pass out, but managed to stay on my feet. I recalled Muhammad Ali talking about how a hard punch to the head delivers you to the "green room," where alligators playing trombones march around you. Slowly the world stabilized. Where was Reyna? I found him near the end of the block. He'd gone to a public phone to call the police. A man leaned out of a window in one of the plain apartment buildings, buildings resembling large air conditioners, lining the avenue and asked us if we needed help. Reyna told him we'd already called the police. But the police didn't come. We took a taxi back to my apartment. As we had so often throughout that summer, we stayed up until dawn, listening to music, sipping *mezcal,* talking about what had happened. A drop of blood fell from my head, maybe from my ear or my nose, I don't know, onto the floor between us. We both saw it land. Reyna said, "Frank, we have to change our lives."

The next morning my skull felt as if it were covered with hard-boiled eggs. There were silvery flashes in the vision of one eye that persisted for over a month. I had bruises and cuts in different parts of my body, which I photographed with my iPhone. But when I went to the hospital a few days later for X-rays and an MRI, I was OK, only badly bruised.

Later my friend Gonzalo said, "Frank, you know this city, you know how to keep yourself out of trouble here, you go places where the people aren't so different from you, and you stay away

from places where they're not. It took a couple of rich gringos to
finally lead you into Mexico *profundo* and almost get you killed."
Deepest Mexico, Mexico *bárbaro*, the barbaric and murderous
Mexico of legend and of all too dispiriting and terrifying fact,
but that Mexico is always happening somewhere out there, not
inside my bubble. Mexico *profundo* had turned out to be a bunch
of daddies' boys—*juniors*, they're called in Mexico—on a party
bus. How had they and the driver known as they pulled away
that my brain wasn't hemorrhaging after so many kicks to the
head? I wanted to do something about it, go to the police, bring
charges against them and the party bus company, but everyone,
absolutely everyone, told me that it would be pointless. I'd only
make more trouble for myself, everybody said. For one, because
of the birthday boy's wealthy and politically powerful father.
Actually that also counted for two and three . . . People like that
have impunity, Frank. There's nothing you can do. (The birthday
boy has a politically prominent cousin who, everybody knows,
it's no secret at all, has gotten away with far worse crimes than
a party bus stomping.) Anyway, some of my friends also said,
the entire incident was at least partly my fault, and I knew that
was true too. And my friends unanimously warned me that if I
went ahead and wrote about it for a newspaper or digital news
site, as I was vowing to do, I would come off like a fool. People
would ask, What was he doing, at his age, on a party bus full
of twentysomething gilded children? They would say that I'd
gotten what I'd deserved, and that I was lucky those *juniors*
hadn't shot me in the head and just left me there, because they
easily could have done that too; just as easily as they'd kicked
me in the head they could have shot me in the head, and the
very same impunity would have protected them. Juanca even
suggested that I should feel grateful to them for not having shot

me in the head. "Sleep with little children," said Juanca, quoting a Mexican saying, "expect to wake up covered in shit." In Mexico people also like to say, "The fish rots from the head down," and in the Mexican society constructed over many decades by the PRI, that is definitely how the fish rots, and has long rotted. The party bus carried a school of *junior* fry and this old turtle had gone for a drunken swim among them. What did I expect?

Less than two weeks later, I was sitting in El Centenario, the cantina in the Condesa, with Falstaffian Juanca, the novelist Yuri Herrera (one of the Mexican novelists I most admire), and Alejandro Páez, the founding editor of the digital news site SinEmbargo.com and a writer too, who talks Joe Pesci–fast, his laughter like machine-gun blasts. We bought a bottle of Herradura tequila for the table. I was still going on about wanting to write about the party bus incident and name names, and Paez said that while he wouldn't really recommend that I do it, he'd publish the piece in SinEmbargo.com if I wanted him to. Juanca, a baritone maestro of sardonic commentary and sarcastic mockery, always punctuated by that booming piratical *harharhar* laugh, started up again about what a dumb backfiring thing it would be to do, to vent my anger and my humiliation in that way, and the others joined in, and I finally began to accept that they were right, and to acknowledge the humiliated pride of my defiance. The summer had been an alcohol-fueled relentless march to the bottom that I'd finally reached as I lay on the pavement, bloodied and nearly kicked to death by a mob of rich children. Somehow I'd ended up where I'd meant to end up. I don't want to impose a retrospective clarity of will on what had certainly been months immersed in a flailing muddle, but if there isn't some truth to the narratives of progress with which we sometimes try to frame our lives, however rooted in desperate delusion, we'd never be able to speak them, certainly not silently to ourselves, with any conviction.

So I spoke about that, my summer's march to the bottom, and then the others began to talk about their own vices and addictions, and their own past marches to the bottom. Except everybody was being extremely funny about it. The bottle of tequila was nearly empty. And we started talking about the party bus again and now everyone was making fun of me, and of Reyna too, for having hit on the birthday boy's teenage sister and for having "run away"—but I'd told him to run, and I'd tried to run too!—and finally the whole incident, from start to finish, began to seem sordidly absurd, pathetic, but also hilarious. Everybody was laughing. I loved my friends, the camaraderie and affection behind even the most loquacious mockery. I felt an ache deep in my sides, one not physically attributable to the party-busers' kicks. What's that? It was the ache of deepest laughter, and I realized that I hadn't laughed this hard in five years, since I'd last laughed this hard with Aura.

Two hours later, we were in another bar, and still in high spirits. I spotted Jovi, a young woman I'd gone out with a couple of times a few summers before, and thought, I really like her! How come I never followed up? Of course, back then, in those years, I never followed up. When she approached to say hello, I looked at her and just knew that she was going to be my new love.

The next day, Juanca wrote me a long e-mail. I'll quote a little of it: "OK, querido Frank. Now that you're hungover after yet another *peda* hard-core with 'the adults,' I'll share these reflections with you, because now that you've called me Falstaff I like the idea of appropriating that character for a moment." It was a long recap, regarding my avowed intention to publish a piece about my party bus misadventure, of all the reasons that, as he put it, "you'd look like a fucking moron if you wrote that shit down."

Juanca numbered his arguments, seven in all. They included, "You were as drunk as they were, and to think that you were inviting just ONE of them to fight is just naive. A crowd doesn't receive communication in the singular. What you do to one of them, you do to all of them." Number 5 was, "Where you are correct is that the wealthy are also violent. The poor don't have an exclusive on violence. Classism is a form of very *cabrona* violence here in Mexico. More: POVERTY itself is a form of violence that the rich impose on the marginalized in so many ways. I could show you videos of how the rich humiliate the poor in this country every day, but in the case of what you just experienced, I don't think it's the same thing. So OK, to sum up I suggest that you try to avoid provoking aggression. Nothing good ever comes of that and in general it's a very suicidal part of your personality that, like I told you the other night in the Covadonga, it seems like you like to tempt from time to time, probably at a subconscious level. I'm glad you admitted it there with Páez and Reyna and Yuri: hitting rock bottom this summer, with so much drinking, to find out if life can punish you, that's a good therapeutic admission, but for it to be a breakthrough or an epiphany it has to be accompanied by a change in your conduct. It could also be a search for a rock bottom that is more bottom than the one you lived a few years ago, but with all the affection in the world I tell you, THERE ISN'T, ONE DOESN'T EXIST that's more *cabrón* and devastating than the one you went through and that we've gone through together these past five years. Sometimes one tries to mitigate a major hurt with a more recent one, but believe me, it's fucking USELESS. You've already done a lot of good in your life and especially in that tremendous 'uprising' you had after what happened to Aura. The prize, your book, your reincorporation into life itself, with women and in the everyday, is an achievement that fills many of us with pride and love. Calm the fuck down, *cabrón*. You're on a good path."

I didn't agree with everything Juanca said, but I was grateful for his message. I acknowledge my culpability in the incident at all levels. Self-debasing calamity or brush with death and wake-up call, it changed everything, or rather, in culminating in that night of sidesplitting laughter nearly two weeks later, it somehow did. I was on a new *circuito* now—"on a good path," at last, I hoped—but with the former one welded forever inside me like the components of a circuit board.

I decided that I'd just drive my rental car to parts of the city that I wanted to see. I wanted to drive on the Circuito Interior, and I wanted to go to Tepito. It was August 31, and the last day I'd have the car. I picked up David Lida, who knew the way to Tepito, in my car at his apartment at the edge of the Condesa, and we got onto the Circuito Interior. A long expressway packed with crawling traffic, that's all. The trick was to know when to get off. We exited to be able to circle through a neighborhood David likes. Then, relying on his sense of direction, we made our way through other neighborhoods to Tepito, the barrio that contains what is said to be the world's largest pirated goods market. If it weren't for the market, I suppose it would resemble any other poor neighborhood in the city—alley-like streets lined with cramped, shabby, cratered tenement buildings; still-standing shells of buildings destroyed by the 1985 earthquake that were never rebuilt—but you notice little of that because the market sprawls everywhere, crowded along the main avenues and on side streets like tunnels, one stall after another selling pirated DVDs, clothing, fabrics, electronics, perfumes, animals, everything, much of it pirated, counterfeited, or acquired in some other illegal manner. David didn't want to get out of the car because he had his iPhone with him and had forgotten to take the credit cards out of his wallet; recently two of his friends who'd come to the market to shop for DVDs had been brutally assaulted and robbed. So I drove, exceedingly slowly and cautiously, through the market's warren of streets, the mercantile bustle and hustle all around us reluctant to part or make way. Finally we emerged from the labyrinth, onto the Eje 1, and I drove to Paseo de la Reforma. Whenever I'm on Paseo de la Reforma, I remember a story Aura told me about herself. How, in predawn hours, she sometimes liked to walk alone there, and sit on the steps of the Ángel de la Independencia, the *glorieta* with the statue of a golden winged angel atop a soaring column. Once, when the Paseo's sidewalks were being repaved, Aura got hold of one of its old paving stones, and somehow transported the heavy slab home to Copilco. It was smooth and marble-hued on top, jaggedly rough on the sides. I used to wish I could have been there with her, walking on the Paseo, sitting on the steps of El Ángel as the darkness lifted, or that I could have helped her lug the stone back to her family's apartment in Copilco. When we moved to our apartment in Escandón, Aura brought the paving stone with her. It must still be there, in the dirt of the patio, hidden by the bamboos.

I turned in my car at Alamo. David and I walked into the Zona Rosa for a beer, and the summer of 2012 was over, and so was my driving project.

7

Interior Circuit Redux

IN FEBRUARY 2013, Jovi suddenly left me. Throughout the fall of 2012 and into the winter of 2013, I'd flown regularly, sometimes on a weekly basis, from Mexico to New York—taking a train to Hartford to teach my class at Trinity College—and then back, sometimes leaving the DF on Tuesday and returning on Thursday, sometimes spending an impatient nine days in Brooklyn, waiting to get back to the DF. After one such week plus two days in New York, I flew back to the DF and discovered, most unexpectedly, that the relationship was over. I was devastated because I was in love with Jovi. But even so my reaction was out of proportion. The sudden loss of Aura had been irreversible and this one wasn't that. True, it actually seemed possible that I might never see Jovi again, but she was still alive, and could still answer e-mails. But my nervous system and subconscious seemed not to recognize the difference, and five-year-old trauma symptoms came flooding back. My Mexico City friends recognized what was happening, and were, once again, by my side. But this also meant a return of desperate insomniac prowling nights and all manner of excess, the only way I knew how to outlast and exhaust and finally quiet, for some hours, enough to get some sleep, the bedlam inside me. I believed, probably mistakenly, that without those nights—I was my own boozy Smoky the Bear on midnight to dawn patrol—mind and spirit might have blazed even more toxically. I still had to manage my schedule of flying back up to New York to teach my classes too. One night I dismissed my seminar an hour early because I felt so bereft that I could hardly speak. On the long bus ride back to New York—the bus didn't get to the Port Authority until nearly two in the morning—I felt the return of the bleak, hollowing despair that had so frightened me five years before.

But this time, I was determined not to go through all that again, not to be swallowed by that abyss. I needed to wrestle myself back onto the "good path" that I'd found myself on at the end of the summer, but without having to reenact that forced march to the bottom first. Instead I decided to retrace my steps through that summer by writing about it. I could use words as my compass to map the route I'd taken and give it a narrative order, a sequence of incident and meaning, and rescue it from being something other than just circumstantial and ephemeral. It was my own life, after all, and now I needed to draw some strength from it. The stories one tells about oneself aren't necessarily true, of course, but I wanted this one to be as true as I could make it. This didn't mean that it all had to be factually true, but I decided that this story needed to be factually true too, a dependable *Guía Roji* of the summer.

In that story a man in at least some ways wrecked by loss and long under the control of grief and its grinding solipsism is determined to find his way out. He finally arrives, if not exactly by his planned route, at a reawakening. He even falls in love again. One thing he discovers—during the writing of it, after having lived it—is that a place, Mexico City, has become an essential part of his own story. He understands the ways in which Mexico City has nourished and invigorated him, and has in certain ways brought him "back to life." But, of course, the city doesn't exist only for him; the city isn't his stage. He understands that he owes the city his attention, and maybe even more than only that. He is curious about the city now in a way that he never was before, hungry for information about it, and to feel a part of it. He wants to celebrate but also defend the city—the same impulse he felt in Aspen when that physician shouted out, "What a bunch of bullshit"—but hopefully he can respond more articulately now, with more knowledge and less innocence.

It was March, a month after Jovi had left me, that I began writing this chronicle. We were exchanging messages again, and began to meet occasionally, at first always in public places, like a couple on the verge of a secret affair. By May Jovi and I were back together, and I was happy and proud that we were. Had I not started writing this chronicle, maybe we, or I, wouldn't have been able to fix our relationship. I'd gotten hold of myself, pure and simple. I was back on that better route. A few words from a Nicanor Parra poem had served as a mantra: *Corazón caliente, cabeza fría.* "Hot heart, cool head."

I finished writing my chronicle of the summer of 2012 in June. At last I could get back to my novel. But a lot had changed in Mexico City since the summer before. Now I knew I also had to write about the summer of 2013.

After Heavens:
Summer of 2013

Tepito is the synthesis of Mexico.
—Humberto Padgett*

---

* "Ofrecen Rosario a la Muerte," *Reforma*, November 2, 2003, quoted in Claudio Lomnitz, *Death and the Idea of Mexico,* p. 496.

IT WASN'T UNTIL THIS YEAR, 2013, that the #Ladies really took off in Mexico, capturing even international media attention. There were a few honored precursors, such as, in 2011, María Vanessa Polo, a former beauty queen who, after being pulled over with a friend for a traffic violation in her upscale neighborhood, erupted in imperious rage, berating two policemen as *asalariados de mierda,* "shitty salary men," and *pinche putos de mierda,* "shitty fucking fags," and flailing at them with her fists. All over Mexico, virtually overnight, she became known as #LadyPolanco.* Andrea Benítez, this past April, was tagged #LadyPROFECO after she threw a fit because she didn't like the table she was given at fashionable Maximo Bistrot in Colonia Roma, and then called in inspectors from PROFECO, the federal consumer protection agency run by her father, to shut the restaurant down. In May, there was Dalia Ortega, #LadyRoma, a wealthy drunk driver who, after running over a female pedestrian in Colonia Roma with her Porsche, indignantly warned police that if they arrested her she would use her family connections with the city government to have them fired. All of those incidents were captured by witnesses with smartphones, whose tweets and posted images and videos went viral, humiliating their subjects and even helping

---

* Watch #LadyPolanco: 20minutos.com.mx/noticia/3188/0/lady-polanco/vanessa-polo-cajica/elude-prision

to exact justice—#LadyRoma was charged with homicide after the woman she'd hit died of brain injuries days later; #LadyPROFECO's father, appointed by the new PRI president to his powerful post, was forced to resign; #LadyPolanco had to pay a fine in order to escape a fifteen-month prison sentence for assaulting authorities and for discrimination. Without those smartphone blitzes, probably none of those #Ladies would have faced any consequences for their actions. They weren't the only #Ladies, though they were among the most notorious.

The *New York Times* published a story about #LadyPRO-FECO and the new phenomena of "broad and swift social media campaigns" through which Mexicans vent their indignation over such high-handed abuse. "Andrea Benítez simply did what many rich, connected Mexicans have always done: she used her influence to step on the lower born," wrote Randall Archibald, the *Times* reporter. He quoted a patron of the restaurant where Benítez earned her hashtag: "'It's such blatant corruption that's right in our faces,' said Max St. Romain, 42, a filmmaker who saw the inspectors slap an enormous 'suspension of activities' sticker on Maximo Bistrot on Friday night. 'It's a connection to the corruption that ruled Mexico for decades—the fact that a child of someone in power can use it just on a whim, on a tantrum.'" Now the corruption that ruled Mexico for decades is back in power. At least those who may have felt newly uninhibited by the restoration of the PRI about flagrantly exhibiting their own moral corruption now have to worry that an offended and alarmed nation lies in wait, smartphones ready.

So that's a bright spot, one of the few in Mexico these days. It's not only PRI elites who have to watch out. The most recent incident was #LadySenado, Luz María Beristáin, a PRD senator who, when she turned up with a female friend at an airline counter in Cancún too late to board her flight to the DF, first tried to intimidate the young female employee who refused her a boarding pass. When that didn't work, Beristáin grossly harangued her. In her parting shot, the senator sneered, "Where did you study?" and her friend chimed in, "Surely in Tepito, *pinche escuincla*, fucking brat."

"The return of the PRI is the worst news that our generation has received," former mayor Marcelo Ebrard told me. "It's in the PRI's genes to restore a semi-authoritarian regime. That's the logic of the PRI." When we spoke in the spring, the PRI not only had regained the presidency, but also held the governorships of twenty-six out of thirty-two states, as well as near majorities in both houses of the Mexican Congress. Ebrard said that since Peña Nieto took office, the PRI's reforms have granted the president ever more control over the country's politics, concentrating power in the "Eagle's Seat" and federal government to create a new twenty-first-century PRI hegemony.

One early manifestation of the PRI's restoration was in the situation faced by journalists, which was dire enough before Peña Nieto's election. Article 19, a human rights group that monitors free expression issues, reported on June 30 that during Peña Nieto's first six months in office acts of violence and intimidation against the press rose 46 percent in comparison with the same period in 2012. Eight of the nine Mexican states with the highest homicide rates during Peña Nieto's first hundred days in office were governed by the PRI.* During the

---

* (1) Guerrero, 463. (2) Chihuahua, 417. (3) Estado de México, 407. (4) Jalisco, 362. (5) Sinaloa, 324. (6) Nuevo León, 261. (7) Coahuila, 216. (8) Durango, 197. (9) Tamaulipas, 167. Guerrero, the only exception, is led by a governor who recently switched his affiliation from the PRI to the PRD (sinembargo.mx/15-03-2013/560479). Michoacán (PRI) and Morelos (PRD) are two more states where violence would explode in the latter months of 2013.

first nine months of Peña Nieto's presidency kidnappings rose 19 percent throughout Mexico, compared with the previous year's rate.* Amnesty International recently estimated that half the disappearances in Mexico occur with the collaboration or complicity of government authorities.**

On July 7, 2013, there was a new round of nationwide elections, this time for state governorships, mayors, *presidentes municipales*, state legislatures, and other local posts. During and after the elections, the PRI's opponents and many voices in the media accused Peña Nieto's party of having waged the dirtiest and most violent campaign in memory, murdering candidates and other opponents, terrorizing and intimidating voters, employing widespread vote buying and fraud, and conniving with organized crime's violent and corrupting intrusions into the campaign on the party's behalf. The PRI's summer campaign was not, as some observers were determined to perceive it, a masterful if ruthless renewal of traditional Mexican electoral tactics that had served the "wily" old party so well during the last century. It was an in-your-face crime spree shielded by the impunity provided by presidential and PRI power. After the elections, opposition party leaders vented angrily for about a week, even threatening to pull out of the "Pact for Mexico," their legislative agreement

---

* animalpolitico.com/2013/09/en-9-estados-el-secuestro-aumento-entre-20-y-70/#axzz2lbAycntp

** "AI states that, out of 152 cases of disappearance that they documented in seven states, 'in at least 85 cases there is sufficient evidence of the involvement of public officials for them [the cases] to constitute crimes of enforced disappearance under international law' (June 2013)." The Mexican NGO El Consejo Ciudadano para la Seguridad Pública y la Justicia Penal (CCSPJP) estimates that police and military authorities are involved "in one third of high impact and express kidnappings" in Mexico. The Council for Law and Human Rights puts the proportion at 70 to 80 percent (ecoi.net/local_link/259326/371897_en.html).

with the PRI on an agenda of proposed political and economic reforms, unless Peña Nieto punished at least those within his party responsible for the most outrageous offenses. But just as with last summer's presidential elections, the mainstream national television networks and major newspapers, rather than investigating or reporting or editorially denouncing wrongdoing in a sustained way, yielded to Peña Nieto and the PRI, and the criminal election campaign evaporated as a news story and issue.

During its twelve years out of national power, the PRI, retooling its machine with the support of its partners—most overtly, Televisa and TV Azteca—focused all of its energies on recapturing the country. Now, the PRI covets the Distrito Federal, the country's richest prize. Everyone knows that; it's openly acknowledged. Of course the PRI wants to govern the DF again, but to do that it would have to win an election there. But the PRI could never win an election in the DF, right? The city—with a demanding, well-informed constituency and an often aggressively activist base—is too smart and too organized for that to happen. The DF takes pride in its defiant apartness from the mediocrity and overt complicity with crime that characterize governance throughout so much of the rest of Mexico. Electoral tactics like those employed nationally by the PRI over the last two summers would never fly in the DF—imagine trying to buy off the city's millions of voters with cash cards redeemable at a bargain superstore chain or threatening them at the polls or even murdering candidates? Hundreds of thousands and even millions would take to the streets, and the media exposure, local and international, would be intense.

In 1997, when residents of the capital were finally allowed to elect their own government, the DF became a leftist PRD stronghold. But the DF has no longtime allegiance to the PRD like the allegiance of voters in México State for the PRI. In its history the state has never voted for any other party. Mexico City's revulsion against the PRI was particularly prompted by the corruption exposed by the 1985 earthquake—the collapsed schools built by contractors who'd bribed officials to overlook building codes, and many other examples of official malfeasance—as well as the nearly legendary criminality of that era's police forces. But 1997 wasn't so long ago, and it's logical to assume that there are still important sectors of the DF where the PRI wields influence. Organized crime has millions upon millions in money to distribute to politicians and officials. And the DF is almost completely surrounded by México State, one of the country's most narco-infested, corrupt, and violent states—a portion of the city touches on the murder and crime inferno of Morelos as well—and now México State's former governor sits atop the federal government. One possible way for the PRI to take back Mexico City would be to undermine the city from within over several years—however many more years the PRI retains the presidency—and so eventually grind down and exhaust its residents' and the crucial business and finance sectors' trust in the governing competence of the left that it might create an opening for an alternative "strong government." One obvious target would be the city's prized security; another would be the water supply, which comes from outside the Distrito; there are others. It's easy to understand how the PRI could have a strategic interest in exploding the perceived "bubble" of the DF as a secure city, for example by bringing some cartel-style mayhem—bodies strung from highway overpasses, beheadings, massacres in nightclubs, young women kidnapped from bus stops, etc.—into the PRD bastion directly from México State. But it's also hard to conceive

how doing so wouldn't also be self-defeating, given the result-
ing inevitable damage to the national economy, for example, if
the capital, home to many of Mexico's wealthiest citizens and
business interests, were to be overcome with violence and chaos.
Months before, when such fears had first occurred to me, I'd decided that to believe the PRI would actually try was only paranoia
exaggerated by my own loathing of Peña Nieto and his party.

But by the summer of 2013, many Chilangos no longer
considered such a scenario so far-fetched. It was what we often
talked about now. The speculations spawned by those fears provided enough conspiratorial plots and subplots to fill a fat le
Carré novel. "Something is happening"—we thought the signs
were already there, if not yet as openly menacing as the Evil
Witch writing "Surrender Dorothy" in the sky. A new consensus
was taking hold, one summed up by my friend Yoshua Okón:
"Over the next six years, *nos van a chingar*," they're going to
fuck us.

"Anytime you want to fall out of love with Mexico, take a bus to
Coacalco, to Neza [across the border in México State] and just
walk around," said Juanca, launching, over a glass of *mezcal,* into
one of his John Belushi–like rants, embellished with his own
thunderous cannonades of laughter. Well, maybe I could do that,
take a bus; to drive I'd need to rent a car, and that wasn't in my
plans for this summer. Juanca works in market research, and
lately had been spending long days in México State. "You won't
believe that shit. The poverty, the filth. People park their cars
inside cages so they won't be stolen. Inside cages on the street, you
have to see that! How can these people vote for the PRI? Because,
after twenty years, they finally have a *pinche* McDonald's? Aside

from all the streets there named after the *pendejos* of the PRI, they name their streets after flowers, in a place where no self-loving flower would ever grow, not even if you paid it money. Any of those teenagers you see walking around would become a murderer for eighty bucks. We pay them twenty dollars for two hours of their time just to tell us why they want to buy the shit they want. Go to Monterrey. They used to have a beautiful historic downtown, all lit up at night, full of people and places to go. Now it's all dark and deserted and bullet holes all over, but they still vote for the PRI. Stop listening to promises, motherfuckers, just look around at where you live if you want to know who to vote for! We look around and see a much better city than we had twenty years ago. But those motherfuckers look at us and say, Those people like their homos and drugs, they're chaotic motherfuckers in the DF. But *you're* the ones who like it up the ass, Monterrey, not us, only when we choose to. We've worked our asses off for twenty years to create this bubble that we live in, and we like it. It wasn't created by God; we worked hard for it. And now that bubble is going to burst; it's already bursting."

The DF's new mayor, Miguel Ángel Mancera, is in his late forties, twice divorced, now single, with a suave metrosexual demeanor despite relatively humble middle-class origins, and is a darling of Mexican gossip and society pages, often described as bearing a resemblance—this really seems to me a stretch—to George Clooney. In 2008, when nine lower-class adolescents and three police officers were killed in a botched and dubiously justified police operation, Mayor Ebrard had moved quickly to quell outrage and regain confidence in his governance by firing both his chief of police and his chief prosecutor. Mancera, a brilliant

UNAM-educated lawyer, took over as chief prosecutor—equivalent to a big-city attorney general or head DA—and in that post came to be seen as an aggressive and innovative crime fighter with a smoothly charismatic media personality. The mayoralty was expected to raise Mancera's profile much more and establish him, like Rudy Giuliani, as a dynamic national political player. Recent former PRD mayors had been nationally competitive presidential candidates: Cuahtémoc Cárdenas in 2000, and Andrés Manuel López Obrador in 2006 and 2012. Some believed that Ebrard would have been a stronger candidate than López Obrador in 2012, though I think Ebrard understood that the populist AMLO was still the more revered figure in the DF and throughout much of the country, especially among the poor, that is, nearly half of Mexico's population. Many assume that Ebrard will be his party's candidate in 2018. But it also seemed obvious that Mancera intended his mayoralty to provide a platform from which to challenge Ebrard in 2018. Some commentators even gave Mancera an advantage, speculating that he would benefit from the spotlight of his office, while Ebrard—who chose not to run for the Senate, as many had suggested he should—would find himself challenged to find a way to remain in the public eye over the next six years.

But Mancera's first months in office as mayor were at best a puzzling disappointment; actually, they were downright weird. Previous PRD city governments had staked their identities on representing a leftist alternative to the federal government's policies, and PRD mayors had sought to be regarded as outspoken opponents of the PRI and PAN presidents. Yet Mancera, who has never actually been a member of the PRD, seemed to have renounced that role. The political agenda and identity of the DF's PRD isn't necessarily the same as that of the national PRD, a party that originated as an offshoot of the PRI. Mancera closed ranks with the PRD national party and legislative leaders Jesús Zambrano and Jesús Ortega, politicians, increasingly bitter rivals of Ebrard's, who'd endorsed the PRI and Peña Nieto's "Pact for Mexico," a controversial, apparently pro forma agenda of reforms, some of them good on paper at least. Mancera pointedly distanced himself from Ebrard, who openly disdains the new president. Peña Nieto could not be more unpopular in the DF, yet Mancera met with him in Los Pinos, the presidential residence. In February, in their first joint public appearance, Mancera presided with Peña Nieto over the opening of an exhibition of military hardware in the Zócalo, called "Passion to Serve Mexico," which offered a more than merely symbolic contrast to the skating rink and dinosaur exhibition that characterized Ebrard's use of this public space. The Zócalo is also the daily site of public protests over every conceivable issue. (Ebrard, during our conversation, called it "Our country's space of liberty par excellence, sometimes in excess, but that doesn't matter. It's our freedom place, a symbol against authoritarianism.") In March, Mancera accompanied Peña Nieto to the Vatican to meet with and attend the coronation of Pope Francis, another gesture that seemed intended to mark a difference from Ebrard, who'd relished his battles with the nationally powerful Catholic hierarchy over such issues as gay marriage and abortion. Mancera must have known that his "Peña Nieto, military, and pope" show would strike many Chilangos as a triple heresy; either that, or else, implausibly, the new mayor simply doesn't understand the city where he has lived all his life and which elected him in a landslide. The heavy-handed response of the Mexico City police to the December 1 protests against Peña Nieto's inauguration—a day of transition that began with Ebrard and ended with Mancera as the DF's *jefe de gobierno*—the beating and arbitrary arrests of young protesters and their subsequent long detentions, suggested, especially in hindsight, that Mancera was bringing a new strictness to the governing of the city; such impressions were enforced by new "crowd control" policies that resulted, on June 10, in 269 arrests during the DF's lesbian and gay parade. Yet throughout the first six months of his term, so far as day-to-day governance was concerned, Mancera seemed to be keeping a strangely low profile. I wondered if I just wasn't paying enough attention and found myself asking friends how Mancera was doing. It seemed as if Mancera had no desire or ability to speak to the city, or as if he'd suddenly lost his fluency in Chilango, which he'd possessed as chief prosecutor. Mancera could justify his closeness with Peña Nieto by claiming it would help procure more federal money and perhaps, eventually, more autonomy for the capital. But cracking down on protesters, trying to buddy up to Peña Nieto, celebrating military force in the Zócalo, traveling to meet with the pope—what kind of strategy was that for governing the DF? It was as if Mancera was actually looking far beyond the city itself and ahead to 2018, seeking to distance himself from the socially militant and urban progressive images of the DF's previous *jefes de gobierno*, instead choosing to embrace more "mainstream" Mexican values that, in recent elections, have triumphed nationally, if only just barely. Whether it was already-backfiring, calculated personal ambition, or just the lack of a clear governing agenda of his own, or something else entirely, some other scheme or problem, that lay behind his confusing and passive performance, nothing would ensure Mancera's failure as mayor or as a future presidential candidate, or even as a relevant political personage, more than the DF's losing its image as a zone free of narco cartel violence and control.

As Ebrard put it, "The mayor has two overriding obligations. To keep the city secure, and to govern in a way that is clearly liberal and progressive. Lose those, and the magic disappears."

On Sunday, May 26, at approximately eleven-thirty in the morning, in the Zona Rosa, twelve young people—initial news reports said eleven—vanished outside an after-hours club called After Heavens,* where they'd been partying since the predawn hours. Almost all of the missing, seven men and five women, were from the barrio of Tepito. They were between the ages of sixteen and thirty-four. According to the only initial witness—a friend of the missing young people who'd escaped the kidnapping—one of the club's owners had suddenly turned off the electronic dance music and told everyone to vacate the premises because there was going to be a police raid. Out on the sidewalk armed men, faces hooded or hidden with scarves, herded the twelve into three vans and disappeared. That sort of *levantón*, literally a "lifting," in this case a mass kidnapping, is carried out by the cartels every day all over Mexico; its victims are rarely seen alive again. But *levantones* weren't supposed to happen in the Distrito Federal, certainly not in broad daylight, in such a prominent and central zone of the city as the Zona Rosa, filled with hotels, restaurants, gay bars, and nightclubs, if also with lots of big-city sleaze—*afters*, *teibols*, prostitution, drug dealing, and the like. The alleged *levantón* had occurred on Calle Lancaster, just a block from the Ángel de la Indepenencia and the Paseo

---

* An unlicensed after-hours bar, it was also referred to in the media as "Heavens After" and "After Heaven" and "Bar Heaven" and just "Heaven." I use "Heavens" because it was the name used by the newspapers *El País* and *Reforma,* and because I simply like that name.

de la Reforma, the DF's Grand Boulevard, which was closed to traffic that Sunday morning for a bike-a-thon, and only a few blocks from Calle Liverpool, where the Secretaría de Seguridad Pública (SSP) or Ministry of Public Security police subsection is located. An international culture fair was also being held nearby in the neighborhood that Sunday morning. There were some 225 police in the area.

But it wasn't until Wednesday that news of the mass kidnapping became public, after family members of the missing, in order to call attention to what had happened, began contacting the media and then blocked the Eje 1-Norte that runs along an edge of Tepito, bringing traffic to a halt. Until that Wednesday, Mancera's prosecutors and police hadn't even acknowledged the case; and it wasn't until Thursday, four days after the twelve young people had disappeared outside its premises, that police finally conducted a crime scene investigation of After Heavens. They recovered some marijuana, psychotropic pills, and beer bottles with fingerprints, and discovered that the security cameras over the club's door were essentially sham, without video or memory, unconnected to any cables. The city's vaunted C-4 monitored security cameras seemed not to have captured images of a commando kidnapping on Calle Lancaster or of vans arriving or leaving. Government investigators and police could offer the public no theory of what had happened. By Friday, Mancera's chief prosecutor, Rodolfo Ríos Garza, was declaring, "We haven't yet determined if it even occurred." The sole witness, Ríos added, was "not locatable." On Monday, the day after the incident, the Tepito youth had gone on his own to the Support Center for Lost and Missing Persons (CAPEA) of the Procuraduría General de Justicia (PGJDF), the chief prosecutor's headquarters, popularly known as "El Bunker," to report what he'd seen, but he gave both a false name and a false address. Because of that, Chief Prosecutor Ríos was now casting doubt on the truthfulness of his statement and on the legitimacy of his person. But the families themselves were one proof, at least, that the witness existed—they'd known within hours that their sons and daughters, brothers and sisters, had disappeared outside After Heavens because the witness, a neighborhood boy they all knew, had phoned many of them that same Sunday to relay what had happened, and then their missing relatives hadn't come home.

The baffling "Heavens" case, the most serious crime to have occurred in the DF in as long as anyone could remember, would dominate headlines for days and weeks, and rattle the city's sense of security like a strong earthquake tremor. In December the outgoing mayor, Ebrard, had declared that the DF was on the verge of becoming one of the safest major cities in the world. Now stories in both the Mexican and the international press, under headlines such as "Fear Arrives in the Heart of the DF," were citing the Zona Rosa mass kidnapping to question Ebrard's claim—many stories quoted him—and to suggest that the DF was no longer a haven from organized crime violence, if it ever truly had been. Mayor Mancera and Chief Prosecutor Ríos were repeatedly insisting that the DF remained free of operating cartels, but those claims now rang hollow. And Mancera was suddenly facing his first political crisis. In a column in Spain's *El País,* the paper's veteran DF journalist Salvador Camarena wrote, "The worse that can happen to Mancera is that the people he governs start to miss the former prosecutor they used to have while at the same time realizing that they don't have a mayor who rises to the level that Chilangos have formed of themselves, whether valid or not: the notion that their city is different from the rest of the country, [a country] ravaged by violence and moral hypocrisy. Mancera's hour has arrived."

On Thursday, the day before the chief prosecutor announced that the only witness so far couldn't be found, while insinuating that perhaps he was no witness at all, Pablo de Llano, the thirty-two-year-old *El País* correspondent, had gone to Tepito. There he met with some relatives of the missing, who put him in touch by cell phone with that same witness, who is known as Toñín. "I told them I wasn't going to give my name," Toñín told de Llano. "I went wearing dark glasses and a cap that I never took off." Toñín repeated what he'd told CAPEA, how one of the owners of the after-hours club—a man named Ernesto Espinosa Lobo—had ordered everyone to leave, and how Toñín himself had escaped the kidnapping by fleeing up a back stairway with some waiters and at least two other youths, and out onto a rooftop; and how, presumably from that perch, he'd seen armed commandos take his friends away in vans. De Llano was astounded that authorities had let Toñín slip away, that they hadn't even offered him police protection. Even while city government officials were still publicly doubting that the *levantón* had occurred, they were also leaking information to the press, which unquestioningly made public whatever was shared. The leaks were intended—their purpose was obvious to knowing observers such as the correspondent from *El País*—to exploit the stigma attached to Tepito, for the Barrio Bravo, or the Fierce Barrio, in the minds of many residents of the capital, evokes practically congenital criminality. Two of the missing Tepiteños, sixteen-year-old Jerzy Ortíz Ponce and his friend nineteen-year-old Said Sánchez García, were the sons of imprisoned Tepito gangsters: the locally legendary

Jorge Ortíz, known as "El Tanque," and his associate Alejandro
Sánchez Zamudio, aka "El Papis." The families and even some
journalists protested that Mancera's prosecutors were already
trying to "criminalize" all of the missing by linking them to two
fathers who'd been in prison for ten years. (Placards held up by
relatives of the missing at their continuing street protests read,
"We want an Investigation, not Criminalization.") Government
officials, including Ríos, denied being the source of the leaks,
and insisted that they were not trying to smear the victims. A
subsequent widely publicized leak suggested that the Heavens
case might be related to, and was perhaps in retaliation for, what
had happened on May 24, two days before the *levantón*, when a
drug dealer had been expelled by the security guards of a Condesa
nightclub and bar known as Black and then executed by men
waiting for him outside; his body was left slumped against a tree
in one of those pretty tree-shaded medians where fashionable
condechis walk their purebred dogs in the morning. By means of
such leaks, Mancera's government, before it had even publicly
accepted that there had been a *levantón*, was already imposing
the scenario that the Heavens case was related to a war among
Tepito gangs and drug dealers—not "organized crime," that is,
not narco cartels—over the lucrative nightlife turf, or *plaza*,
of Delegación Cuahtémoc and especially of its three bordering neighborhoods: the Zona Rosa and *colonias* Condesa and
Roma, the DF's golden nightlife triangle, drawing young drug
consumers from all over the city and beyond. But also leaked to
the press during that first week were images captured by security
cameras of a pair of vans circling through the neighborhood.

Along with the two adolescents Jerzy Ortíz and Said Sánchez, the abducted included Eulogio Fonseca Arreola, twenty-
six; Alan Omar Atiencia Barranco, twenty-six; Gabriela Téllez

Zamudio, thirty-four; Jennifer Robles González, twenty-five; Monserrat Loza Fernández, twenty-eight; Josué Piedra Moreno, twenty-nine; Arón Piedra Moreno, twenty; Rafael Rojas Marines, thirty-three; Guadalupe Karen Morales, twenty-five; and Gabriela Ruiz Martínez, twenty-five.

On Saturday, June 1, I went with Pablo de Llano to Tepito. One of the reasons he invited me along, both on that day and on subsequent visits, is that Tepito is a notoriously unsafe neighborhood for an obvious outsider—especially a tallish, thin, fair-haired young man like Pablo—to walk around alone in. Tepito's place in Mexico City lore is unique, and not just because of its reputation for violence and criminality—Iztapalapa and a few other neighborhoods have a similar reputation. For hundreds of years, Tepito has been regarded as a uniquely insular, tight-knit, obstinate barrio that operates according to its own codes, hostile to law and authority. Some residents of the capital take a paradoxical vicarious pride in the barrio, regarding it both as the outlaw heart of the city's iconoclastic, tough, hustling spirit, and as a dreaded place of violence and crime that they'd like to keep walled in. In the colonial era, Tepito was a poor indigenous neighborhood and market area whose residents despised the Spaniards and were always looking for ways to dupe them. Near the neighborhood there was a customhouse through which *pulque*, the alcoholic drink made from fermented maguey sap, entered the city, and much of it ended up being sold in Tepito. By the nineteenth century the barrio had also become notorious for its drunkards, robbers, pimps, and whores. During the Mexican-American War, residents waged a scrappy resistance against U.S. troops, hurling rocks and debris from rooftops, luring soldiers by night into traps—it isn't hard to imagine what sort of traps—and murdering them, and General Winfield Scott ordered the barrio razed. On December 1, 2012, the day of the anti–Peña Nieto disturbances, young protesters fled into the neighborhood and Tepiteños took to the streets to block pursuing riot police from entering.

Tepito today is a neighborhood of pirates, contrabandists, gangs, gangsters, drug use, and drug peddling, its danger and pockets of despair somewhat disguised by its teeming, feverish mercantile activity, for more than anything else Tepito is, and has always been, about buying and selling. The barrio gives the impression that there is nothing on earth that isn't bought or sold in its twenty-five-block labyrinth lined with *tianguis*— market stalls—and plastic tarp–covered streets and alleys, or that isn't counterfeited in small clandestine factories or warehoused behind the scarred walls of its *vecindades,* the two- or three-story tenement complexes where most Tepiteños live, and other buildings. It is estimated that seven out of ten pirated goods, especially copied CDs and DVDs, that are sold in Mexico come from Tepito. A steady river of *fayuca,* or counterfeit products, from China arrives in Tepito daily direct from Mexican ports, though a great deal of *fayuca* is produced within Tepito itself. Koreans supply knockoff and cheap clothing turned out by their own Mexican *maquiladores* and sweatshops, and Jews control the market's textile trade, and there is a strong contingent of Middle Eastern vendors as well, but most of the stalls are owned and worked by people from the neighborhood. Tepito is also the source of at least half of the drugs sold in the DF's *narco-menudeo,* or street trade; it's the city's narcotics warehouse. The Sinaloa Cartel is now reputed to be the main supplier, but Tepito gangs and dealers control and sell into the city's *narcomenudeo.*

The emblem of the Tepito subway stop is a boxing glove, symbolizing the many fighters who've come from the neighborhood, including national hero "Kid Azteca." After being roughly expelled out a subway car's doors by a rugby scrum of hard-shouldered passengers, Pablo and I climbed station stairs lined on both sides with vendors, and emerged as if through the gates of a medina directly into a tarped, shaded, crammed tunnel of market stalls, most selling pirated DVDs in gleaming cellophane envelopes for the equivalent of three U.S. cents apiece. I saw a young man coming toward me with a tawny baby hawk perched on the stick he held out; a cage holding small parrots and owl chicks hung from a strap around his neck. For a moment I imagined bringing a hawk back to my Brooklyn apartment in the fall to hunt mice.

Police, needless to say, are not beloved in Tepito. A private police force hired by the Tepito merchant association patrols the market, on the lookout for thieves and robbers. Most of these, Pablo de Llano told me, are former DF policemen who were purged for corruption or other violations. Pablo had already established good relations with a number of the merchant police, and they'd provided an entry into the neighborhood and put him in touch with relatives of the missing young people who owned *tianguis* and worked in the market. The merchant police communicate with each other by walkie-talkie, and keep their pistols tucked inside their belts, hidden by their top garments. That Saturday afternoon Pablo and I spoke with Raúl, a short, stocky man in a black utility vest. Despite his paramilitary demeanor, he was articulate and friendly. Raúl told me later that he'd gone to high school in a small town in California, and I wondered if that was the source of his mix of TV cop earnestness and laid-back garrulity. Most of the relatives of the abducted twelve weren't in Tepito that day; they'd traveled together into México State in response to news reports that corpses of three of the victims had turned up there. But Pablo had already checked this out, and the México State authority he'd spoken to by phone had denied that any bodies had been found. (Whether any bodies were actually found or not, the reports about some of the missing Tepiteños turning up there did prove false.) We went behind the row of stalls into an area covered by laminated roofing, and, standing together near the mouth of an alley leading back into a long concrete warehouse building, spoke about the case for a while. Raúl shared our initial incredulity and skepticism, and amplified it: a Sunday morning *levantón* in the heart of the Zona Rosa, only blocks from the SSP's headquarters, and police all over the neighborhood? And then it wasn't until four days later that the prosecutor's office finally sent investigators and police into After Heavens? In the meantime, the club's owners, security personnel, and waiters hadn't even been questioned, and now, apparently, couldn't be found? *¡No mames!* The chief prosecutor claimed that the witness, Toñín, also couldn't be found, but Raúl knew that he was hiding out right there in Tepito—of course Toñín was terrified!—protected by family and friends. All over Mexico, when cartel commandos are going to carry out a *levantón* like that, they inform the police first, so that the police will know to stay out of the way. Raúl said that such an operation, in the heart of the DF, was inconceivable without at least the connivance if not the active complicity of police. But who'd carried out this one, and why? The Heavens *levantón*, he opined, couldn't have been orchestrated without the involvement of authorities, and only someone high up could have given the order. Higher up than just a local police commander, he said. How high up? I asked. Very high up, he said. Someone at the very top. One of the top three. As high up as the chief of police, he said, or the head of the judicial police—that high up. We discussed various scenarios, including that the kidnapping could have been in retaliation for the murder of the drug dealer outside of the bar Black, a young man said to be from México State. Raúl suggested that whatever else was involved, the operation seemed likely to have a political motive. Mancera was the most obvious target, Mancera and the PRD. Who would gain from striking such a blow? The PRI, for one. Could that mean, I asked, that the PRI had a mole in Mancera's government, someone very high up, such as the chief of police or chief prosecutor? That seemed like at least a logical possibility, we all agreed. Moments later, walking with Pablo through the market, I said, "If this were a le Carré novel, the PRI's mole would be Mancera himself." That idea excited me. Our conversation with Raúl had consisted of speculation mixed with commonsense deduction, fortified somewhat, though not necessarily or absolutely reliably, by the former Mexico City policeman's knowledge of "how things work." Still, all that afternoon, my thoughts kept returning to the implications and possibilities of that exciting and scandalous story, Mancera as PRI mole. But, of course, this wasn't a le Carré novel. Most probably this was mass murder, almost inconceivably cruel and, like almost all similar murders that have been occurring throughout Mexico in recent years, unlikely ever to be fully solved or punished. In Raúl's opinion, the kidnapped victims were probably already dead. Most people one spoke to, even in Tepito, apart from the family members, said the same. A crime like that impatiently begs for a narrative, and when authorities seem unable or unwilling to provide a credible one, imagination, presumptuous, even vain, tries to provide that narrative on its own, reading and deciphering the circumstances according to its own propensities. Rumors, speculation, and extremely divergent interpretations of what little information and evidence exists fill the vacuum, in the media and in people's conversation, as was already profusely happening in the Heavens case. But usually, in such cases, after enough time has passed, indifference sets in, and confusion becomes boredom or resigned skepticism: "We'll never find out what happened there." Other stories seize headlines. People begin to forget, and often that's just what authorities count on, waiting for it to provide an escape from accountability. Of course there are always those who can't forget, such as victims' family members, lovers, and friends, though usually, in Mexico, they are condemned to anguished solitude and silence. But over the coming weeks it would at least initially seem that the banded-together families of the missing Tepiteños were not going to lapse or be intimidated into resignation and silence. Sometimes there are other people, totally unrelated personally to the victims and their families, probably without the least bit of personal feeling for their plight, who have their own reasons for keeping a case such as "Heavens" simmering in the public eye.

A banner hanging in the Tepito market:

¿Les has visto? Have you seen them?
Said Sánchez G.
Sex: Male. Age: 19 years. Height: 1.85.
Identifying characteristics: Devil tattoo on right shoulder.
Jerzy Ortíz Ponce
Sex: Male. Age: 16. Build: Robust. Height: 1.85. Skin:
Light brown. Face: Round. Mouth: Small. Nose: Flat. Eyebrows: Full. Lips: Thin. Chin: Pointed. Type and color of

eyes: Large, dark brown. Type and color of hair: Straight, black. Identifying characteristics: Tattoo in the form of a diamond on the outer part of right wrist. His name tattooed in Hebrew letters. On inside of right wrist a tattoo of the letter J, a heart, and the letter L. Both ears pierced with earrings, piercing on the top of one of his ears.

Adjacent to each description was a color photograph. Said Sánchez's photo, showing the smooth face of a solemn and slightly frightened-looking boy, must have been taken several years earlier. Jerzy Ortíz's was of a bull-necked, flushed-faced, pugnacious-looking teenager wearing a baseball cap.

At the bottom of the banner a three-line prayer summoned the compassion and mercy of God, Jesus Christ, and the Holy Spirit, amen.

The banner hung inside the spacious *tianguis*, deep within the Tepito market, owned by María Teresa Ramos Uruttia, maternal grandmother of Jerzy Ortíz, son of Jorge, El Tanque. Ramos owns two other adjacent stalls, operated by family members. One sells women's sandals, tattoo sleeves, and other adornments; the other sells cell-phone chips. Ramos's stall features embroidered and spangled rocker T-shirts, the Misfits, Janis Joplin, Kiss, Megadeath, John Lennon, and others of superheroes, and also hair accessories, gaudy bracelets, earrings, and the like. Ramos has lived in Tepito for all of her sixty-six years. She is a diminutive woman with hair dyed an orange hue, and a softly leathery, puckishly animated face; her eyes, at least on that afternoon, were as puffy and slitted as a boxer's after a fight with a hard-jabbing opponent. She wore a baggy brown T-shirt, and jeans. Tears overflowed her eyes and she intermittently broke into sobs as she spoke to us, and at moments her entire body seemed to be trembling. Jerzy was the youngest of her six children, she told us, though she meant grandchildren. Ramos has four sons and daughters, including Jerzy's mother, still married to his father. After El Tanque went to prison, Ramos, along with his mother, raised Jerzy. Jerzy and Said, son of El Papis, the two youngest of the missing, had been friends since childhood. Physically Jerzy was said to be a replica of his hulking father. In a photograph that I saw in a newspaper, taken when El Tanque was in police custody, he looked like a professional wrestler, naked from the waist up, massive upper arm turned to the camera and sporting two big tattoos, one of a demonically laughing skull, and the other of a chubby-cheeked baby, a realistic ink portrait of his first daughter. It was hard to believe that at sixteen Jerzy could be a consequential figure in any organized crime group, or that he'd already inherited his father's mantle as a feared Tepito gangster, though some believed he possibly was being groomed to be one, a crown prince of Tepito crime. Jerzy, Pablo de Llano would learn a few days later, still slept at night with his mother in her bed. When Pablo asked her why, she answered, "He's my youngest, my baby."

Jerzy's grandmother was incensed over how the Tepito angle had been played in the press. "I've been living here for sixty-six years," she said, "during which nothing like this has ever happened before. Whenever they find a dead person everyone wants to say he's from Tepito and that that's why, but that's a lie. There are killings and robberies here, yes. And, yes, the barrio is dangerous. But that Jerzy's father was a narco doesn't diminish the importance of finding the *muchachos*. The boys' fathers, they're paying for their crimes. Jorge, they've taken him all over the republic," she said, referring to the different penitentiaries in which El Tanque has served time, in the DF, in Durango, and, currently, in Hermosillo. "None of my children is a *ratero*," a thief. "None use drugs. All of us are workers. I haven't moved from here for anything. We have nothing to hide. Let them investigate us all they want."

Ramos said that on the day when the police came to arrest El Tanque on charges of drug dealing and extortion, he was right there at the family's complex of stalls—at his, he'd sold exercise equipment—fixing six-year-old Jerzy's bicycle. She said that one of the police held a gun to the boy's head. "Now Jerzy works with me here," she said. "He was in high school. He went to school with his sister, but when she got pregnant, he dropped out." One of Ramos's grandchildren is a chef, and another, she said, studied communications, and was spending all his time on the Internet, contacting the media. "If Jerzy didn't want to study," she said, "he had to be a merchant, because that's our trade." I asked her what Jerzy's working hours were, and she guilelessly answered, "Ohhh, Jerzy was our spoiled grandson. He came to work at whatever hour he wanted."

While, on this Saturday, the authorities had yet to confirm that any of the missing had even been in After Heavens, Ramos knew that Jerzy and Said had been in the club because another friend who'd gone with them had been denied entrance, but said that the other two had gone inside. She exclaimed angrily, "How could they have allowed a sixteen-year-old into that place!" News reports described After Heavens as a dark, three-story space where drugs were openly sold. A sister of one of the missing women, who'd often gone to the club herself, said that it had a "heavy atmosphere." People came armed, she said, though nothing ever happened there, unlike other places she'd been to in the city, where gun battles had broken out. A woman who sold candy at her little stand on Calle Lancaster described for a reporter the young clubgoers' expensive cars and their intimidating attitudes, and how they would sometimes park where they weren't supposed to. An employee of a hotel on the block told a reporter, "We'd see women and men come out of that bar very drunk, usually around eleven in the morning." Ramos said, "Whoever owns that club, and whether they sold drugs there, none of that interests me. I just want them to give back the *chamacos*. Were they taken by aliens from outer space?" How could it be, she asked, that the nineteen security cameras supposedly filming Calle Lancaster, including those of the hotel and of a bank, hadn't captured anything?

Ramos confided that the stress and anxiety provoked by the disappearance of her grandson had nearly killed her. She's diabetic and suffers from hypertension, and both her glucose and her blood pressure had risen dangerously. She was weeping again. A sad-eyed, sturdily built gray-haired man spoke to her from across the stall. This was Ramos's husband. Her expression cleared, and she gestured with her hand. "Go and get the T-shirt," she said. "We have to keep selling." He obediently headed off.

Violence, dread, death, and the imperative to keep selling; that's the way of Tepito, I thought later. "Tepito is blessed!" exclaimed Ramos. "There's nothing that can't be bought or sold here." The merchant matriarch's expression turned beatific, and her eyes opened wide. "This barrio is so beautiful, it's miraculous, you have no idea." She told us how neighbors had rallied around the families of the missing, helping however they could, bringing food, going out into the *eje* to stop traffic, something they would do again, but for now, she said, the families of the missing were asking for calm. They were going to meet with Chief Prosecutor Ríos the next day. "We don't know what he's going to say," she said. "We have to give them an opportunity to do their work."

One line of investigation that the DF police would obviously have to pursue was whether Jerzy Ortíz's and Said Sánchez's parentage did, in fact, have anything to do with the kidnapping. Even if it turned out that it did, they would need to find out why the other ten were taken. Not all of the Tepito market stall merchants we spoke to that day seemed indignant or even disturbed by what had happened. Some said that the kidnapped youths must have "owed something"—implying that they had crossed or taken something from a rival group—or else that Jerzy had been on *un mal camino,* headed down a bad path. I don't know if those merchants actually knew something about whatever Jerzy or any of the other young people had been up to, or had themselves been influenced by press coverage that implicitly criminalized the victims without providing any proof, or by their own personal memories of El Tanque or legends of his fearsome reputation. When El Tanque was arrested in 2003, it was for drug dealing and extortion; he has claimed that he was just a dealer in the *narcomenudeo* and that prosecutors had inflated the charges to make it seem a more significant operation than it was. Four years later, on February 14, 2007, Mayor Marcelo Ebrard ordered a predawn raid of six hundred police commandos on the enormous *vecindad* or residential complex at Calle Tenochtitlan 40, also known as La Fortaleza, where the imprisoned El Tanque's gang, known then as the Tepito Cartel— it no longer exists—ran a drug supermarket and had its center of operations. One hundred forty-four families were expelled out onto the streets while police used sledgehammers to smash down doors and walls. According to John Ross's account in his book on Mexico City, *El Monstruo,* "350 kilos of marijuana, 3.5 kilos of cocaine, and 80 tons of pirate CDs were retrieved from the caves and tunnels inside the Fort." As the "tenants huddled on the sidewalk in the chill February dawn . . . Marcelo sent the coffee wagon around." The Fortaleza was razed and bulldozed, and the city government expropriated the property. The Community Development Center that Ebrard promised to build on the site opened in 2011. It has sports facilities, including a boxing school and a pool where lessons are given in swimming and even scuba diving; adult education and job training courses whose curriculum was designed by a committee of Tepito residents; a part-time high school degree program for working youths; and supplementary classes and activities for gifted children. The center means something to a neighborhood whose residents, according to what Ebrard told me, have the highest incarceration rate in Mexico: out of 38,000 Tepiteños, he said, 1,600 are in prison. There was a guy, thirty or so, with a pirate's black beard and swagger, who sold DVDs from a cart at the edge of the pavement on Avenida del Trabajo and was the type who "hears about everything that goes on here"; Pablo regularly checked in on him. He had no regrets over the razing of the Fortaleza. "Have you seen the new center?" he asked. "*Está poca madre*." In Mexico City slang *poca madre*, literally "little of mother," or "motherless," means something like really fucking cool.

The day before Pablo and I went to Tepito, Mayor Mancera, in his hour, had stridden into the glaring spotlight of a press conference to take questions about the Heavens case. The mayor declared that the twelve missing young people should be considered not forcibly "disappeared," but simply "absent." He called the incident "an isolated one" and insisted, "There are no cartels operating in the DF."

Today is July 25, one day shy of two months since the morning the twelve young people were kidnapped—forcibly disappeared—from outside After Heavens. All twelve are still missing. There has been no indication of any sort that they could still be alive. Maybe some are alive, maybe all are, or maybe none are. Nor has there been a counterattack by any criminal group with whom some number of the missing twelve might have had links, as would seem certain if they indeed had such links. Maybe a violent counterattack is in the offing; who knows? It's possible a ransom was demanded, not of the families but of some such criminal group, but we don't know if there's any truth to that, it's just one rumor among many. There have been some arrests in the case, but they haven't provided any information beyond what we knew early on, that the after-hours club's owners and some staff played a role in the kidnapping. Yesterday the families met yet again with the chief prosecutor, Rodolfo Ríos Garza— they've met with Mayor Mancera too. In an e-mail last night, Pablo de Llano, who has been closely following the case and reporting on it for *El País*, wrote: "The families haven't exploded yet, but some of the mothers have reached their limit. Today they've again come out of a meeting frustrated. As for your question, why those twelve?—it still makes no sense to me either." Two months later, and still no reported or leaked evidence or hard allegations that any of the missing were involved in organized crime activities, though two of the young Tepito men had served prison terms for robbery.

Today, July 25, is also the sixth anniversary of Aura's death. At tonight's Mass in the church on the corner, the priest will again pronounce Aura's name during the prayer for the departed. Hopefully he'll pronounce it correctly this time, though I suppose it won't matter much, as only I'll be there to notice. Naty is staying in with five-year-old Aura, my goddaughter. She couldn't get a babysitter. Her husband Sam says he'll meet me after the Mass. Juanca can't make it—he'll be out of the city for work—and Fabis is in Baja California. Apart from them, I didn't inform anyone else about the Mass. I only told Jovi about it yesterday. She asked me why I'd told so few people. I said, "I just don't need people to show me that kind of care or support anymore, and don't want them to feel obligated." She nodded as if she completely understood, and I liked the way she looked at me, with something affirming in her softened, grave expression. She won't go to the Mass, but will meet Sam and me after it.

One of the things I am thinking about today is how different this summer has been from the last one. A year ago I'd wanted some sort of epiphany from the Mass, anything that I might just pull from within myself during an hour of concentration and maybe even prayer to help me understand the persistence of grief and how to honorably break its grip on me. Now here I am just a couple of weeks short of the first anniversary of my relationship with Jovi. I tell myself that I want nothing for myself at tonight's Mass, only a space for intense reflection, and to do what feels right. But anniversaries, of this sort anyway, are not like other days. The wound is tender today. Nostalgia, sadness. In the morning I spent about an hour reading Aura's book. This year, unlike last year and the four years before it, I don't observe my private and hellish stations of the cross, thinking that at this hour you were in that horrible rural hospital, at this hour we were in the air ambulance, etc. I feel myself drawing back from horror and trauma. I will not take the day off, I have work to do, I need to finish writing this part about Tepito and the summer of 2013.

But last night, in bed beside Jovi, I woke at about three in the morning, flooded with anxiety, thinking about what Aura was going through at that same hour six years ago, in the emergency ward, in that unspeakably terrifying and heartrending void that I can never reach, alone as she faced her death, only hours away. During that long night and morning when the hospital staff wouldn't let me into the emergency ward to see her. When I could be of no help, when I would never be able to be of any help to her ever again, when my love could not have been more futile.

What is it like, what has it been like, for the Tepito families, as they ponder the fates of their missing? What are they going through, when they wake at three in the morning?

That same Saturday, after we'd met with Doña María Teresa Ramos in her *tianguis,* there seemed to be no one else for Pablo and me to speak to; the families hadn't yet returned from México State. But it turned out that it was the day of the monthly Mass for La Santa Muerte: St. Death or Holy Death. In the DF's working-class barrios and in many other parts of the republic, La Santa Muerte, a gowned skeleton, often wearing a princess's tiara, usually carrying a scythe and globe, has become a figure of popular devotion nearly as iconic as the Virgin of Guadalupe, and in some communities may even have overtaken the Virgin. In the DF there are numerous Santa Muerte shrines, including one in nearby Colonia Morelos tended by a "priest" who is also a dentist, but the most important one is in Tepito. The monthly Mass draws thousands of worshippers. A few of the merchant police offered to walk us over there, and to get us inside so that we could speak to Doña Queta, the famously formidable "priestess" who presides over the shrine and the Mass. Pablo had interviewed her before, and he thought that if anyone had a feeling for the pulse of Tepito, it was Doña Queta. She is one of the most well-known and respected personages in the barrio. Surely she'd heard something or had some insight into the Heavens case. The faithful confided in her, confessed to her, and sought her blessing every day.

The Santa Muerte shrine is on the outskirts of Tepito, on Calle Alfarería, away from the market, on the other side of Avenida del Trabajo, in an area of dilapidated streets that seem relatively quiet and are mostly lined with *vecindades*. If these blocks look somewhat bombed, that's partly because the 1985 earthquake hit the neighborhood hard, inflicting damage everywhere, and many collapsed buildings were never rebuilt or replaced. The vacant lots and ghost buildings are not necessarily uninhabited—through some paneless windows you spot laundry hanging in the blackness inside, or cartons piled high. I kept thinking, during the first visit and then even more so on subsequent ones, that the sky from Tepito, looming over the urbanscape's low uneven contours—concrete rooftops, peeling paint and whitewash, rusted corrugated metal sheets, empty gaps—looks different than it does from other neighborhoods. The sky seems to crouch over the neighborhood as if worried for it, helplessly gazing down from on high, but also hoisting its skirts up away from it. Or else, I thought another day, it's like a Paul Bowles sky, which makes Tepito feel like an ancient walled city in the desert, and accentuates its busy, tense, and ominous insularity.

That Saturday, Calle Alfarería was packed for blocks on end with devotees of the Santa Muerte cult. Over loudspeakers, we could hear Doña Queta's intense, somewhat harsh and relentless voice pronouncing prayers or a sermon. The scent of marijuana pervaded the air. On a strip of trampled grass and dirt along the edge of the avenue, vendors were selling all manner of Santa Muerte figurines, statues, images, amulets, and other merchandise, but some were also selling small busts of Jesús Malverde, the outlaw patron folk saint of the narcos, especially in northern Mexico. As San Judas Tadeo, at the center of another phenomenally popular Mexico City cult, is the patron saint of lost and desperate causes, and also is believed by some, mainly by prostitutes I suppose, to especially protect prostitutes, the Santa Muerte is considered the protector of thieves, and is generally associated by those outside the cult with criminality. La Santa Muerte apparently has centuries-old cultural roots that some researchers trace to sixteenth-century Chiapas and Guatemala, but the contemporary version of the cult, much metamorphosed, didn't become known in Mexico City until around 2000, and then burgeoned. The death saint's current mystique, the root of its popularity, seems to have spread from the country's penitentiaries. A former girlfriend, Verónica, back in the 1990s, used to photograph the Islas Marías federal prison and its inmates, spending weeks at a time on the legendary prison island, and I remember her telling me about La Santa Muerte, and how only one prisoner at a time was allowed to have the gowned skeleton tattooed on his back, and how another prisoner might try to murder that one to seize the honor for himself. When Claudio Lomnitz, in *Death and the Idea of Mexico,* quotes a follower of the Santa Muerte who says, "She's miraculous, but she is also very jealous . . . because you can only believe in her. . . . And if you don't, she takes you with her," I remember how furious Verónica was with me when she discovered that I'd slid a tiny prayer card with an image of the Santa Muerte into my wallet next to one of San Simón, another folk saint-divinity attractive to criminals, and to many others too, from Guatemala, with divine ancient Maya roots. I only had the cards because I liked them, but she insisted La Santa Muerte would harm me if her image had to share my wallet with San Simón, and she made me throw the card away.

Now Santa Muerte images, and tattoos, are all over the place in Mexico, especially among the more marginalized groups in the city and country. Daniel Hernández, in *Down and Delirious in Mexico City,* reported that a taxi driver told him, "The local narco capos bring their automatic assault weapons to Doña Queta's on Halloween so that the tools of their trade can be blessed by Death." Pablo said that when he was reporting his piece on the cult for *El País,* some heavy-looking men, in mobster suits, carrying walkie-talkies, had turned up while he was interviewing Doña Queta, and that their presence had clearly embarrassed her. Raúl was accompanying Pablo and told him they were Federales, PGR federal police, often the same as crime capos anyway. Claudio Lomnitz describes a Mexico City "brotherhood of policemen and criminals that has the cult of La Santa Muerte at its core." Lomnitz situates the cult as prospering in a spiritual space left vacant in Mexico by the receding of the "sanctity of the state," and by implication the sanctity and authority of traditional Catholicism too. He writes that while the "cult seems to have begun on the fringes of the state—among the criminal element and the police—[it] has only recently begun to work its way into the mainstream," attracting law-abiding followers and those who, like many Tepiteños, live in circumstances where the line between illegality and lawfulness is commonly blurred. La Santa Muerte now has millions of followers in Mexico, but this has less to do with whatever association with criminality the saint may have and everything to do with what any criminal has in common with every other person, and that is that someday he or she will die. So here, again, was the Mexican idea of a skeleton, of Death, as an equalizer between rich and poor, powerful and powerless, and criminal and law-abiding. "We believe in you because you are just," goes a prayer at the dentist's shrine. "You don't discriminate. You take the poor and the rich." Mexico's Catholic hierarchy condemns the Santa Muerte cult as paganism, and in parts of Mexico authorities have had Santa Muerte shrines destroyed, and the faithful have marched to defend their "freedom of religion." In the DF, in 2009, as Hernández reports, they marched right up to the doors of the Metropolitan Cathedral on the Zócalo. But La Santa Muerte really works more like pure Catholicism, if far from doctrinally pure—in Catholicism, praying to the saints, "God's most gracious advocates," is another way of praying to God. That's what one of the merchant policemen was explaining to me as we walked over there. "It's not the worship of death itself," he said. The faithful, he said, pray for the intercession of La Santa Muerte with God as they might similarly pray to the Virgin or to any saint. But La Santa Muerte is especially powerful because she shares with God the knowledge of when death will call us. Our destiny is death, but we still have lives to endure. La Santa Muerte knows how much time we have left and can ask God, who also knows, for help on our behalf. It seemed easy enough to understand when explained that way.

But I was far more curious about what Doña Queta might have to say about the Heavens case and the missing Tepito young people than I was about La Santa Muerte. Many years spent in Central America had long ago used up whatever fascination I'd once had with folk religions. We went around to the back of the shrine, where the merchant association police passed us off to a teenager who was waiting for us and who led us through the packed, jostling crowd to a beefy, smooth-faced young man who turned out to be Doña Queta's son. Most of the faithful carried their own framed portraits or statuettes of La Santa Muerte, many of these inside backpacks slung backward over their chests, draped skulls poking out the tops. Some hauled along life-size or even larger figures of La Santa Muerte, made of lacquered papier-mâché; one that I saw was winged like a giant bat. People pulled figures or portraits of La Santa Muerte from their bags while others crouched in front and blew marijuana on these images—a rite, I suppose, that I saw repeated several times. We were taken into a roped-off area alongside the altar, at the front of the *vecindad* where Doña Queta lives. She was finishing her sermon, I caught very little of it. Inside its windowed altar, the life-size Santa Muerte stood in her radiant blue gown, a matching satiny *chal* draped over her head, which is a human skull, with hollow eyes and a grin of yellow teeth, wearing a shoulder-length brown wig. Her long, brown-boned fingers were also those of a human skeleton. Doña Queta regularly and dotingly changes La Santa's color-coordinated vestments and adornments. Perched near the feet of the saint was a chocolate-skinned baby mannequin, dressed like a little king, a Santería figure—Doña Queta is a devotee of that Afro-Cuban folk religion too. There were all kinds of other stuff in and around the altar, including banks of fresh flowers and a platter of red lollipops. People had formed an extremely long, winding line for their chance to visit one-on-one with La Santa Muerte. Doña Queta was helping to direct traffic, letting people through the little gate, shouting, "One at a time . . . wait your turn . . . don't push." Her coarse black hair is splotched white, as if by a paintbrush, just over her forehead, and she has a handsome brown face, with a strong jaw and sharply winged brows over heavy-lidded, intense black eyes. Pablo said later that she seemed in an especially testy mood. A tall blond man standing in our area was a

Danish anthropologist, and while Pablo spoke to him, I went to the front, as close to the altar as I could get. Then a mariachi band began playing right behind me and for the next hour or so I was trapped there. Not only their clothing, hairstyles, and worn facial features but also something in their anxious, passionate expressions suggested that most of these worshippers were poor. Though most were clearly urban working people, they reminded me of Maya peasant worshippers in Guatemalan highland villages for whom the religious statues inside a church are not just representations of this or that saint but literally divine and powerful in themselves. They approached Doña Queta, the grand holy lady, with nervous docility, and then went forward to beseechingly stand, bow, and pray before the holy skeleton, holding out their own Santa Muerte figures and images, kissing their fingers and pressing them to the glass unless Doña Queta sharply told them not to. Some took photographs. The priestess hurried them along, because there were still hundreds of people waiting their turn. Those who wanted to leave a lighted candle or a gift—a bouquet of roses or a fistful of lollipops—had to carry their offerings into the small room off to the side. Some of the young men were clearly drunk or on drugs or both. Some of the women looked like prostitutes, the very poor ones who line the streets outside the Merced market. I saw countless Santa Muerte tattoos. One inebriated youth, bedraggled but muscular, who was being unruly in line, approached Doña Queta. I was surprised by how attentive she was as he spoke to her, and then she seemed to speak sternly but kindly to him—she knows his mother, I thought to myself—before prayerfully blessing him, her hand over his forehead. He stumbled forward to the altar, and then stayed too long and became agitated again when he was told to move on, though he finally did. I watched Doña

Queta speak with and bless several of the faithful as she had done with the inebriated youth. All of the people I watched approach the altar were there to ask for something that they believed or hoped Holy Death could deliver to them from God: protection, health, money, love, an end to loneliness or to misery, success in one endeavor or another. And who is to say that asking in this way, concentrating on what you want, summoning what you believe to be some greater power to strengthen your own endurance or will, might not be of help? Why do humans pray? And does it much matter who or what you pray to? Just reciting or reading a poem can be a prayer, I knew from my own experience. Poetry is faith, devotion, and desire too; sometimes it's a spiritual humbling, sometimes an uplifting. After Aura died a friend, Sharon, brought me an inscribed copy of Joan Didion's *The Year of Magical Thinking*. Didion's advice to me, in a separate note, was to "read lots of poetry," and I did.

Doña Queta remembered Pablo from their interview and greeted him enthusiastically, and he introduced me. When he asked her if she knew anything, or had heard anything, or had any opinion about the Heavens case, her expression hardened. She said she had heard nothing, and she turned away from us.

Lomnitz writes, "Although the cult of La Santísima Muerte appears to have begun in that no-man's-land between society and the state that is organized crime (including its connections among the police), it is extending to working people of various classes. As a local Tepiteño intellectual has declared: 'They want to scare the Mexico City public about Tepito, without realizing that Mexico is becoming the Tepito of the world. Tepito is the synthesis of Mexico.'" This idea of that intellectual, Humberto Padgett, a well-known journalist, interested me more than La Santa Muerte itself. Of course, Holy Death is a part of the synthesis, but not necessarily, I would come to think after a few more visits to the shrine, in so spiritual a way. But then again, it isn't always evident what's spiritual and what isn't. For some crime can be spiritual, or can be an essential component of life's spiritual fabric.

Even though he was no longer mayor, Marcelo Ebrard still had his security detail, all of its members selected from various branches of the Mexico City police. Almost always there was at least one of his *guarura* in our lobby, and frequently, when Ebrard was in the building but going somewhere soon, there was a whole team. At night some always slept on cots in a little room carved from a storage area in the lower-level parking garage. The *guarura* in their black suits stood out in front of the building by the attendant row of SUVs, and staked out the corners of the park and side streets. I'd gotten to know a number of them over the past year. I didn't have a television in my apartment and sometimes went downstairs to watch *fútbol* matches with them on the cheap television set with bad reception behind the doorman's reception desk. Fernando looked like a prototypical *guarura*, a burly hard guy with a mustache, probably in his forties. Reading *The Mongolian Conspiracy*, Rafael Bernal's classic novel about the veteran Mexico City police *pistolero* Filiberto García, I kept picturing Fernando. It was always kind of touching to see the surly-looking Fernando out front in the park mornings or evenings, walking the Ebrards' prim little schnauzer. Some of the other security men looked like college professors or lawyers. Fernando told me that one of the tests given to applicants trying to qualify for the security corps is to have their jumping ability measured on a trampoline. This is to ensure that they have the leg strength and agility to hurl their bodies into the air to shield or even catch a bullet meant for their charge. It can be a treacherous job, being an official *guarura* in Mexico. Once I was watching the news with Fernando when a story came on about a team of bodyguards who were ambushed and assassinated after letting the man they protected off at the airport in Coahuila. Fernando said that sometimes—though not necessarily in this case—a corrupt politician or businessman will set up his own *guarura* to be killed because they've witnessed or learned too much about his dirty deeds.

As a former Mexico City chief of police, Ebrard doubtless chose an elite, trustworthy group of men to protect him. When I came back from Tepito that Saturday evening, I found a number of them crowded onto the leather couch in the lobby, including one I thought looked like a law professor, a trim man with black-framed eyeglasses, always in a crisp white shirt and suit, who seemed to be their unit's leader. He seemed not only intelligent but also shrewd and sharply alert. We spoke about the Heavens case. I told them what the merchant policeman had said about the *levantón*, that it was unlikely that any such commando operation could have been carried out in the heart of the Zona Rosa without police complicity. The professor agreed, and said that it wouldn't be the first time something like this had happened in Mexico City over the years. Only this time it was front-page news. He laughed, and so did his companions.

"Do you think there was a political motive behind it?" I asked. "Do you think the PRI could have an infiltrator high up in the police?" "It's possible," said the professor. He looked amused, but his expression was knowing. I asked, "What if it's Mancera who's the infiltrator?" The professor laughed again and said, "Stranger things have happened in Mexico."

*   *   *

July 25: At seven in the evening I go down to the Jesuit church
on the corner, to the Mass at which Aura's name will be spoken
during the prayer for departed souls, and sit alone, near the
front, choosing a spot that offers a direct view of the Virgin of
Guadalupe's side chapel off to the right of the altar. Because of
Aura's professed devotion to La Guadalupana, whenever I step
into a church or cathedral anywhere now, I always pray, in my
manner, at least briefly to the Virgin, and ask her to look after
Aura. It's a different priest this time, not the ancient, jovial
one who officiated last year. This priest is younger, seventy or
so, silver-haired, European, his cheeks rosy; he seems pleasant
enough and leads a crisp, straightforward Mass. Although this
year I'm alone, as I'd wanted to be, my mind is all over the place,
I can't concentrate at all. I can't even sustain my silent beseech-
ing prayer to the Virgin. I am thinking about Tepito, the case,
this *crónica*, my impatience to get back to my novel, everything
I need to do to prepare for the move with Jovi in September
to Brooklyn, my own inability to concentrate, and whatever
else. *Concentrate, cabrón*! But today I have the attention span
of a goldfish, darting after every drifting thought-crumb. Then
I hear, almost like a continuation of my own thoughts, "Aura
Estrada de Goldman" . . . and then other names. The priest is
offering the prayer for the departed much earlier in the Mass
this year than in others, practically at the beginning. And I've
missed it! I slump back in the pew, fuming. What the fuck! The
way I've thought about these yearly Masses is that I should be
able to at least build a silent altar for Aura inside myself and
sustain it there until that climactic moment when her name is
spoken, along with those of others, during the prayer for the

departed. Now what? I stand when the rest of the congregants stand, and sit back down when they sit, and stay seated when they kneel. I don't cross myself, and I remain silent when the others recite their parts of the prayers or sing along with a hymn. My concentration doesn't improve. I feel bored and restless. I'm not a practicing Catholic, not a practicing anything, what am I doing here? I get a call on my phone from Yoshua and hurry outside to tell him I'll call him after the Mass. For a moment I stand on the church steps and consider not going back inside but heading to the bar across the street. I have the novel I've been reading with me.

But I go back inside, and sit in the same pew, and find myself still unable to concentrate or listen to the Mass. Then I hear again, just audibly enough to surprise my attention, "Aura," and a run of other names—the priest is apparently reciting a second prayer for the eternal souls of the dead, as if somehow he knows that I missed the first one, but this time naming the departed only by their first names. "Sacred Sacrament," he says with finality, among other words, when he is done. I feel totally flummoxed. I've missed this prayer too. When the congregants again drop to their knees, onto the narrow planks at the bottom of the pews in front, I drop to my knees too. Why did I do that? Inside the moment and later, I honestly don't know. I just did. I have a bad knee and it aches sharply against the plank. I clasp my hands atop the pew in front practically just to hold myself steady as I shift my weight and try to position my knee so it won't hurt. And I also reflect that, really, I never find myself in this particular posture, of humility or submission, down on my knees. When was the last time? At Aura's funeral, which I barely even remember, I was so out of my senses that day? In this posture faithful Catholics humble themselves before or open themselves to their God. I don't have a God, but the posture itself works like a genetic muscle memory imprinted by millennia of religiously faithful ancestors. I don't know how else to put it, really—I feel Death pressing down on me. I feel Death's weight in my bones, feel clamped and pinned by it, there as I kneel. Finally I'm absorbed by what is happening, all senses focused on this one event, which is a humbling before Death, the Truth and fact of it. It happened. Six years ago today, death altered my life in a way I had never imagined anything could alter it. I am filled with a heavy sensation of resignation, and even something like exhausted but grateful submission, like that of someone long on the run from the law who finally turns himself in. There's no shaking you, Death. I'm not who I was before I met you, and now we go everywhere together. It's my duty to know you, Death. In the moment I understand all of this almost wordlessly. I've unexpectedly supplied my own rite, made it with my body by kneeling, which opened me for what came. I kneel before Aura's death like a medieval knight kneeling before his queen to make a vow. What vow? Just to keep going, but also to try to live responsibly with my knowledge of Death, and to try to be good, and also fearless when it counts. I'll fail, but not always. Try to quit smoking again, I think, but that comes under trying to be good, as does so much else. Those are my vows.

We are all back in our seats again. We are nearing the end of the Mass because it's the part, which I always like, when you stand and wish peace on your neighbor, shaking hands with whomever you can reach. I shake hands with a diminutive elderly lady dressed in black, and her smile is wonderful. When I sit down again, I shift my gaze to the Virgin of Guadalupe and the words, silently, come out of me, Take care of Aura, take good care of her wherever she is, Virgencita, and help her to be happy

if you can, if she knows what happened to her, if she's conscious
of all that she's missed out on, if she knows, please help her Virgencita, and tell her that she's always with me. . . . A sweet-sad
gush of prayer is what that felt like—the priest says the Mass is
over, and I'm getting up to leave—and I look back at her again
and think that I truly am fond of the Virgin of Guadalupe and
that if I were much younger, I'd even get myself a big radiant
tattoo of her image. But I instantly reject the idea, out of some
awkward sense of filial duty to my late Jewish father. This only
reflects how conventionally my mind can work, since what has
my father or my age to do with it? And then I think I should
get the Virgin of Guadalupe tattoo, if only on the chance that
someday, in a morgue, I can befuddle a coroner or medical ex-
aminer who with the reflexes of his own conventional mind will
suppose that the wrong name tag has been affixed to my corpse's
toe. And then what will he do? I leave the church grinning.

Minutes later, in the bar across the street from the church,
sitting at a table outside, sipping my first *mezcal,* I write all this
down in my notebook.

On May 26, Sunday afternoon, within hours of the morning's
levantón, and on the next day, family members from Tepito, individually and in groups, had gone to CAPEA, the Procuraduría's
missing persons office, to report the kidnapping of their sons
and daughters. The spokesman for the Procuraduría, the chief
prosecutor's office, told Pablo de Llano that the reason four days
had passed before the possibility of a mass kidnapping outside
the after-hours club on Calle Lancaster was even acknowledged
by his boss was that in CAPEA it was initially assumed that those
missing persons reports weren't connected to the same place or

to any one group of people. Just an honest mistake, according to the spokesman. But the family members knew that their missing had been taken from Heavens, and had told this to the people at CAPEA. On Monday, June 3, Pablo and I went to the Federal Human Rights office in Coyoacán—believing we might find the families there, since that morning in Tepito we'd been told that this was where they were—and spoke to a woman, Guadalupe Cabrera, who was assigned to the Heavens case. Members of ten of the families had met with her that morning, she said, but now they'd left. Cabrera had copies of their original CAPEA statements on her desk, and after a bit of badgering by the two of us, she confirmed that the family members had individually reported that the young people had been in the after-hours club, and that they had vanished together.

From the start, the Mancera government's handling of the case, in both actions and statements, established a pattern that constantly left you suspecting either incompetence or malfeasance. On Thursday, June 6, after an armed commando group assassinated four people in a Tepito gym called Body Extreme, the sense grew that the city was reeling out of control. The media fanned that impression, and not just in the pro-PRI Televisa and TV Azteca mainstream. On June 9 the cover of the influential left-leaning weekly magazine *Proceso* blared the headline "The Emergence of Criminal Violence. The True DF." It was accompanied by a color photograph of Mayor Mancera, whose ears stick out, looking less like George Clooney and more like Gollum in a suit and a tie, forehead sweaty, eyes reddened and glaring, lips sharply pulled down at the corners. Inside there was another photo of the mayor, flanked by his chief prosecutor and police chief, seated at a press conference, looking pale and despondent, staring down at the floor. In its cover story, *Proceso* revealed, as did other news reports that week, that in 2010 groups of armed young men had begun turning up around midnight at Condesa and Zona Rosa nightspots, telling owners and managers that they were there to sell drugs, and threatening reprisals against those who refused them entrance. "Any owner who opposes their coming inside gets lifted," a man told another newspaper, "*y le dan en la madre*"—and they fuck you up. Ismael Rivera Cruces, president of the National Association of Owners of Licensed "Discotecas, Bares y Centros de Espectáculos," told *Proceso* that about 150 of the 250 nightspots in those two neighborhoods received such visits. (Heavens was one of hundreds of unlicensed clubs in the zone.) "The drug dealers had to abandon many of the places because there was little business," said Rivera Cruces. He spoke about the problem to officials in Ebrard's government, including Rodolfo Ríos Garza, who was personal secretary to then Chief Prosecutor Mancera; and to Jesús Rodríguez Almeida, then a sub-prosecutor and now Mancera's chief of police. He said he received little response. But, he said, "Curiously, [the drug dealers] retreated for a while and the space was tranquil throughout 2011."

In November and December 2012, when Mancera took office, the dealers came back in force. Now sometimes as many as twenty or thirty arrived at the clubs and bars in old automobiles, carrying assault weapons. "They were armed and told the business owners that if they didn't let them work they'd kill them or burn their places down," said Rivera Cruces. As a warning, some establishments received funeral wreaths with the owner's name; others received decapitated dogs' heads. Now the drug dealers were hitting places not just in the Condesa and Zona Rosa, but in the Roma, in the Center, and in other *colonias*. Rivera Cruces told *Proceso* that he didn't know who the dealers were, whether they were with a cartel, or whom they worked for. Two months before the Heavens *levantón*, Rivera Cruces went to speak to Chief Prosecutor Ríos about the worsening situation; he said that Ríos told him the owners were obligated to denounce the drug dealers to the police, because if the owners let them in, they became accomplices. "I told him, sure," said Rivera Cruces, "and we'll pay for those denunciations with our lives." The "delinquents," he told the magazine, never partied with the other clients; they just stood and watched, while others stayed outside, observing the people arriving, "how they paid, if they wore watches, etcetera." I couldn't recall seeing people like that, or drugs being sold openly, at the Colonia Roma after-hours club Reyna and I frequented last summer; but when the club was shut down by the city for a few months this spring, the rumor was that drug dealing on the premises had something to do with it. Now the place is open again, though I haven't been there this summer. The usual clientele there ranged in age from the twenties to the forties, and it was obvious that there was plenty of drug use. "How else are people going to dance until seven in the morning?" said Reyna, when we talked about it the other day.

In the weeks following the Heavens *levantón,* reports of a few other apparent kidnappings from nightspots appeared in the press. One of those had occurred in April, when five young men had disappeared from Bar Virtual, in Colonia 18 de Marzo. Their families came forward only after they saw how quickly the media and authorities responded to the Tepito families stopping traffic on the Eje 1. Neighbors from Colonia Pensador Mexicano (Mexican Thinker) and other *colonias* near the airport blocked the Circuito Interior in protest against the authorities' indifference to the disappearance of an eighteen-year-old boy from a bar the week before. The press also began to report on the workings of the *narcomenudeo* in the city. According to the SSP, the public security ministry headed by the chief of police, there are five thousand *narco-tienditas,* places where you can buy drugs, operating in the city. But a study carried out by the DF's legislative assembly put the number at thirteen thousand and concluded that they operated "with complete impunity." One delegate said, "It's easier to buy coke powder in the DF at night than Coca-Cola," which doesn't seem like much of an exaggeration to me.

Mancera appointed a special operations force to conduct an investigation into the Heavens case, parallel to those being carried out by the Procuraduría's anti-kidnapping police and other police units. And he flooded both the Zona Rosa and Tepito with heavily armed police patrols. Bars and clubs were raided and shut down. Mancera announced a plan to shut down all after-hours clubs in the city, though that didn't seem likely to happen. On June 4, Chief Prosecutor Ríos announced that the kidnappers had belonged to a *pandilla*, a gang, and not to an organized crime group, i.e., a national or transnational drug cartel. For the first time since the disappearance, Ríos made mention of La Unión, supposedly founded in 2010, a Tepito gang that allegedly controlled, or wanted to control, the Zona Rosa–Condesa–Roma drug *plaza*. From then on La Unión would remain at the center of official accounts and speculations about the case. However, the same day, Mancera declared that there was no proof—in the form of "witness, scientific, or documented evidence"—that the missing twelve had even been in After Heavens that night. A few days later, when another young man was gunned down in Tepito, becoming the ninth person murdered in the barrio in the first eight days of June, Mancera declared that it was "the same situation we've always had in Tepito." The mainstream newspaper *Milenio* published, probably as a result of a leak, that this last slain youth "possibly could have worked for a relative of 'El Tanque.'"

Meanwhile prosecutors and police had been going over images from the private and city security cameras on Calle Lancaster, and had discovered footage that showed seven of the Tepito young people arriving at the after-hours club at four in the morning in two vehicles: a dark red compact car and a taxi. They had come to After Heavens from Bar Cristal on Avenida Cuahtémoc in Colonia Roma. Bar Cristal was promptly searched by police and shut down; it was reported to be a hangout for La Unión gang members. The next day, June 7, the prosecutor's office announced the discovery of footage showing the actual *levantón* as it occurred, which, after sharing it with the families of the missing, Ríos unveiled at a press conference. The images, filmed from a distance and blurry, showed about seventeen men pulling up in front of the club in eight cars, mostly compacts. The men milled around and walked up and down the sidewalk and street in front of Heavens. They appeared to be unarmed, and their faces were uncovered. According to Ríos, the footage showed nine of the missing young people exiting the club, and docilely getting into the waiting cars. But according to some, including Josefina García, the mother of Said Sánchez, "You don't see the *muchachos* getting into the cars." And neither Jorge Ortíz nor Said Sánchez was visible in the video. So, no assault weapons, no commandos with their faces hidden, and no vans, as the first and so far only publicly known witness, Toñín, had reported to CAPEA. Chief Prosecutor Ríos said at the press conference, "We discount the participation of a commando operation. What we can credit is the intervention of a gang that arrived in various vehicles." There had been no "violence"; it had been a peaceful *levantón*. Ríos ascribed the mass kidnapping to a conflict between two rival Tepito gangs. He added that there was "a connecting thread" between the Heavens kidnapping and the slaying of Horacio Vite Ángel, the drug dealer murdered outside the bar Black in the Condesa two days before.

During those days the first arrests were made in the case. Heavens' head of security, Gabriel Carrasco, "El Diablo," was captured along with his driver-bodyguard, Andrés Henonet González, and the wife of one of the club's three owners. The next day, apparently in response to his wife's capture, that owner, Mario Rodríguez Ledezma, "El Moschino," turned himself in. El Diablo had told his interrogators that a few days before the kidnapping, El Moschino, along with another of the bar's owners, Ernesto Espinosa Lobo, "El Lobo," and the club's manager, Ismael García, "Polo," had told him and other employees to be ready to help out with a *levantón* at the club that Sunday. "Which is to say," he said, "they were going to put some subjects, apparently from Tepito, in place to be lifted." He said that he'd understood that Jerzy Ortíz, El Tanque's son, was the operation's target. El Moschino mentioned to his interrogators that the club's manager, Polo, had told him that the kidnappers included members of La Unión. According to El Moschino, dealers from La Unión had sold drugs inside Heavens. When the police studied the phone records of the drug dealer executed outside the bar Black in the Condesa, they revealed that he'd been in regular telephone contact with Heavens' manager, Polo. It might be that the dealer, Vite Ángel, worked for Polo, who'd told him when and where to sell his drugs. At least one newspaper reported, apparently on the basis of the detained owner's testimony, that dealers from La Unión had told Polo that he would be killed in retaliation for the dealer Vita Ángel's murder unless he helped to deliver the people they wanted from Tepito. But according to another report I came across in the press, Polo had boasted that he was the one who'd murdered Vita Ángel. So Polo was obviously a key figure, but he was a fugitive. The two other owners, Ernesto Espinosa, El Lobo, and El Moschino's brother, Dax Rodríguez Ledezma, were fugitives too.

In Tepito, on June 9, a youth was murdered and another wounded, when they were gunned down by men who'd chased them through the streets in an automobile. The next day *Milenio* had a headline quoting Mancera's exhortation: "Speak Well About the DF." At almost the same time as the shooting in Tepito, Mancera made an appearance in the Metropolitan Cathedral on behalf of a family assistance program, accompanied by Cardinal Norberto Rivera and Rigoberta Menchú, the Guatemalan Nobel Peace Prize winner, who resides in the DF. Addressing the press and the others assembled there, Mayor Mancera said: "Mexico City is all of us, and Mexico City is stronger today. It's strong and it's alive and therein is the proof of our strength. Let's speak well about Mexico City, let's talk about all the good things that happen in this city every day, and our government will take care of the rest, and in that we have many allies. Our most important ally is our social fabric, the strength represented by the men and women of this capital."

Mancera spoke that day, or tried to speak, as a DF mayor is expected to, confidently cheerleading for the city and the competence of his own government. But his words were also patronizing and somewhat Big Brotherish. Over the coming days and weeks, Mancera was more visible than before, frequently speaking out in that exhortatory and optimistic way, and presiding over a group same-sex wedding. Mancera repeatedly emphasized that, despite the Heavens case and the violence in Tepito, the DF's overall murder and crime rate had not gone up at all. Mancera was not wrong about that, though news stories, in the national and international press, precisely because of the Heavens case, were suggesting the opposite. But Mancera still needed his government to solve the case and to find out what had happened to the twelve missing young people. Mancera had already fired the head of CAPEA over its perceived bumbling of the case in the first days. And now he publicly warned both his chief prosecutor and his chief of police that they should not consider their jobs secure if they couldn't produce results.

Mancera was still insisting that there were no "organized crime" groups operating in the city. If he were to acknowledge that these existed, then the Heavens case would become the responsibility of federal prosecutors and their police investigators. Though Mancera had asked the PGR, the office of the attorney general of Mexico, for help in finding the missing twelve wherever they might be in Mexico, he was determined to keep the case tightly under his government's control. After all, what big city in the world doesn't have local drug gangs that sometimes turn violent or go to war against each other?

On June 29, while conducting an antinarcotics operation in the city that *was* under the jurisdiction of the PGR, federal police busted a drug den—a house where drugs were sold and consumed—in Coyoacán. There, they found and arrested one of the two fugitive owners of After Heavens, El Lobo, Ernesto Espinosa. El Lobo was allegedly involved in running the Coyoacán den. That night he was driving a yellow Hummer, and was, reportedly, on drugs. The feds turned El Lobo over to city prosecutors.

The investigation seemed to be advancing. But El Lobo's capture raised disconcerting questions. Mancera had a special task force assigned to the Heavens case. The Procuraduría's anti-kidnapping force and the SSP's Mexico City police were at work on the case, combing the streets. And who should know the streets of the DF and the workings of its criminal underworld better than the police? Not only do Mexico City police know criminals; many police are in league with criminals. But there are also internal affairs units that monitor the police—several hundred police have been sent to trial and prison in recent years.* A lot of people had been involved in the After Heavens *levantón*, at least seventeen kidnappers for starters, and people talk—criminals to other criminals and to their friends, to police, to people who inform for the police; police among themselves; and so on. With informers and security cameras everywhere, no part of the city should be impenetrable to the Mexico City police, and those whom the police really want to capture should never be impossible to find, so long as they are still in the DF. So then how could it be that El Lobo, running a drug den, driving his yellow Hummer around the DF, while on drugs no less, had eluded the Mexico City police during the month when he was one of the most wanted men in the city? And how could it be that, of the seventeen men who prosecutors had said carried out the kidnappings, who had arrived at Heavens in eight cars, captured by security cameras, not a single one had been arrested? Didn't it defy logic to believe that merely a gang of

* "In two and a half years, 415 judicial and preventive police were brought before the criminal courts for involvement in some activity outside the law. . . . According to the Public Information Office of the Chief Prosecutor of the Federal District (PGJDF) the 415 agents were involved in crimes such as abuse of authority, aggravated robbery, sexual abuse, bribery, deprivation of liberty, express kidnapping, murder, malicious wounding, covering up crimes, unlawful exercise of public service, [and] aggravated rape" (*Crónica*, February 11, 2013).

local drug dealers, many of whom were probably adolescents, could carry out such a cartel-style *levantón* at eleven-thirty on a Sunday morning in the heart of the Zona Rosa? Wouldn't they have known that such an audacious and unprecedented crime in the DF would be likely to attract the focus of the national and even international media, and inevitably trigger a major police investigation and manhunt? Why would a local Tepito gang, in cartel terminology, so *heat up the plaza*, and bring all of that heat down on themselves?

On July 2 three charred bodies turned up in the municipality of Huitzilac, in Morelos, a state that has become a gruesome war zone contested by rival cartels, a part of which borders on Mexico City. One corpse was that of the third Heavens owner, Dax Rodríguez Ledezma, brother of El Moschino, and the other two belonged to two women: his cousin, Heidi Fabiola Rodríguez, thirty-three; and his girlfriend, Diana Guadalupe Velasco, an eighteen-year-old university student. They'd been snatched after coming out of a movie theater in Iguala, Guerrero, also one of Mexico's most violent, narco-contested states. According to the federal attonery general's office, the victims had been tortured and murdered in Guerrero, and their bodies had been transported to and left in Huitzilac, hundreds of miles away. That is to say, the bodies had been planted—somebody had wanted them to be found in that place.

This orchestrated triple homicide did not seem like the work of a local Tepito gang. However, in the DF, Chief Prosecutor Ríos did not make much of it; he merely lamented that now his investigators would not be able to interrogate the third owner of Heavens. Mancera's government said that the murder was under the jurisdiction of police in Morelos, because that was where the bodies were found. In Morelos that claim was rejected—the police there said it was the DF's case to investigate. And so, at least as of this writing, no further investigation had been made into the murder of Dax Rodríguez Ledezma and the two women.

A city judge had already dispatched El Diablo, along with his chauffer-thug and Dax's brother Mario, El Moschino, to prison on pretrial kidnapping charges. The club's manager, Polo, and all the kidnappers remained at large. Only two weeks after the crime, in June, the Tepito families had publicly called on President Peña Nieto and the federal government to intervene in the case. During the second week of July the families finally met with federal prosecutors to ask them to take over. But they were told that the PGR couldn't do so until the DF declared the involvement of "organized crime" and formally requested help or handed over the case. Those the families spoke with at the PGR confided that they did believe "organized crime"—a national narco cartel—was involved, but added that they couldn't say so publicly. However, two or three days later, the families' lawyer shared that opinion with the press, making it seem as if it was his own.

I wondered: if the families knew about any of the missing young people's involvement in criminal activities that could have provoked such an extreme retaliation, or if city prosecutors and investigators had shared any such information with them, would they so openly and insistently be pressuring to push the case forward? The families, especially the mothers, clung to the belief that the victims were still alive, and these relatives would do anything to get them back, whatever they had been involved in before. At a press conference, a female journalist directed a question to the families as a whole, skeptically asking if they really believed that their missing relatives could still be alive. One of the mothers responded, "Do you have children?" The journalist answered that she didn't. The mother said, "Then you don't understand the question you're asking."

By mid-July, the Heavens case was fading as a news story. Since the murder of Dax Rodríguez Ledezma, there really had been nothing new to report. Perhaps this allowed Mancera to feel that he was bringing the situation under control. Meanwhile, President Peña Nieto and his government, including federal prosecutors and police, had maintained a wall of silence regarding the Heavens case and the situation in the DF. My own best off-the-record source, a man with years of experience in the government of the DF and the Mexico City police, said, "The PRI could have rung the bell, Here come the Apaches! They could have had Mancera's head. Instead they went forty-five days without opening their mouths. They didn't even bite during Mancera's weakest moment."—i.e., during the first days and weeks after the *levantón*.

Then, on July 11, forty-five days after the abductions, Peña Nieto's commissioner of national security—something like his chief federal police investigator—Manuel Mondragón, broke that silence. During an interview with the television news show *Primeras Noticias*, Mondragón said that organized crime "was getting a little out of control in the DF," and that in some zones, such as Tepito, it had "crystallized." The interviewer asked him if he meant that there were national drug cartels, such as the Sinaloa Cartel or the Zetas, in Mexico City, and Mondragón responded, "Not overtly, except in some areas as in this case we're talking about [Tepito]. There it is manifesting itself, and we're seeing the results of that." Apparently referring to a Tepito "gang," or gangs, he said, "I believe they must have . . . it's possible that they have connections with other cartels from outside, but they are there in the city, with naturalization cards." Twice during the interview he repeated that figurative mention of naturalization cards, implying that the cartels' presence was known and accepted. Mondragón had been Ebrard's chief of police and the two were close; when Mondragón accepted the post under Peña Nieto, Ebrard even publicly wished him well. In the interview, Mondragón had spoken carefully, as if reluctant to put the DF's current mayor in a difficult spot. But his words instantly became the day's top story and Heavens was back in the news, in bold headlines. "Mondragón Sees Cartels in the DF" and, beneath it, "Mancera Denies It" were on *Milenio*'s front page, and the headlines in other newspapers were similar.

"What's happening in the Distrito Federal?" Salvador Camarena of *El País* asked when he interviewed Marcelo Ebrard in late June.

Ebrard answered, "I'd better not get into that, not now. I've already been *jefe de gobierno*."

"They say you're moving the new mayor's chair"—that is, undermining or even conspiring against him—said the journalist.

"What would I gain by moving his chair? That would be putting the city at risk; it would be opening the way for the PRI."

"It appears that the current *jefe de gobierno*, Miguel Ángel Mancera, has many enemies."

Ebrard didn't deny it. "I'm not among his enemies," he said. "On the contrary."

One plausible element in a strategy for the PRI to eventually take back the DF would be rendering the PRD defunct or irrelevant as a national party, and thus "opening the way for the PRI." The PRI might be able to accomplish that now by simply watching the party self-destruct. The PRD was drubbed in Mexico's summer local elections. In one year, it fell from being Mexico's main opposition party, a serious contender for power, to being the country's third party, behind the PAN. Many blamed the losses on party leaders Jesús Zambrano and Jesús Ortega, PRD insiders who gained control of the party in the wake of Andrés Manuel López Obrador's defection to form his own political organization. The pair, with whom Mayor Mancera had cast his lot, are known as "Los Chuchos"—Chucho is a common Mexican nickname for people named Jesús. It was Los Chuchos who negotiated the PRD's participation in Peña Nieto and the PRI's "Pact for Mexico." There's nothing wrong, of course, about an opposition party working with the party in power on reforms—of the education and tax systems, of media and labor laws, and so on—to improve a country. It made sense that to withdraw from the Pact for Mexico would strip the PRD of legislative influence, an argument Zambrano often asserted. But by going all in on the Pact for Mexico before Mexico and even the PRD's congressional delegation knew what all of its agreements were, Los Chuchos seemed to have abdicated their party's political identity, which is one that provides a critical opposition voice from the left. On June 17, when Peña Nieto was in the United Kingdom for a G-8 meeting, the *Financial Times* published an interview with him in which he announced a plan to reform the constitution to permit a privatization of Pemex, the behemoth national petroleum industry. In the interview, Peña Nieto said that the opposition parties, including the PRD, who'd signed the Pact for Mexico had already agreed to the potentially historic reform. Ever since Lázaro Cárdenas nationalized the oil industry in 1938, expropriating U.S. and Anglo-Dutch companies, Pemex has been an icon of Mexican national sovereignty.

Extremely corrupt, troubled, and dysfunctional as Pemex unsurprisingly is, poll after poll shows that the majority of the population opposes its privatization. Many Mexicans may be less against a reform of the national oil industry that could include some privatization than they are against giving the PRI, with its obvious legacy of patronage and corruption, the opportunity to carry this out. Nobody has forgotten the squalid crony enrichment of the PRI privatizations carried out by President Carlos Salinas and his government.

The *Financial Times* story kicked up a storm. "Chucho" Zambrano denied that he'd secretly agreed to the Pemex constitutional reform, but members of Peña Nieto's cabinet and PRI senators came forward to say, adamantly, that he had. The controversy opened the way for Marcelo Ebrard's return to the political spotlight. He challenged Peña Nieto to a public debate over what to do about Pemex, and insisted that any proposed constitutional reform of the petroleum company be voted on in a national referendum. Ebrard called on the PRD to pull out of Peña Nieto's Pact for Mexico.

In a column in SinEmbargo.com titled "The Chucho Train, the Mancera Train," Alejandro Páez Varela, the digital site's founder and editor, wrote of Zambrano and Ortega, "[T]heir 'enemies' are multiplying by the hour . . . the overwhelming majority of Mexico City's congressional delegation has decided to sign a letter that says NO to the PRD leadership's intention to negotiate an energy reform that includes an opening to privatize Pemex . . . This train is losing steam. And its engineers are all alone. . . . 'Los Chuchos' conspire and search for allies. They discover that every day they have fewer. They cling to the other engine that is losing steam day after day: the Jefe de Gobierno's. Now it's two engines that are going nowhere. . . . Mancera is paying the price for having gone to bed with 'Los Chuchos.' So the Jefe de Gobierno shuts himself inside his four walls. He can't face his voters. How, if the twelve *chamacos* from Tepito are still 'absent'? He can't face the leaders of the left. How, if he's already been bought by another band?"

On July 20, at a public event packed with PRD politicians and supporters, Ebrard announced a new movement, the Progressive Movement, to renovate and change the party's direction. The event itself signaled Ebrard's ambition to take control of the PRD, and to oust Zambrano as its leader. "We are going to be a counterweight to the excesses and abuses of the PRI," declared Ebrard.

"In Mexico Machiavelli couldn't even get elected to a local leadership post," Ebrard said of Mexican politics when we spoke again in the summer of 2013. "Nobody here reads his books because they're too obvious, they're like folklore." Ebrard said, "The party's leadership is a disaster. They just want to be a little moon of the earth," the earth being Peña Nieto, whom Ebrard also compared to a monarch. "People need us to be their voice. But these leaders are with the Bourbons, and Paris isn't represented anymore."

The proposed privatization of Pemex had handed Ebrard a "line in the sand" issue. "The people who tell us not to be nationalistic are two of the most nationalistic countries in the world," he said, "the United States and the United Kingdom. Of course we need to be nationalistic; finally that's what this is all about, what kind of project can we carry out as a country, or not. How do we maximize our profits from petroleum? Their basic argument is that we don't have the technology and we don't have the resources, and so we have to open up and share a majority of what's ours. They say, Don't be ideological—but their ideological argument is the worst because they say privatization is always the best, and that argument is nothing more than the last remnants of Thatcherismo. You listen to Peña Nieto, his life story is from Atlacamulco [the president's birthplace] to Thatcher."

Pemex needs major reforms, said Ebrard. "[Pemex's] union is extremely corrupt, but the PRI doesn't want to reform it, because it's an ally of the PRI." The union is a sinkhole of corruption that squanders millions upon millions of dollars every year, through its contributions to PRI election campaigns and in other ways. "Pemex's administrative council is madness, filled with political appointees," said Ebrard. "So, Pemex is bad because we're Mexicans and this is how we do everything, and so we'd better sell to Exxon? Of course we can do better. The argument that we don't have the resources is scandalous." It was a decision, he said, not a preordained destiny, not to reform and invest. "We can have technology, but we have to make that decision. It's a decision."

Ebrard didn't want to speak much, on the record, about his successor's troubles as mayor and about the Heavens case, though he did say the latter was likely to have lasting repercussions.

One Sunday, June 23, one day short of a month since the Heavens *levantón*, I'd again accompanied Pablo de Llano to Tepito. At the subway stop we were met by Juan, the younger brother of Alan Omar Atiencia Barranco, twenty-six, one of the missing youths, married to Karen Morales Vargas, twenty-five, also taken from Heavens that Sunday morning. Their two families live in the same *vecindad* on a street a little outside the Tepito market area. We hadn't walked very far when we noticed that a kid, about fourteen, small and wiry, had fallen in step just behind us. He was wearing a bright yellow and blue América *fútbol* team jersey. Sometimes he pulled alongside and looked at us, his stare moving from one face to the other, and then fell back again. Pablo wondered if maybe he was a relative of the Atiencia Barrancos, but Juan hadn't greeted or even acknowledged him. When we reached the *vecindad* the kid followed us through the open doorway, down the tunnel-like entrance alley that led to a small courtyard, where there was a glass shrine strung with Christmas lights, and with statues of the Virgin, San Judas Tadeo, and El Niño de Antorcha inside. Most of the *vecindades* have such shrines in their courtyards, paid for and tended by their residents. Another alley, to the right of the shrine, led to a larger courtyard in back. A steep concrete staircase led to Karen Morales Vargas's family's home, perched like a cave dwelling in the wall above the smaller courtyard. With a smirk that was mocking, or maybe deranged, the kid glanced at us and left, back down the alley to the sidewalk. Later Pablo asked if I thought the kid was a *halcón,* a falcon: that is, in the vocabulary of contemporary Mexico, somebody who works for a cartel or another crime group as "eyes and ears" in the streets, reporting on strangers who enter its territory.

The Morales Vargas apartment consisted of probably two low-ceilinged bedrooms that we didn't see but where, in the manner typical of the *vecindades*, beds were likely to be shared by children and even adults at night, just off the small living room, with an adjacent tiny kitchen. Inside the apartment, Karen's mother, Ana María Vargas, was seated on the living room couch along with a few of her grandchildren and a Chihuahua. Ruth Marines, the mother of Rafael Rojas Marines, was sitting in an armchair next to the couch. A teenage girl sat at a small table absorbed in her laptop. Pablo and I sat on low plastic stools like the one the girl was sitting on, and Juan stood leaning in a corner. Bureaus and cabinets filled with religious statues and other souvenir-like objects crowded the room, which had the playroom clutter of a home where numerous small children reside, though there were actually few toys to be seen. A large television sat atop one cabinet. Family photographs and religious images covered the walls. One of the photographs, inside the largest frame, was of a handsome young man in a *fútbol* shirt, his name, Cesar Adrian Morales Vargas, in calligraphic lettering in the poster matting alongside the photo, with "5 Julio 1984–19 Agosto 2011" and some phrases such as "rest in peace . . . forever in our hearts," though I don't recall the exact words. Karen's mother was a diminutive, pretty fortysomething woman, in a sweatshirt and jeans. Ruth Marines, in a dark dress, was taller and more heavyset, with a good-natured face that also suggested a strong character. Both had the classic Mexican features: prominent cheekbones, full lips, vivid dark eyes, and seemingly ageless brown skin. The mood in the room was warm and friendly. It didn't feel like sitting down with two mothers who were facing the possible death of two children in the most horrific of circumstances. Mexican politeness, I thought, a nearly obliging levity, and also, maybe, the way mothers know they need to be when there are small children in the room. We talked about the Chihuahua, who was named Pecas and belonged to Karen's younger sister Jéssica, the eighteen-year-old sitting at the computer. Karen's Chihuahua, Chiquis, was Pecas's mother, but as Karen was not there to take care of her, Chiquis had been sent to stay with in-laws. Karen and Alan Omar had three children.

Ana María, Karen's mother, owned a little sidewalk stand outside the *vecindad* where she sold candies, popsicles, and *chicharrones*.

That was now providing the family with what they had to live on. Karen had worked selling lingerie and bikinis from a stand out on the *eje*. Karen and her mother had an especially close bond. Pablo told me that Ana María did not hide even from her other children that Karen was her favorite. The last time Ana María saw Karen was at one in the morning on the Sunday of the *levantón*. She'd just packed away her candy stand, and was carrying out trash, and Karen came down the stairs and helped her. Alan Omar and their friend Monse—Monserrat Loza, also one of the disappeared—waited out on the sidewalk. Karen was wearing beige slacks and matching beige heels, and a loose black blouse embroidered in front with rhinestones. She was carrying a black bag with a golden chain strap—Jéssica piped up from the corner to add that the bag was studded. Karen had ironed her black hair even straighter than it already was but hadn't put in a flip curl over her forehead, as she usually did when she went out for the night.

Alan Omar worked at a stand that repaired cell phones. Though married to Karen, he lived with his mother, María Victoria Barranco, in a neighboring apartment in the *vecindad*. The two families were tight-knit, sharing the duties of raising the three children. Alan Omar's father was a merchant seaman from Ecuador who'd turned up in Tepito one day and stayed; now he was gravely ill. A fair-haired, light-skinned little boy, one of the children on the couch in the living room, had inherited the Ecuadoran's features. Alan Omar was a devoted fan of América, the *fútbol* team that on Sunday night, May 26, would play Cruz Azul for the Mexican League championship. Alan Omar had planned to watch at home, and had asked his mother, before going out for the night with his wife and Monse, to have his favorite snacks ready. That Sunday afternoon, María Victoria prepared his platter of snacks for the championship match. The match, which América would win, was to begin at eight. As the hours went by and Alan Omar didn't appear, she grew uneasy. Then she, along with the other families in Tepito, received Toñín's terrible message.

Rafael Rojas Marines, thirty-three, sold sunglasses from a stand in front of the Tepito church. In 2004, he'd gone to prison for six years for robbery. He lived with his mother in Tepito. Ruth Marines sat up in her chair and spoke, with a slight smile that seemed both a little chagrined and resigned, about that Saturday night when she'd last seen her son. She knew he was headed out to an *antro,* as nightspots are called, and tried to talk him out of it. "You're going out to fight," she said. "Those places are full of trouble and you get crazy when you drink." But Rafael had been in a bad motorcycle accident six months before, and surgeons had put metal plates and screws into his shattered arm and shoulder. "Don't worry, Jefa," he told her, "I'm going to behave, I couldn't fight now even if I wanted to." Later Marines would tell another interviewer, "When I saw my son leave, I felt something really bad, and I wanted to call him back so that he wouldn't go out." Only two days before his abduction, Rafael had finally had the money to pay a dentist to implant false teeth to replace the three he'd lost in the accident.

"My son Cesar Adrian never set foot in prison," said Ana María, referring to the young man in the memorial photograph on the wall. "He never gave me any trouble. *Era un chavo tranquilo,* an easygoing boy." He was a devotee of San Judas Tadeo, who is the "wholesome" saint, in comparison with La Santa Muerte. But two summers before, on August 19, 2011, Cesar Adrian had gotten into a fight out on the street not far from home. Another youth went to fetch his brother, and quickly it was three against one. Ana María, at her candy stand, heard the volley of gunshots. Cesar Adrian had received nine bullets yet managed to come running down the sidewalk to his mother. "Don't worry," he told her, "I'm going to get out of this, I can do it, I can. Don't cry Mamá, I'm going to get out of this." There was no ambulance at hand, so "*luego luego,*" she flagged a taxi and rushed him to the nearest hospital, but he did not survive his wounds. Three months later, police arrested one of the youths who'd killed her son. The other two, though everyone knew who they were, remained at large. "And the one who was arrested," said Ana María, "wasn't even the one who'd fired the most shots."

Now Jéssica stood up from the computer in which she'd been quietly engrossed throughout our conversation. She was entrancingly pretty, fresh-faced, cheerful. In the United States, I thought, she might be a classic cheerleader type, the kind of girl who always looks as if she must smell of soap and laundry detergent, her shimmering hair newly shampooed. A swath of brown belly showed in the space between her pressed T-shirt and spotless pale tight jeans. "He was shot nine times," she said animatedly. "Four in the chest, and four, no three, in the back, and one in his *pompas,*" his butt. "That's eight," said her mother. "Twice in his *pompas,*" Jéssica added quickly.

"They left five children in the street," said Ana María, referring to her slain son's children. Two were now living with her, three with other families. Ana María has eleven grandchildren in all. "I was in really bad shape," she said. Two of her son's killers were free, but she was afraid to press charges, fearing for the lives of her other children. A psychologist provided by the city finally convinced her, and an arrest warrant was issued for the two, but nothing happened. "They're still walking around these streets."

Another teenager came into the living room. If possible, Brian was even more beautiful than his sister Jéssica. His features resembled hers and his long dark hair was just as lustrous. He was muscular and lithe, covered with tattoos and piercings, but shared his sister's air of pulchritude, even if his T-shirt, "Rebel Fondue" printed on it, and fatigue pants were fashionably ripped. (I remembered Barbara Patterson in *The Savage Detective*s ranting about her boyfriend, that all he does is take showers, "because if nothing else Rafael is clean, like practically all fucking Mexicans," an anthropological observation that, in my experience, is right on the mark.) Just that morning Brian had been let go from criminal detention, where he'd been held for three days for robbery. From the apartment his mother had heard screams down in the street and, heart in mouth, had run outside and seen the police taking her son away. A lady, Brian calmly explained, had accused him of stealing a cell phone and two hundred pesos, equivalent to about seventeen dollars, which he said he hadn't done. The police wanted to charge him with aggravated robbery and *pandillarismo*, gang violence. But the woman hadn't turned up to formally press charges, and so he'd been released.

The conversation turned to another photograph on the wall, of a young woman whose softly sensual face, with large almond eyes, was the most beautiful in the room. Pablo had mentioned to me before how struck he was by the beauty of many of the women he saw while walking around in Tepito. He'd been coming to Tepito several times a week, meeting with families, preparing a piece for *El País* that would include photographs and short profiles of each of the missing twelve, to be published a few days before or on June 26, which would mark a month since the *levantón*.* The woman in the

---

* Pablo de Llano's stirring two-page spread of profiles was published on June 25 (internacional.elpais.com/internacional/2013/06/25/actualidad/1372189257_835177 .html).

photograph was named Nayali, and she'd been the only child of Ana-María's sister-in-law, and a cousin of Jéssica and Brian. She'd been killed, seven years before, in Tepito, at age twenty, by a stray bullet.

It was as if the young dead on the walls had joined us. It was as if they—along with the missing, Karen, Alan Omar, and Rafael; and the certifiably living, mothers, brothers, a sister, orphaned grandchildren; Pablo and me—were conversing in this crowded *vecindad* living room. "Don't cry, Mamá"—as if the photograph on the wall had spoken those words in sync with his mother. We were in the *Pedro Páramo* world of the murmuring, whispering, talkative dead. But this wasn't Rulfo's austere ghost poetry, just as bustling, dangerous Tepito hardly resembles abandoned, desolate Comala. This was more like Aura's *Pedro Páramo,* I thought. She'd had an idea for a novel in which she was going to reinvent *Pedro Páramo* as a modern reality show. In Rulfo's novel, Juan Preciado comes to Comala to look for his father, Pedro Páramo, not yet understanding that everyone he meets in Comala is dead, and that if he's come there, it's because he's dead too. Aura had an obsession with her absent father and in her novel the protagonist's search for her father was to be the subject of a reality television show set in contemporary Mexico. For her novel to be a credible reimagining of *Pedro Páramo*, she would have needed to make the dead be also alive, and vice versa, and, it being set in contemporary Mexico, maybe Aura would have found voices for those who, in the manner of the "disappeared," seem to exist in no definable condition. Maybe her novel, I thought, would have had some resemblance to the conversation—by turns antic, melancholy, disconcerting, even humorous—we were having in this living room in Tepito.

Now thirty-four-year-old Gabriela Téllez, also kidnapped from Heavens, and her nineteen-year-old daughter, Danae Téllez, "joined" the conversation in that room. In the morning Pablo, by phone, had arranged to meet with Danae in Tepito later that afternoon. But since morning she'd stopped answering her cell phone. Sometimes it rang and she didn't pick up, and sometimes it was turned off. Pablo was desperate to meet with Danae for his piece of individual portraits of the twelve missing, because he'd now spoken to and collected photographs from members of every family except Gabriela's, and he was running out of time. Danae was Gabriela's only relative who could really tell him about her. They'd been inseparable. Night after night, mother and daughter had gone out to the *antros*, the bars and clubs, together. They were regulars at After Heavens. Danae had escaped being kidnapped along with her mother because that Saturday night, after going first to Bar Cristal, they'd returned to their Tepito apartment when Danae had felt tired, or unwell. Long past midnight, when friends had phoned Gabriela telling her to come to Heavens, Danae had begged off, saying she wanted to sleep, and her mother had gone alone. Gabriela worked at a computer store in the center, and that was how she'd maintained her household, which included Danae, two other much younger children, and an elderly mother in poor health who'd recently had a knee operation. Ana María and Jéssica knew the Téllezes. Danae wasn't in school, they told us, and had never worked a day in her life. Her mother had always doted on and spoiled Danae, they said. Now she would have to somehow support her younger siblings and grandmother. Danae was described as flighty and immature; she behaved as if she were even younger than Jéssica. She didn't seem to have grasped the reality of what had occurred, or of her new situation. That was also the impression Pablo had taken from his few brief conversations with her, when the families came out of meetings with the chief prosecutor, or held a vigil or stopped traffic. "A typical teenager," he'd told me. Danae was lively and scrappy-seeming, he'd said, quick to laugh, and extremely pretty.

Jéssica suggested that we look at Danae's Facebook page. Pablo and I bent over the computer. Almost the first thing I noticed was that Danae had more than 2,700 Facebook friends. A teenage girl, not in school, unemployed, residing in Tepito, with nearly 3,000 social network "friends." The world is a mystery to me, I thought. We looked at her favorite music: Moenia, Da Fresh, La Rolledera, El Komander. Her favorite movies included *Dead Poets Society* and *El Cartel de los Sapos*, a cable series about a drug cartel. Pablo was clicking through Danae's posted photographs, and enlarged a close-up of her and her mother together: Danae with her cheek pressed against her mother's cheek, her hand on her mother's shoulder. Gabriela, who doesn't look much older than her daughter, with blondish hair and pleasant features, just short of plump, gazes with a composed expression into the camera. Danae's face is all teenage drama. Long messy bangs fall over big glossy dark eyes, which stare passionately, almost sorrowfully, into the lens. She is wearing lipstick and her lips are long, full, and slightly pulled down at the corners, as if to transmit soulful earnestness. A strapped black top bares her shoulder. In the photo, at least, she really does look as if she could be an actress.

We scrolled through her posts, most written in social networking shorthand. Only hours before, Danae had posted this: "aunke todo sto ha sido muy difícil no dejo de recordar ke smp l pasabamos super by T AMO ♥ y smp stas n mi mnt y n mi corazon u eres l amor de mi vida mami!" Translated, minus shorthand: "though everything has been very difficult I don't stop remembering that we always had a super time bye I LOVE YOU ♥ and you're always in my thoughts and heart you're the love of my life mami!"

Danae had given Pablo a vague address, Calle Plomeros, near the Circunvalación, a diagonal avenue cutting through an edge of Tepito. We decided to walk there. Danae still wasn't answering her phone, but Pablo would keep phoning, and maybe a neighbor would be able to tell us where she lived. At the edge of the market, far down Avenida del Trabajo, we asked a woman working at a *tianguis* for directions. She gave them to us, but then said, "Take a taxi, don't go that way, *está canijo.*" *Canijo* is another of those Mexican words with several meanings but was originally a term for a bad person. She looked anxious. "Or walk around the long way," she said. We walked there because the Santa Muerte shrine was nearby and Pablo wanted to talk to Doña Queta again. Earlier, Pablo had remarked, "The more time you spend in Tepito, the more dangerous you realize it is."

We crossed the avenue, passing by a small plaza with a bare concrete crucifix that seemed to serve as a local garbage dump, and a hangout for people who sniff paint thinner. A man in blackened, filthy clothes sat at the base of the crucifix, holding a paint thinner–soaked rag to his nose. A few other younger addicts, expressions glazed and stuporous, milled about. It was quiet at the Santa Muerte shrine, but Doña Queta came out to speak with us. Pablo again asked her if she knew anything, had heard anything, about the Heavens case, and asked what people in the neighborhood were saying about it. Just as before, her expression turned cold. She said she knew nothing. "I don't talk about things I don't know about," she repeated a few times. Her fierce eyes bored into mine. "People shouldn't talk about things they don't know about," she said. She held my gaze in a way clearly meant to challenge me, and I returned it. For some reason, I didn't feel at all discomforted.

"I don't talk about things I don't know about," I said, though of course I sometimes do.

"Good," she said, and her expression relaxed a little.

Pablo had told her where we were going and why. Doña Queta also warned us, "Be careful walking around there."

We continued down Calle Alfarería, past Panaderos (Bakers). There, its two stories rising above other buildings midway down the block, we saw Extreme Body, the gym where four Tepiteños had been assassinated nearly a month before, and we went past Peluqueros (Barbers), Pintores (Painters), to Plomeros (Plumbers). The streets had a Sunday quiet. Few people were out on the sidewalks. Pablo was supposed to phone Danae when he reached Plomeros and the Circunvalación, but again, she didn't answer. If she lived on this corner, said Pablo, her neighbors must know her. We spoke with a couple in a small *tienda*, asking if they knew Danae Téllez, the daughter of Gabriela Téllez, one of the Tepiteños who'd been taken from outside that *after*. No, they answered, they didn't know her. We walked up and down the block, and when we passed the *tienda* again, the man came out to tell us that he thought he knew of a Gabriela who lived one street over, on Carpintería. When we were on that street Pablo stopped at the wide-open entrance of what seemed to be a mechanics garage of some sort, and inquired again about Gabriela and Danae. There were about eight men seated inside, in a loose circle of chairs amid machinery and benches, many of the men grimy with black grease, most in T-shirts, with *cuayamas*—liter bottles of beer—on the floor between their feet. But the tall, muscular man who came out to speak with us didn't look like a mechanic. He was wearing what seemed to be a blue ski sweater, and he was distinctly Aryan looking, blond, with a flushed face, and vividly bloodshot blue eyes. His fleshy pink lips were wrenched into an amused leer that didn't seem at all relevant to the matter of whether or not he knew if Gabriela and Danae Téllez lived around there. He grabbed Pablo by his skinny arm with his two big hands and tried to kiss him on the mouth. Pablo jerked his head away and struggled to pull free and the man pulled back harder, trying to kiss him again and telling him to come inside, cajoling like an insistent lover for him to do that, promising a good time. The other men, like orcs sitting in a dark cave, watched. I didn't want to do anything to provoke them. I was frightened that if I were to go to Pablo's aid—and do what? punch the blond giant?—the orcs would rise and charge outside and then it would be extremely violent, we wouldn't stand a chance. So I stood frozen, nearly at Pablo's side but helpless. While the man pulled on him, Pablo shouted that he was a reporter for *El País*. But it was over quickly. Pablo wrenched free, or else the man finally just let go, and we hurried away, around the corner, with nobody chasing after us. A group of homosexual Tepito mechanics sitting around getting drunk on a Sunday afternoon, was that what they were? We agreed that it was hard to imagine a face more depraved-looking than that blond giant's.

We gave up on Danae. Pablo had another idea. Jacqueline, the sister of Jennifer Robles, another of the missing, was a close friend of Gabriela Téllez. Jacqueline often went out with her sister and Gabriela and Danae, but, like Danae, she also hadn't partied on into the morning hours on the Saturday night that ended with the Sunday *levantón*. Pablo had already interviewed Jacqueline about her sister for his piece, and thought that she would be able to talk about Gabriela. Pablo had described Jacqueline to me before, giving the impression of a tough, funny girl who said what she thought, and I could tell he liked her a lot. After he'd phoned her, we caught a taxi. By then evening had fallen and it was dark. Jacqueline lived just outside Tepito, in a small *vecindad* in Colonia Morelos, in a neighborhood considered distinctly a notch below Tepito in the city's social gradations. When she came down to let us inside, she wiggled a finger through the hole in the black sheet metal sliding door where a lock should have been, and said, "This is our combination security lock." Jacqueline is twenty-six, a striking woman with an ample figure and a sultry, self-possessed manner. Very rickety metal stairs led upstairs to the apartment, which was small and dark. It belonged to her grandmother— whom Jacqueline always referred to as her mother—and doubled as her workplace. The Robles sisters' grandmother sews stuffed animals and figures that are sold in the Tepito market and by street vendors. Currently she was making felt dolls of Mike Wazowski, the one-eyed monster from the *Monster Inc.* movies. Green and white felt limbs, big-eyed heads, and some fully assembled Mike Wazowskis were spread over the workbench along one side of the room. Jacqueline sat down at a low plastic table. With the back of her T-shirt riding up, you could see some of the Santa Muerte tattooed over the small of her back. She was in a sullen mood, and gave not very descriptive answers to Pablo's questions about Gabriela. "*Muy tranquila, muy noble*, always willing to help a friend . . ." Yes, affirmed Jacqueline, Gabriela always went to places like Heavens and Bar Cristal with her daughter. Mother and daughter both liked to dance to electronic music, house, *progre, minima.* When Pablo pressed her for an anecdote, some special memory of Gabriela that she could share, she shrugged and repeated her generic words of praise. In the photograph that would appear above Jennifer's profile in Pablo's *El País* piece, the two sisters stand close together inside a nightspot, in pretty club dresses, Jennifer's arm draped around Jacqueline's shoulders. They wear identical sunglasses with huge white frames and both have their hair bleached peroxide blond. But Jacqueline had dyed her hair dark, her natural color, within days of her sister's disappearance. Later Pablo would speculate that Jacqueline was so reticent that evening because she was probably hungover from drinks or drugs. Maybe she was, but to me her mood, which filled the room, seemed familiar, a murky, exhausted, locked up inside grief and trauma mood. We must have seemed to her as if we were speaking from another planet, and I remembered Iris Murdoch's famous remark, "The bereaved have no language with which to speak to the unbereaved."

The families we'd spoken to earlier that day hadn't wanted to talk about the Heavens case itself, the progress of the investigation, or what Chief Prosecutor Ríos had told them at their last meeting. Pablo told Jacqueline that he'd heard the chief prosecutor and his people had been pressuring the families not to talk to the press about the case, and he asked if that was true. She nodded affirmatively. But what did she think? Did she believe, I asked, that the *levantón* had in some way been directed against El Tanque?

"It's been ten years. El Tanque isn't anybody now," she said. "They don't have anything." She was dismissive of the scenario of a turf war between two Tepito gangs as the motive for the *levantón*. "It's not just any idiot who is going to do something like this," she said. I asked her who, then, she thought was behind it.

Jacqueline, staring down at the tabletop, said sullenly, "The government."

"The city government?"

"Peña Nieto," she said. "They want to control the *plazas*, like they do in México State."

Mexican drug cartels are in the DF and have been for years. In SinEmbargo.com in June, Humberto Padgett wrote that a U.S. Congress report, prepared by the Congressional Research Service in 2011, identified seven drug cartels operating in Mexico City: the Sinaloa Cartel, the Zetas, the Beltrán Leyva Cartel, the Juárez Cartel, La Familia Michoacana, El Cartel del Golfo, and the Tijuana Cartel. Any more recent report would have to add Los Templarios, among others. It must be noted, though, that that report was on greater Mexico City, all those parts of it outside the borders of the DF. In the DF, it's an open secret that the Sinaloa Cartel has been the main supplier of the local *narcomenudeo*, along with the Beltrán Leyvas; the 2011 CRS report confirmed that. La Familia Michoacana, according to Humberto Padgett and also to what you just hear around, entrenched in Neza, abutting the DF, is said have penetrated the Tepito *narcomenudeo* market. Padgett also reported, in that piece, the arrest of a narco religious leader of a Santa Muerte cult, though he didn't say where in Mexico City it had occurred. Capos and other major cartel figures have always kept homes in the DF. The cartels do big business in the city, laundering money through the banks, investing, and so on. Over the last ten years, I've only very occasionally gone to the *teibols*, the strip clubs, but I still have a few women friends who work in those places—one, for example, who has worked for twenty years to raise her son and put him through school and into a university—or who have until recently. One of them told me this summer, "As you know, Frank, all kinds of people come to a *teibol*." When she'd worked in a *teibol*, she'd met men from the Sinaloa Cartel, and knew girls who'd gone out with them. "They like to live in the Condesa," she said. These aren't crack-addicted *sicarios*, assassins, that she was talking about, but criminals higher up in the food chain, who, if they live in the Condesa, look, at least, as if they fit right in. "Los Sinaloas," she told me, were men who could talk about books, movies, politics; they'd been to college. She knew a girl who'd gone out with a Zeta too and that had ended as one would expect a romance with a Zeta to end, with a violent beating, and now nobody had heard from the girl in a long while. Another *teibolera* friend had recently told her that a customer, a man who seemed to know what he was talking about, had warned her to be careful because there was going to be an outbreak of violence in the city, probably with assassinations and gunfights occurring in nightspots, including *teibols*. This was not long before the killing of the drug dealer outside the nearby bar Black, followed two days later by the Heavens *levantón*. But those events did not seem a part of, or had not subsequently triggered, anything like an all-out narco cartel war. Humberto Padgett wrote, "However narco-executions have been going up in the Mexican capital. According to . . . the newspaper *Reforma* [March 12, 2013] during the first 100 days of president Enrique Peña Nieto's government . . . the Distrito Federal was the scene of 73 executions between December 1, 2012, and March 11, 2013."

Surely Mayor Mancera knows what is happening in his city, yet following the mass kidnapping at Heavens, he said, "I have no information that any cartel is in the DF," and, "The Federal authorities haven't reported to me that any cartel is operating in the city, and they're the ones who map that situation." Why would he speak that way? Because as long as the cartels aren't warring violently with each other in the streets, as the cartels do throughout much of Mexico, as long as they are not massacring each other and each other's police, to say nothing of innocent bystanders, as the cartels do throughout much of Mexico, as long as they are not leaving corpses strung from overpasses and strewing decapitated bodies and heads all around the city, as the cartels do throughout much of Mexico, as long as they are not kidnapping girls and women off the streets and selling them into sexual slavery or taking them to torture-rape safe houses and tossing their corpses away like trash, as the cartels do throughout much of Mexico, as long as they are not killing reporters and bloggers in the DF or terrorizing media into complete silence about their activities, as the cartels do throughout much of Mexico, as long as they are not trying to *take over* the city through extortion and terror, burning down businesses or murdering their resistant owners and their families, steeping the city in violent death and savagery in order to terrorize its citizens into submission, as the cartels do throughout much of Mexico, as long as they are not upsetting the equilibrium of the city, of nearly everyone's daily routines, as long as people aren't afraid to leave their homes to travel to work or school or to go out at night, as people are throughout much of Mexico—then it is *as if the cartels are not there*. Maybe Mexico City's *narcomenudeo plaza*, profitable as it may be, is not big enough, a speck compared to the vast *plaza* over the border, to actually go to war over. The cartels know that, for numerous reasons, they could never take over the DF in the way they can México State and a *municipio* like Neza, or cities like Torreón, Nuevo Laredo, Acapulco, and so on, drug trafficking points of entry and departure, leading north. The city's real powers, many of them multinational—banking, finance, big media, telecommunications, industry, construction, superstore commerce, and so on—need the DF to be stable, and because the cartels also make money in the DF and want to be left "in peace," stability even seems to suit them. When the cartels take over a city or town, their control makes it resemble Lovecraft's "Innsmouth," occupied by venal frog-fish-men fathered by monstrous creatures, the Deep Ones, who come ashore from their secret citadel under the ocean. The Deep Ones offer treasure in exchange for human sacrifice and immortal life to their hideous offspring, who eventually subsume the town. A stranger coming upon Innsmouth quickly senses its stifling menace and corruption. Everything "reeks."

The DF isn't like that, but maybe that's what going on in the sky over Tepito: something like the hovering shadow over Innsmouth. Maybe the Deep Ones are already in Tepito. But it's not as if narco executions didn't happen in the DF before. Jorge, one of former Mayor Ebrard's younger security guards, told me that once, when he was a beat policeman, he'd had to recover the bodies of some decapitated men, load them into a police pickup, and bring them to the morgue, but this had freaked him out, had left him, he told me, deeply shaken and with nightmares for weeks. So it wasn't the usual thing, something that a DF policeman would expect to encounter as part of his normal duties, as it would be for his counterparts throughout much of Mexico. But 73 narco executions in the DF over three months is a shocking number, a rate, Padgett reported, comparable to or higher than that in some of the most conflicted narco states, though México State and Coahuila, over the same period, had 209. But what is disconcerting is this: I didn't notice that those narco executions were happening, and hardly anybody I knew mentioned it. That most excellent journalist Marcela Turati did; I do remember now her telling me, months ago, something like this. But mostly the press, if it did know about the executions, sounded no alarm, nor did anyone else in a position to know. And I recalled what Ebrard's *guarura*, the "professor," had told me one afternoon in the lobby of our building, that if police were involved or complicit in the Heavens *levantón*, of course the same kind of thing had happened in the DF before, only this time it had become front-page news.

Pablo and I both had our own off-the-record sources, men with direct lines into the highest levels of the city government and police, his in the Mancera camp, mine in Ebrard's. Sometimes we got together and shared our notes, and tried to construe from our different mixes of information and speculation some idea of our own about what lay behind the Heavens case.

Pablo's source, though he was officially "with" Mancera, said it was a police problem. Mancera had lost the internal control over the Procuraduría's investigative police—formerly known as the judicial police, or *judiciales*—and the SSP's Mexico City police that Ebrard, said Pablo's source, with thirty years of experience in city government, had known how to exert. Since Mancera had taken office as *jefe de gobierno,* said Pablo's source, in the DF there had been an "empowering of criminals protected by the police," manifested in attempts by the Tepito drug gang La Unión to control the *narcomenudeo* in *colonias* Condesa and Roma, the Zona Rosa, and other parts of the city. In Mexico City the police constitute, and long have constituted, an autonomous culture, and the police there, especially the notorious judicial/investigative police, *are* organized crime. The police are what the DF has instead of aggressively operating cartels, Pablo's source emphasized. Throughout the DF, all the places where drugs are sold and distributed are protected and controlled by police who guarantee their dealers' impunity. La Unión, said Pablo's source, began in 2010 as a Tepito gang of extortionists and *sicarios*, assassins for hire. But now, he said, La Unión is a drug gang led by police and former members of the police, and the same is true of the city's other drug gangs. And it's not just city police who are in on the action: in the heart of Tepito, said Pablo's source, there's a post where federal police conduct their business with their own dealers or factions of La Unión. The city's stability, said Pablo's source, rests on a long-established pact between the business powers and the city government that "nobody wants to see broken." One of the most important responsibilities of the *jefe de gobierno*, in exchange for the ongoing support of that *clase empresarial,* is to keep the police under control. The challenge to Mancera now was to attack his own police, and deactivate at least one of its factions, without provoking a disastrous war within the police. Should the city begin to see *levantones* of police, "the next step," said Pablo's source, then it would know that war had begun.

And so while Pablo's source did not think that elements within the PRI itself had orchestrated the *levantón*—as part of a strategy, say, to fray that pact, and destabilize the city—he asserted that the crime had "great political capital" and had become a "political weapon." That source said, "Everybody knows the PRI wants the DF." Whoever had carried out the *levantón*—La Unión or some faction of the gang, or some faction of the police, or some combination of these—had done so imitating the style of a cartel because they thought they had protection. The police protect the local drug gangs. But the overriding question, said Pablo's source, is: Who protects the police?

When I spoke to my source, I asked whether it was true, and if so how, that Mancera had lost the control over the police that Ebrard had been able to maintain. One mistake Mancera made, said the source, was that when he was chief prosecutor he'd hired as a sub-prosecutor Jesús Rodríguez Almeida, a lawyer and veteran of the federal police, the federal investigations agency, and the federal attorney general's office. Then, as mayor, Mancera had appointed Rodríguez Almeida to head the SSP as chief of police, the post Ebrard had held under AMLO. As a federal officer and official, Rodríguez Almeida had worked in the north, in narco-controlled states such as Chihuahua, and, said the source, when he came to the DF "he brought all that pollution with him." Nobody has ever described the notoriously corrupt federal police and justice forces, especially those in the most violent narco zones, as anything much better than at least passively complicit in the criminal activities of the cartels. Such an explanation certainly fitted with the scenario of drug gangs empowered by police factions described by Pablo de Llano's source. Not every present and former federal police officer or investigator is dishonorable, obviously; hundreds, even thousands, of corrupt Federales have been purged in recent years. In the last year alone, under Rodríguez Almeida, hundreds of police were detained for corruption and other crimes and purged from the Mexico City police. But should it ever be exposed that a DF police force of ninety thousand, led by an official formerly associated with the federal police, had fostered, or protected, a faction or factions of police engaged in cartel-like crimes, nobody is going to fall over in surprise. Nor would there be much surprise if one of those factions came, with or without his knowledge, from Chief Prosecutor Ríos's investigative police.

To my source, a key to the Heavens case lay in the murder of After Heavens' owner Dax Rodríguez Ledezma, whose burned and tortured body had turned up with those of his cousin and adolescent lover in the municipality of Huitzilac, in Morelos state, some distance from the Pacific state of Guerrero, where they had been kidnapped and murdered. This occurrence, though it would obviously seem to be of major importance to those trying to solve the Heavens case, had been at least publicly forgotten by Mancera's government, by his chief prosecutor, and by most of the Mexico City press. The source said that he had heard that Dax Rodríguez Ledezma had been tortured and murdered because he'd been talking to police—whether federal or from the DF or elsewhere, the source didn't specify. There is a rumor that Dax Rodríguez left behind a video, recorded by himself, in which he revealed what he knew about the *levantón*. It was also being said that the other two owners of After Heavens, in detention, beyond admitting and describing their own roles in setting up the Tepito youths to be kidnapped, were keeping silent about whatever else they knew regarding the case.

Huitzilac, in Morelos, said the source, hadn't been chosen at random. He said Huitzilac, because of its history and also its geography, is a symbolic place in Mexico, representing "the gate to the city" from the Cuernavaca side. Controlled by the Beltrán Leyvas, the territory was described by one Mexican newspaper as the cartel's "paradise." The municipality of Huitzilac is where, on August 24, 2012, in the town of Tres Marías, gunmen later identified as federal police suspected of working for the Beltrán Leyva cartel ambushed two agents of the CIA who were traveling with a Mexican navy captain in a car with diplomatic plates.

Two and a half years before, acting on information provided by U.S. authorities, a Mexican navy commando team—the navy is considered by far the least corrupt branch of the Mexican armed forces—had hunted down and killed the cartel's leader, Arturo Beltrán Leyva, "El Barbas," in Cuernavaca. The August 2012 ambush of the CIA agents and the Mexican officer was apparently in revenge for that killing. One hundred fifty-two bullets were fired at the car, piercing its armor, but the passengers, though wounded, survived. It was widely assumed in Mexico that the agents were in Tres Marías that day staking out the terrain for an attempted capture of Héctor Beltrán Leyva, "El H," now the cartel's leader. The attack exposed CIA involvement in Mexico's drug war, creating a furor that raised tension between the U.S. and Mexican governments, and embarrassed President Felipe Calderón. Eventually fourteen federal police were arraigned for the assassination attempt, and now await trial. But Héctor Beltrán Leyva, El H, remained free.

Another possibility is that the bodies of Dax Rodríguez Ledezma and the two women had been placed in Huitzilac precisely because it was Beltrán Leyva territory. Then it would have been a message intended for El H and his allies, most likely the Zetas, sent by a rival such as the Sinaloa Cartel.

During the first weeks after the Heavens kidnapping, when the Mexican press was filled with speculations about the case, a rumor turned up in some reports that a few years earlier, a truck shipment of cocaine, worth $2.5 million, belonging to the Beltrán Leyvas had gone missing in Tepito. My source also mentioned this rumor and seemed to credit it. In this version, the *levantón* had been a settling of accounts, by El H, for that apparent theft. The youths lifted from After Heavens, or some of them, or else people they were associated with, had kept, or stolen, the Beltrán Leyvas' cocaine. But others said that the stolen cocaine had belonged to the Sinaloa Cartel. Another rumor, said the source, was that the kidnappers had asked for a ransom double the worth of the missing cocaine, but if so, who had they asked and who was supposed to pay it? But if the *levantón* was directed against the "sons of La Unión," possibly including, say, Jerzy Ortíz, the son of El Tanque, then why take all the others? Why not settle the manner in some quieter way, with a direct narco execution of whoever had been directly involved, or of their sons or daughters? Because whoever had sent that message didn't mean or want it to be discreet. Such a message, said the source, could also have been a testing of Mayor Mancera, to see how he and his government would react to such an incursion and challenge. If the message came from El H, said the source, it would also have been a taunt: "I don't care if you come looking for me." The source said that El H most likely wouldn't have attempted such an audacious strike, in the heart of the DF, if he hadn't felt sure of federal protection. El H wasn't punished by the federal government even after the attempted assassination of the CIA men. "If you don't do anything against Señor H," said the source, "it's because of some pact you've negotiated with him."

The source had heard a rumor that the twelve abducted young people had already been taken to the *pozolero*. *Pozole* is a corn and meat stew; usually it is made with pork, or sometimes chicken, but the cannibalistic Aztecs cooked it with human meat. A *pozolero* is a drug cartel specialist who melts bodies essentially down to nothing in vats of acid. That would be another kind of message, said the source. When a cartel wants its enemies to know it means to destroy them, then those it takes are never found. They vanish into an acid stew.

But when bodies are found hacked to bits, or tortured and burned, as in the case of the bodies of Dax Rodríguez and the two women in Huitzilac, that, explained the source, says: "There is somebody giving orders and that somebody is not afraid." If El H was that somebody, then the federal government, the PGR, would have to go after him in Morelos. "It's strange, isn't it, that the government can capture Z-40"—the Zeta leader taken near the Texas border in July—"but it can't get H Beltrán?" The source said that Manuel Mondragón, Ebrard's former chief of police, now leading the federal government's investigative unit, "knows that he has people working for him who work for them," i.e., work for the Beltrán Leyvas.

"We're never going to know what happened," Pablo de Llano, whose editors were pressuring him to "solve" the case, often said. "The truth is probably never going to come out." And I agreed. Recent Mexican history was full of such high-profile cases, which drew a lot of attention for a while but were never solved. But we both felt convinced that much, or some part, of the truth about the Heavens case lay embedded in the accounts of our sources. You could fit various pieces together in different ways—criminal factions of the Mexico City police, El H, or another cartel—and have them make sense. But there were always questions left dangling.

On July 15, 2013, the digital news site AnimalPolitico .com published a report titled "Terror in Tepito." It described the anonymous interviews given to Radio Nederland by residents of the barrio about the Zeta-like way that La Unión reigns over the barrio. Regarding the After Heavens *levantón*, the piece said, "The families of the disappeared say nothing except that they have faith in God and the authorities. At first, the relatives of the victims were noticeably anguished and desperate, but then their attitude changed, as if the authorities had given them good news in exchange for silence. Nevetheless, there are others who prefer not to keep silent, a group of neighbors of the disappeared, also from Tepito." That was perhaps unfair to the families, but the article gave the impression that their silence had an immediately local cause. The neighbors contradicted the perception that the missing young people were criminals just because some of their parents had been: "*Chale,* that's not hereditary," one said. "You shouldn't criminalize the youngsters." But La Unión, the neighbors said, had been running rampant in the barrio, extorting and killing at will. One of the interviewed men had a list of thirty Tepiteños he accused the gang of having murdered. "Why does La Unión kill? To eliminate rivals?" he was asked. "No, only to control Tepito by terror. Without any motive, without a word, they come and shoot people, whoever . . . Many people never denounced these crimes out of fear, and the authorities come and say the same as always, that it was a settling of scores between rival gangs, and they don't verify or investigate, and nothing happens. . . . The police know, and they don't do anything." Another interviewed man said that La Unión was founded and is led by "Ricardo López Pérez, alias 'El Moco' (The Snot), a former federal police agent. . . . He armed Tepito vagabonds and teenagers in Tepito." They took over local extortion rackets and the *narcomenudeo*. "El Moco and his henchmen kill people just for the fun of it and so that people will know they're in control. Nobody opposes them." Another of the men interviewed brought up the Beltrán Leyvas and the missing cocaine shipment. To retrieve bundles of cocaine dropped into the ocean off the Pacific coast, said the interviewee, Arturo Beltrán Leyva had preferred to hire young Tepito gang members rather than local scuba divers. (I wondered if that could have any relation to the scuba diving lessons at the new Community Development Center in Tepito, where local residents helped to design the curriculum.) When Arturo Beltrán Leyvas was killed, the Tepito scuba diving gang was left holding the cocaine while others fought for control of the cartel, with El H eventually emerging as leader. Another person who was interviewed described the members of La Unión as devout Catholics and followers of La Santa Muerte, and said that some even went on pilgrimages to Santiago de Compostela in Spain.

During those same weeks undercover reporters for *Universal* had ostensibly gone shopping for drugs in the *vecindades* of Tepito, at the drug supermarkets and secret vending "safe houses" that are tended by dealers armed with assault weapons. In their newspaper report they described the apparently congenial relations between police and dealers, and wrote of the police, "The few arrests they make are of people who come to Tepito to buy drugs for the first time and in small quantities." They also described how closely monitored those streets are by *halcones* working for the drug dealers.

These pieces did not do much to clarify my understanding of the After Heavens case, but they did make me understand why some had urged Pablo and me not to walk around in those streets. The "silence" of the families about the case made more sense too, as did Ana María Vargas's reluctance to pursue the capture of her son's murderers. And the kid in the *fútbol* shirt who'd followed us to Ana María's *vecindad* that day probably was, as we'd suspected, a *halcón*. Tepito, in the center of the DF, a figuratively walled-in barrio, had become, I now realized, a place, like so many of Mexico's darkest places, where people live terrorized by organized crime that they don't dare or can't speak out against, for fear of their own and family members' lives, and because they know the police are in league with their tormentors. "I don't talk about things I don't know about," Doña Queta, the Santa Muerte "priestess" and *santera,* had said. Doña Queta's hard stare into my eyes now seemed especially disturbing if also enigmatic, both confiding and a perhaps complicit warning. Her stare was Tepito's stare.

Pablo de Llano was again in touch with Toñín by phone, trying to get him to agree to an interview. Toñín was still in the barrio, but lying low, afraid to talk. Much as DF authorities had seemingly discarded the murder of Dax Rodríguez as a focus of their investigation, Toñín's account, which he'd since repeated after he'd finally been tracked down in Tepito by police assigned to the Heavens case and hauled in to give an official statement, had also been forgotten. He'd described his friends being abducted from After Heavens by men armed with assault weapons, some with their faces hidden, and then driven away in vans. Back on June 12, Martin Moreno, a columnist and reporter for the mainstream newspaper *Excelsior,* had published a piece in the "Red Publica" section of SinEmbargo.com, in which he wrote, "This 'Red Publica' is in a position to declare that the video shown last Friday to the families of the abducted Tepiteños by the chief prosecutor in the DF, Rodolfo Ríos, was incomplete." According to Moreno, the blurry video was *mocho,* that is, it had been cut or altered. "At its end," wrote Moreno, "[the tape] registers how three vans arrived to take the kidnapped from Heavens. One van is blue. The other white. One wasn't filmed. Why did Ríos hide that?"

Moreno republished the piece on another digital site, Ciudadanosenred, and sometimes retweets it, as he did, recently, during the last week of July. I don't disbelieve that Moreno was shown the missing piece of video by somebody, or was at least told about it by somebody he trusted who'd seen it. I can certainly understand his reluctance to reveal these details, because whoever had showed it to him or told him about it, if identified, would certainly be endangered. But I doubt that anyone who tried to find this piece of video now would succeed. Moreno also wrote that Ríos had "discarded the testimony of three witnesses." Those three statements are verifiable because they are in the official case file as "Preliminary Inquiries."* Other crime and court beat reporters, but only a few, also read and wrote about the statements. They were given by three young people who had escaped the Heavens *levantón* by fleeing up the club's stairs and out onto the roof. From one of those statements: "I come out of the bathroom, and I see two *chavos* and two waiters running up the stairs, but the *chavos* went into the ladies' room, and as you go up the stairs you pass a dog [statue] like all lit up with lights and there's a glass door, and when you open it you see a spiral staircase that goes up to the second level and the owners' offices, and running behind the waiters were Toño [Toñín] and Zoé [when Toñín had first gone to testify at CAPEA he'd given Zoé's name], and at the moment I turned around, as they went past, I saw a subject, tall, robust, dark brown skin, a red scarf covering half his face, very short hair, wearing a long black gabardine, and holding in his hands a type of assault rifle, and behind him was another person I didn't get a good look at and he was holding what seemed like a pistol, and when I saw that, I turned and ran."

---

* Averiguación Previa DGAVD/CAPE/T2/891/13-05.

Another witness: "And at that moment as I was coming down, I saw like seven people armed with rifles or machine guns, and so I didn't want to go outside so what I did was slam the door shut and run back inside the *antro*."

And the third: "I've already told you that things got heavy because a commando had come to the *antro* and taken a lot of people, and also I said that there were *patrullas* [police] and that, it seemed, there were Federales, and they went in blue vans and a green Suburban and also a gray van. . . . I don't know if they were local [police] or Federales but they were armed. . . . One of the men was very brown, with short hair, wearing civilian clothes, and what seemed a white bulletproof vest."

But Chief Prosecutor Ríos, on June 7, had declared, "There was no commando or armed persons," and had said that the missing young people had been taken away in private automobiles. Ever since, that has been the official story.

"Princess, I'm going now," Gabriela Téllez told her daughter, Danae, who was already in bed. "I love you, my princess. I won't be long." Those were the last words her mother spoke to Danae, just before she left their *vecindad* apartment to go to After Heavens. She was wearing fluorescent green pants, recalled Danae, black shoes, and a black jacket, and had her hair in a ponytail.

New information on the Heavens case having dwindled to nothing, or nearly nothing, Pablo de Llano thought that maybe he would publish a story about Danae. This time we took a taxi to meet her. The address she'd originally given Pablo that Sunday a few weeks before turned out to be not very close to where she actually lived. Now, going to meet her, we drove down a street lined with auto body garages that were, according to the

taxi driver, "chop shops" where stolen cars were fixed up, sometimes with new paint jobs, and sold cheap. At the large *vecindad*
where Danae lives we waited a long time before she finally came
downstairs with her older cousin. She said that she didn't want
to take us into her apartment. She said that she didn't want our
conversation to disturb her little brothers, one nine and the other
four. And her cousin said that they felt "watched by dangerous
people" and didn't think it was a good idea to bring reporters
into her apartment. It was raining lightly, but we sat outside
on the curb, partly shielded by a small bus shelter. In person,
Danae looked much younger than in her photograph. Her face
was a child's, perky and pretty, and she wore braces. Her figure,
however, was womanly, with long legs sheathed in tight orange
jeans. She wore a hooded gray sweatshirt that belonged to her
little brother. She spoke like a child, in high-pitched bursts of
breathy excitement.

"We had total trust in each other," said Danae when we
asked her to describe her relationship with her mother. "I confided everything to her. We always went out together, we did
everything together. We hardly ever fought—well, only, say, if
she didn't want me to go out with a man I liked, like this one
who was fifteen years older than me."

Danae said she had no idea who her father was. She didn't
know the identity of the father of one of her brothers either.
Her other brother's father was shot and killed during a robbery.
Danae said about her mother, "I do have faith that she's coming
back. I can't imagine my life without her."

She wasn't in school now, and had never held a job. But she
said she'd like to go back to school, to study international relations. "You know, to work in an embassy, that kind of thing. I
like languages." In high school she'd studied English and French.

Though she had only a year of high school left, it didn't seem likely that she'd be going back. Not now, when she was going to have to find a way to support her little brothers and elderly grandmother. An uncle had been helping them out, she said. She didn't like to cook, she said. But she did use to help her mother with the laundry.

Danae was full of a restless, ebullient energy. When a neighbor passed with her small daughter, she sprang off the curb to fuss over the child, squealing, "*Ay, mi vida!*"

While we sat talking, the four of us arrayed along the curb, teenage boys passed behind us on the sidewalk, staring. They came back several times, and seemed to want to make sure that we saw them looking at us.

We spoke about that last night she'd spent with her mother. At Bar Cristal, she said, the deejay was Chris Fortier, from the United States. But she'd had a headache, and that's why, Danae said, they'd come home early, and why, after a friend phoned and told them to come, she hadn't gone with her mother to After Heavens. Jerzy Ortíz, she said, never went to After Heavens. He always went to Bar Cristal. That night must have been the first time, she said, that he'd gone to Heavens. Danae and her mother went to the Zona Rosa after-hours club all the time. Admission was two hundred pesos, but she and her mother never had to pay. "We went Friday, Saturday, and Sundays," she said, "and we wouldn't come out sometimes until six the next evening." Then they'd return later, after midnight. And what did she do there? "Dance dance dance," she said, "and sleep and dance." She took naps at a table. "No, we didn't get bored. I'd sleep, and then I'd wake up, and then I'd dance some more."

But Danae and her mother did more than just go out to bars and after-hours clubs. Her mother sold computer games at work, and had brought a Play Station home, and the family liked to gather around it, playing Super Mario Brothers.

"We haven't accepted what's happened," Danae said. This was the closest she'd come to acknowledging the final consequences of what had happened, or might still happen, to her mother. I can only imagine the terror and sadness that she seemed to be trying to shield herself from with her bright manic talkativeness. "I'm always calling out for my mother," she said. "I come home and shout out to her, or I ask where she is."

An old woman with a cane and two little boys were walking down the opposite side of the street. These were Danae's grandmother and her brothers. She got up and went to them. While they were speaking, she took off her sweatshirt and exchanged it for a red one with the taller of the boys. She bent over the smaller boy, kissing him, and then crossed the street back to us.

We spoke just a little while longer. Danae and her cousin were going to another meeting with the families at the Procuraduría, "the Bunker," with Chief Prosecutor Ríos, who, according to later newspaper reports, would tell the families that evening, as if to convince them of his good faith, "I might lose my head over this case," by which he meant his job.

On the way back to Colonia Roma, in a taxi, Pablo and I talked about Danae and about her mother, Gabriela, who, night after night, had taken her teenage daughter to After Heavens, where drugs were sold openly, and where people came armed. There Danae had met a man, fifteen years older, whom her mother hadn't allowed her to go out with. We speculated about what that man must have been like, if it was over *him* that her mother had turned disciplinarian and protective. Well, nobody could stop Danae, assuming she might still want to, from going out with him now.

*   *   *

Today is August 2, and the Heavens case has disappeared from the Mexico City media as a news story. The press, for the most part, seems to accept the Mancera government's explanation that the *levantón* was an isolated incident in the context of a turf war between two Tepito drug-dealing gangs. Some newspapers repeatedly describe La Unión as El Tanque's gang—a description that prosecutors and police never use. But people in the city, insofar as they still pay attention to the case, seem to accept that too.

"The only divinity around here is corruption," says Pablo, disgustedly. He is referring not just to the Mancera government's and the police's handling of the case. It's long been known in journalistic circles that much of the establishment media, even in Mexico City, have yielded to pressure from the Peña Nieto government to stop running stories about narco violence in the country. Some of Mexico's most renowned print journalists have personally told me about editors turning down stories that they would once have been eager to run and ruefully citing pressures from above. Something similar may be occurring with the Heavens case. The pressure may be coming from the Mancera government, but also from other powers and interests that want to protect the DF's reputation as a city shielded from violent organized crime by its competent government and ever-improving police. After all, a lot of wealth, a lot of investor and consumer confidence, depends on the perception that the city is a secure place. Pablo is going home to Spain for a few weeks, but when he comes back, he's determined to take the Heavens case up again and to interview Toñín. If Pablo can persuade Toñín to tell his story in *El País*, it could put a crack in the wall of complacent silence that now seems to surround the case. He and Toñín have been in regular contact by phone, and Pablo is trying to convince Toñín that an interview in an international newspaper like *El País*, rather than in a Mexico City newspaper, would raise his profile and provide him with protection.

Mancera, Pablo says, is probably being perceived as having done a good job handling the Heavens case. And looking at it in a certain light, maybe he has. For instance, the mayor made no aggressive move that could have provoked a war among police contending for control of the *narcomenudeo*. And if Mexico City works in ways "that nobody wants to see broken," Mancera seems to have retained the crucial support of the finance and business sectors. Yet if the mayor appears to have defused the crisis, it is likely that he and his prosecutors and police have done so by covering up, willfully ignoring, and maybe even tampering with evidence in the case, and this seems like a ticking time bomb. He has handed his foes, or his challengers, weapons that can be deployed against him. Those behind the Heavens crime—whoever they are—may feel now that they've achieved what they wanted, and that they now have an even stronger hand.

Today, August 2, is also the first anniversary of my "party bus" experience—being kicked nearly unconscious by *juniors* celebrating the birthday of a friend whose father was a pharmacy king and a pal of Peña Nieto's. That incident is now famous among my friends as the night that I completed last summer's journey to rock bottom. As if to help me observe the date, all week AnimalPolitico.com has been promoting an online discussion of the question: *¿Podrán las redes sociales poner límites a la influencia y el poder de los 'juniors' mexicanos?* "Can social networks impose limits on the influence and power of the Mexican *juniors*?"—*juniors* being what rich-kid daddies' boys are called.

#Juniorpartybusmob: I wonder, What if Reyna or anybody else had managed to film that incident with a smartphone? How would it have gone over on the social networks? Just the video itself: a dozen or so young *juniors* standing over a man in his fifties laid out on the pavement, kicking him in the head. (Yes, I should never have been there in the first place, but that was *last* summer. It could never have happened *this* summer.) When those hearty lads climbed back onto the music-spouting party bus, did they share a round of cheers and toasts, as in some corny beer commercial?

Whenever I go to the movies in Mexico and watch the commercials interspersed with trailers, all I see now are party-busers: adolescents and young men and women who look just like the people on that bus. Seeing them is like enduring a nightmare flashback. In Mexican-made commercial after commercial, for Telcel, for Pepsi, and so on, *juniors* and young *ladies* are the only image of "Mexicaness" ever shown, at least to movie viewers in this country. There is not a single even light brown or *mestizo* face in any one of those commercials, not even in the particular commercial that shows about a hundred scantily clad cheerfully romping Mexican party-busers at a swimming pool party—not *one* among a hundred. I sit there muttering, snorting, and cursing and Jovi, next to me, hushes me. But sometimes I hear people in a nearby row reacting the way I do. When a Gatorade commercial, obviously made in the United States, filled with black and brown as well as white athletes, comes onto the screen, I feel a moment of ridiculous self-righteous pride. All of this makes me recall that day a month ago when Jovi woke with a painful sore throat, and we went to a nearby private hospital with an inpatient clinic. I sat in the waiting room watching the television affixed high on the wall. It was a Televisa daytime talk show, with eight hosts—four men and four women—who stood in a row talking at each other all at once, keeping up a steady stream of frivolous, gossipy, arch banter; waving and flapping their hands; jumping around. The men, especially, instantly reminded me of the younger *juniors* and *mi reyes*—"my kings," as these types are also called in Mexico—on the party bus. Televisa must assume, or know, that these only slightly older party-busers, acting out the high-spirited good life, appeal to their daytime viewers all across the republic. But I don't know any Mexicans who are anything like those people on TV; the closest I've ever actually come to any social interaction with them was on the party bus.

The talk show cut away to a special segment: one of the young *ladies* was standing in an empty field. This turned out to be the place, in Monterrey, in December of 2012, where the pop singer Jenni Rivera, "La Diva de la Banda," died along with four others when the private Lear Jet they were traveling in crashed. The man who owned the jet had been under investigation by the DEA for presumed ties to El Chapo Guzmán and the Sinaloa Cartel. In February 2013, a protected witness testified that Rivera used to perform at private narco parties thrown by Edgar Valdez Villareal, "La Barbie," a notorious *sicario* and capo of the Beltrán Leyva cartel until his arrest in 2010. The witness's testimony confirmed persistent rumors that Rivera, like other Mexican artists, used to give private performances for narcos. The witness described one occasion when Rivera had consumed so much cocaine and so many pills that she could barely perform, and La Barbie came onstage to mock and humiliate her, and even kicked her. The television showed wooden crosses erected in the dirt where Rivera and the others had died, and the flowers and tinsel baubles her fans had left there. Then there were images of yellow butterflies, and a close-up of water dribbling from a patch of parched earth and rocks. A barely audible sappy song, probably one of Rivera's, was playing. According to the television talk show *lady*, miracles had been occurring at the spot where Rivera lost her life. *Lady* was pitching the idea that Jenni Rivera, in death, had become a saint or a benign magical spirit that attracted butterflies and made water spurt from the desert. So this was the drivel with which Televisa was sentimentalizing Jenni Rivera, the psychotic murderer La Barbie's coke jester, for Mexican viewers. Well, if you can turn the enabler of Atenco's murders and rapes into a Ken Doll president, why not turn Jenni Rivera into a saint? But how could *lady* be sure that it wasn't one of the four others killed in that crash whose magical spirit was responsible for these "miracles"? I mean, why not even acknowledge that possibility? The show returned to the chorus line of Televisa actors and actresses playing at being *junior* and *lady* party-bus hosts.

Someone spoke to me, and I looked over. A tall Mexican man, sixtyish, balding and with a mustache, was looking at me with a polite restraint that failed to completely mask his disdain. "Do you mind if I change the channel?" he'd asked. "Yes, please, go ahead, I didn't know you could!" I blurted. He switched to a *fútbol* game. Mexico was playing Spain in the world sub-twenty youth team championships. When I'd left our building, Ebrard's *guarura* and David had been watching the match in the lobby, and Mexico was ahead 1–0. It would be a desperately needed morale-boosting victory for Mexican *fútbol* if Mexico could hold on to win. While we watched in the hospital, Spain quickly tied the score, and then, in the last minutes of regulation, scored again and won, and Mexico's astonishing *fútbol* summer of humiliating failure in international competitions, including World Cup qualifying matches, continued.

*   *   *

Last night, August 5, I met a friend for drinks in a small bar just off the Plaza Río de Janeiro that serves excellent cold draft beer, the best I've found in Mexico, and of course *mezcal,* and where you can sit outside. It's been "my place" this summer, a calmer summer than the last one. My friend has been working in Condesa *antros* and bars for years. He grew up in one of the city's poorest neighborhoods—he is so worried about being identified that I've promised not to even name which one—and went to a university and makes a good living now. We'd arranged to meet because I wanted to ask him about the *narcomenudeo* in the nightspots of the Condesa. His personal stories about intimidation by drug gangs and police collusion confirmed what I'd already heard and read, and the specific details he shared with me, which I promised not to reveal, were bizarre and terrifying. Ten or more years ago, around the time the valet parking services were proliferating around the Condesa, he said, was when this problem began. It was one of the valet parking groups that "initiated the *plaza,*" selling drugs to young people going into the bars and clubs. Their ringleader, a Tepito youth, was arrested and sent to prison, where he met a *narco padrino,* or godfather, also from Tepito, known as "El Rafa." After they both got out of prison, in 2009, they opened a *narco tiendita* in the Condesa, on Avenida Nuevo León, the main commercial avenue; it operated out of a van parked in front of the *antro* popularly known as El Mojito. "They sent *chicos* to sell drugs outside and inside the bars and clubs," he said. A year ago, in 2012, El Rafa was arrested for an attempted kidnapping in the Zona Rosa, and was sent back to prison. But, as other *antro* owners and managers had described over the past months, the pressure from the gangs had since grown. Nightclub security guards have been beaten savagely; sometimes the guards, as soon as the gangs conveyed their threats or warnings, simply fled their posts. Obviously, many of the Condesa clubs and bars are extremely lucrative, but their owners and managers have lately been consumed by stress and fear, not only for their own lives, but because even a misunderstanding with the gangs could provoke, for example, on any night, a machine-gunning of clients and staff, such as occurs all over narco-controlled Mexico, but hasn't occurred, yet, in the DF.

Many of the young Tepito drug dealers wear Santería necklaces and sometimes they leave esoteric Santería graffiti, as they did on the walls of a washroom of a club in the center, to mark their turf or to leave messages that only somebody familiar with Santería symbols would understand. That would seem to express a belief in magic powers, but also in the spirituality of Santería— like the Santa Muerte cult, the Afro-Caribbean folk religion has a syncretic relationship to Roman Catholicism—and a faith in the holiness and even the redemptive potential of crime. It would be an expression of their surroundings too, something that they'd learned "in the neighborhood," and that maybe they'd been manipulated into identifying with. The Tepito residents interviewed by Radio Nederland had described La Unión gang members as devout followers of the Santa Muerte who even go on Catholic pilgrimages to Spain. At Doña Queta's Santa Muerte shrine in Tepito, Santería divinities are also venerated. If the *chicos* who belong to a Tepito *narcomenudeo* gang really are devout in some way—if their Santería trappings are not just gangster pretense and vanity—then they may even see themselves as holy warriors on a violent pilgrimage through a cursed land, rife with injustice, corruption, and hypocrisy, which must be purged of all enemies and made submissive to their will.

In the middle of our conversation, my friend received a phone call from a Mexican woman now living in Paris. They were having an affectionate, friendly conversation. Then I heard my friend saying enthusiastically, "This city has a volcanic energy. . . . Yes, next time we'll trade stories about the city. . . . It's really beautiful here. Here, it's *poca madre*, really fucking cool." Even someone working in a bar menaced by a drug gang, who'd just shared horrifying stories about his own experiences, hadn't lost sight of the greater city. Like so many others, and like me, he is in thrall to the DF. While I waited for him to finish his conversation—now he was recommending that she read a book by Edmond Jabes—I thought, So is all this just one more DF story? And then I thought, What do I care? Let them fuck around with the Condesa etc. *plaza*, I don't go to those clubs, and neither do most of my friends; as long as they don't harm innocent people, let them sell all the drugs they want. Anyway, my drug-using friends all order their drugs over the phone, to be delivered. It's not as if the dealers stand around in the Covadonga, or ordinary cantinas, or a little bar like this one we're in now. This way of thinking has some justification, every megacity breeds crime in one form or another. But, of course, innocent people *have* been harmed, I thought. Maybe not *all* of the missing Tepito young people were "innocent" of any kind of involvement in the drug trade and of the potential consequences of that in Mexico, but surely some were, and maybe they all were, because no one has provided any evidence to the contrary. Their families have been harmed. Ana María Vargas, Ruth Marines, Jennifer Robles, and Danae Téllez have been harmed.

When my friend got off the phone, I asked him what was happening now in the Condesa. He said that what he'd been hearing from other *antro* owners and managers was, "It's a period of realignment for the mafia capos. The PRI wants the city. Peña Nieto's drug gangs are coming in to take over the *plaza*. The PRD gangs are being pushed out. That's what people are saying."

Peña Nieto's drug gangs? I thought, If people keep saying that sort of thing, it can't be coming from nowhere; there must be at least a symbolic truth to it. Mentions of the federal police had cropped up in the Heavens case: in one witness's statement, for example, and in the conversations that Pablo de Llano had with his source, and that I had with mine. PRI drug gangs, logically—with the federal government now ruled by the PRI—would be protected or led by Federales, along with local police allied with them; PRD gangs by Mexico City police. But is that all the PRI "wants" the city for? To sell drugs in Condesa *antros*? But drug gangs provide deep and dangerous penetration, especially of the police, I thought. Such penetration brings the capos—those for whom not only the gangs but also the police ultimately work—closer to those they most want to corrupt, and this spawns upwardly climbing chains of corruption. The drug gangs hold a key to the city's stability. If what the city's true powers want most of all is stability, then it will be "Peña Nieto's drug gangs" they'll have to placate, and the police and politicians who protect those gangs. I felt depressed about the city's future. I felt I was beginning to understand more than I wanted to understand, and could prove nothing. This is what my obsession with the Heavens case—a case I'd begun to follow on my own, rather than as a journalist with an assignment—had brought me to.

My friend said that the situation in the clubs and bars had calmed since the After Heavens *levantón*. That drug gang's van, he said, which for years had operated from in front of El Mojito, was gone now. Police, at least for the time being, were closely

monitoring the adherence of clubs and bars to closing hour regu-
lations. No more laissez-faire "let them have a few more hours,"
said my friend. "What was that club doing anyway," he said of
Heavens, "staying open like that until noon?" He thought the
Heavens case was part of the "realignment among capos" that
he'd mentioned, the elimination of one gang by another, or else
a "settling of accounts." He told me he'd heard a rumor that the
missing twelve had already been taken to the *pozolero*. I told him
I'd heard that rumor too. It was terrible to think about in every
way, twelve young people, including five women, boiled away
to nothing in a vat of acid. An emphatic vacancy. The Heavens
case is a synthesis of the terrible tragedy that has befallen Mexico.
The Heavens case is as Mexican as *pozole* itself.

A friend of his passed by on the sidewalk and stopped to
sit at our table. This was the newspaper *Reforma's* renowned
cartoonist "Camacho," whose graphic history of President Calderón's disastrous *sexenio*, published earlier this year, had become
a Mexican bestseller. The waitress announced last call, and he
ordered two whiskeys. Camacho, who looked to be in his late
thirties or early forties, told me that he'd read my book about
Aura. In 2006, his wife, five months pregnant with their first
child, had died of cancer. Seven years later, he was still alone,
still trapped deep inside his terrible loss. He said he'd met me,
or nearly met me, a couple of times several years ago, not long
after Aura had died. He'd shied away from talking to me then,
he said, sensing that I wouldn't want to talk, and that a conversation would be too difficult for both of us. He showed me, on
his smartphone, a newspaper column recently published by a
friend of his. In the column, titled "Defeats," his friend, Juan
García de Quevedo, reflects on the suffering of someone close
to him, someone who provokes worries about suicide: "There

are moments in life when you are chased by the black dogs of depression and uninterest in life. . . . On the way home, soaked by the rain, you come upon a bar and stop in for a whiskey to warm your body and soul. One whiskey follows another." Camacho and I had a moving conversation, there in the little bar. He spoke without self-pity. We spoke like two friends who know what they're talking about.

Now it is the next morning, August 6. This morning's headline in *Reforma*: *Cerca crimen a la Ciudad*, "Crime Closes in on the City." The subheadline: "A Wave of Violence on the Periphery." A colored map, headed "12 Bands Operate in the DF," shows where around the city each band, or gang, is based. The story's lead sentence: "Organized crime is coming ever closer to the Distrito Federal." Most of the gang violence, the paper reports, is in the México State municipalities adjacent to the DF. In the last four months, there have been 208 killings there. The national cartels, La Familia Michoacana and the Gulf Cartel, are disputing this territory, according to the newspaper. Other organized crime groups, including cells belonging to the Beltrán Leyva Cartel, are also fighting for "control of the drug trade and extortion from businesses, such as bars and nightspots," in those municipalities. Restaurant-bars have been machine-gunned and burned. Inside a bar in Neza, two men and two women were executed. The story makes no mention of the Heavens case.

On September 9, Jovi and I will be moving up to Brooklyn, maybe for as long as ten months. She wants to learn English. I feel sad to be relinquishing this beautiful apartment on the

Plaza Río de Janeiro, but we don't need three bedrooms and three bathrooms, and with its high rent—Jon Lee gave up his share of the apartment in May—keeping it makes little sense. Hopefully, when Jovi and I return to the DF, I'll be able to buy an apartment, a place near this one. The DF is home now, whatever is going to happen here. The other day, as we were walking through the Plaza Río de Janeiro, Jovi said that the *David* statue's *pompas* looked like chewed gum. A few afternoons ago, we were just coming into the plaza when we saw a young man in a tracksuit with a whiplike arm motion cast a weighted net, like those people use to catch fish close to shore, to swoop up pigeons gathered over the corn kernels he'd tossed onto the paved path. He walked swiftly away, carrying his loudly warbling captives in a tightly netted bundle under his arm, looking back nervously at us over his shoulder. Two old women, in their own warbling voices, were reprimanding him, and one was near tears. Jovi wondered if what he'd done was illegal and if we should call for the police. I had no wish to give him a hard time. People will do what they need to do to feed their families, even kidnap pigeons from parks.

    One recent afternoon a photographer who was taking my picture for a Chilean magazine made me stand in front of a Spanish colonial home tucked in deep shade into a corner of the plaza. The house's owner, an enormous, lightly bearded man, came out and asked us what we were doing. The photographer told him. Then, just like that, the owner invited us in for lunch and wine with his friends. He is an artist, originally from Sonora, and he'd prepared a delicious Sonoran lunch, with a *machaca* casserole and flour tortillas. He was generous with his wine too. He regaled us with stories of his youth, when he'd spent five years exploring South America by bicycle.

This morning, in the plaza, I saw the elderly man who practices Asian swordplay, and who looks like a grizzled Pablo Picasso, tutoring a student, a girl of about ten, in *Kill Bill* moves.

A woman in the plain habit of a missionary nun—denim dress, white coif—stops me on the sidewalk on Calle Durango. She has a pleasant, young face, bright and lively dark eyes. A white adhesive strip wrapped into a tight tube around the tip of her nose makes it protrude like Pinocchio's. She has traveled all over the world, she tells me, evangelizing, spreading the Word of God. It was Barack Obama, she says, who revealed her calling to her. She and Barack Obama grew up together, she tells me, in El Paso, Texas. Even then, she says, Barack Obama never went anywhere without a Bible under his arm. He was so noble, so good, so polite, so dedicated to God, she says. Barack Obama told her that he wished he could go out into the world to spread the Word of God but even back then he knew that he couldn't, knew that he was called to do other things. But you, Sister Catalina, Barack Obama told her, you have to go out into the world and spread the Word. And so she did. All over the world, to so many countries. Which countries? I ask. She's been to Sinaloa, she says. She's been to Sonora, to Tamaulipas, Tabasco, and Chiapas, she's been all over the world. But the people in Chiapas are selfish and mean, she says. Such poor people, such hard lives, so in need of God, but they are greedy, those *chiapecos*. What have you brought us? they asked her in Chiapas. Money? Food? Nothing, she said, only God and his Word, his message of love, and the *chiapecos* told her that if she had nothing more to give them, she should go away.

The other night Jovi and I talked about the Heavens case. Jovi is, as they say here, *muy barrio*. When she moved at seventeen with her father and younger brother from Veracruz, they lived in México State, in one of those places that Juanca doesn't like, where streets are named for flowers, and where her family and many of her friends still live. She finished high school and when she started studying at the UAM, not so very long ago, she moved on her own to Iztapalapa, another ancient Indian barrio nearly as notorious as Tepito. There she spent the rest of her adolescence and her early twenties. She never wants to go to Tepito with me, not even to buy DVDs. I get the feeling she doesn't like Tepito much, though she's never explicitly said so. She always says, "Be careful," when I go there. The vox populi in the barrios, Jovi told me, is that the missing Tepito young people must have done something to provoke the violence that befell them, that they owed something, that it was a settling of scores, and that this explained the apparent *valemadrismo*, the indifference, of people in the city regarding the case. "You know how this city is," she said. "People will come out to march over anything; it doesn't have to be about something that happened here." But in this case, only the families were marching. "Why do you think that is?" she asked. She understands the city, its underlying energies and dynamics, as I never could. I feel sad that the stigma attached to Tepito, manipulated by the Mancera government and the media in the Heavens case, has come to so define the kidnapping of twelve young people, like a quarantine wall around it. But I am beginning to understand how this city conserves and balances its diffuse and wild energies, waiting for what its many communities recognize as a real emergency to coalesce around it, as it did last summer, sending a million-voiced howl of protest and warning to the world, when faced with the election of Enrique Peña Nieto as president of Mexico.

Jovi agrees that Mancera's handling of the Heavens case, at least as I've described it to her, is wrong and should be exposed and condemned. But the city is larger than Mancera, she tells me, and it is larger than the police, and it is larger even than the cartels. Any cartel that actually tried to take over the DF would be hopelessly outnumbered and overwhelmed. Just with all the universities, the activist groups, the anarchists, and so on, said Jovi, the streets would fill; there'd be barricades, and every kind of resistance. People would fight to save the DF. What cartel would be even crazy enough to try, with all the forces it would find arrayed against it? But the PRI represents a more realistic threat than the cartels to the city's spirit. "Even if Mancera is a total failure as a mayor," said Jovi, "that doesn't mean people are going to vote for the PRI." The city has no automatic allegiance to the PRD, she said, but the people in this city are smart, and they'll vote for whoever offers the best vision and ideas for the city, probably someone from Morena, AMLO's new party— who knows? "The people in this city," insisted Jovi, "know how to force the city government to answer to them." The other night my friend the artist Yoshua Okón said something similar, grounded in the character of the city in which he has lived all his life, but with a note of warning. "The PRI took the federal government back through a dirty and sophisticated campaign of disinformation and fear," said Yoshua. "It won't surprise me if the PRI tries the same tactics here. Mexico City is the only hope left to us in this country against the total hegemony of the PRI. The PRD's only chance is through the wide and loyal support of the population. To win that, it had better abandon its corrupt practices and defend the rule of law and the public space that little by little it has been selling to the private sector.

That's the only way it can recover its credibility and support from the people of this city."

Sunday night Jovi and I were returning late, around midnight, from a restaurant on Alvaro Obregón. We were walking down Orizaba, only a few blocks from home. The street, like all the other side streets in Colonia Roma at that hour, was dark and nearly deserted. Suddenly we heard screams, and saw a young woman running down the sidewalk. Ahead of her we saw a police car that had just turned the corner nearly bump up alongside a black car, which accelerated away, police in pursuit. We ran after the girl, and a young man who was packing up a sushi stand on the corner grabbed a delivery bike and took off. He reached her first, and then rode ahead, after the two automobiles. When we caught up to the girl she was hyperventilating and crying. She'd been robbed, she told us. A man had leaped from the black car we'd seen, threatened her with a pistol, stolen her purse and phone, and then gotten back into the car, which another man was driving. Jovi was talking to her, trying to calm her. A small crowd had gathered. A police car suddenly swooped to a stop alongside us. A policeman jumped from the passenger seat, opened the back door, looked at Jovi, and shouted excitedly, "Get in!" Jovi pointed at the other girl. "Get in! We caught them!" The people on the sidewalk broke into cheers and shouts of congratulations. The girl climbed inside, and as the policeman was getting back into the front passenger seat he glanced at us with a gleeful and proud grin that still hadn't faded as the car sped forward.

Saturday, August 10. Alejandro Almazán, the multi-award-winning writer and journalist, throws a barbecue for his birthday in the apartment he shares with Manuel Larios, "Meño," also a journalist, just around the corner, on Calle Puebla. They're Covadonga tablemates, regulars at last summer's revels in my apartment. There are lots of Mexico City journalists at the party. Some are beat reporters, directly covering the city's politics; others are long-form *cronistas* who publish in magazines. I'm surprised to discover that they are just as alarmed by and suspicious of Mayor Mancera as I am, since I know that I tend to exaggerate my contempt for public figures I take a dislike to, and sometimes become fixated. "Mancera is just here to hand the city over to the PRI," says one of the city's most prominent daily political reporters. "Somebody has Mancera by the balls," says another; "the question is who?" So far, I learn, Mancera hasn't sponsored one single initiative to improve city life in the manner of his *jefe de gobierno* predecessors; even the popular *ecobici* bicycle sharing program hasn't been expanded. Magalí Tercero, the celebrated urban *cronista*, tells me, "We had twelve years of heaven in this city, but now it's gone."

It's been an eventful few weeks in Mexico, one dismaying headline replaced by another before the significance of the former has had a chance to be fully absorbed. On July 19, Raúl Salinas de Gortari was exonerated of charges of illicit enrichment when a federal judge ruled that seventeen million dollars in frozen wealth and thirty-one confiscated properties should be returned to him. Salinas—"the inconvenient brother of the impure president," the magazine *Proceso* called him—is a symbol of the rampant patronage and corruption of Carlos Salinas de Gortari's PRI presidency (1988–1994), years during which Raúl, the older brother, amassed a vast and publicly flaunted fortune, with hundreds of millions stashed in overseas accounts. Following his brother's presidential term, Raúl had spent a decade in jail on charges of embezzlement, tax fraud, and money laundering, and for the 1994 homicide of his brother-in-law, PRI Secretary General José Francisco Ruiz Massieu; but during twelve years of PAN rule judges had absolved him, one by one, of each of those charges. Now Raúl's seventeen years of legal embroilments seemed finally to have ended. In *Reforma,* the esteemed political commentator and writer Denise Dresser wrote of the Salinas de Gortaris, "They're a family that exemplifies how politics function in this country, and the rottenness of those politics. They're a Mexican mafia."

Days later, a federal judge in Guadalajara delivered an even more surprising and disturbing ruling when, on the basis of a "judicial technicality," he ordered the release of the notorious drug lord Rafael Caro Quintero from a federal penitentiary. Caro Quintero, accused by the U.S. government of having masterminded the 1985 slaying of DEA agent Enrique "Kiki" Camarena, had twelve years left of his sentence, and was likely to face further charges in the United States. The Obama administration responded to the surprise release, of which it received no advance warning, with outrage, and pressured the Peña Nieto government to recapture Caro Quintero so that he could be extradited to the United States. But the sixty-year-old capo immediately vanished on leaving prison and good luck finding him now. "In the days following the capo's sudden liberation," wrote a reporter in *Proceso,* "in the U.S. embassy offices in Mexico City, comments such as this were prevalent: 'It would have been better if they'd just let him escape from prison; that wouldn't have been so blatant or offensive.'"

The Monterrey-based journalist Sanjuana Martínez wrote in SinEmbargo.com: "The Enrique Peña Nieto government's agreements with major drug cartels in Mexico cannot remain hidden or backstage. These agreements include the distribution of territories and their respective domains for drug trafficking. Within these agreements surely there is a commitment to free the illustrious drug lords, those who've given their lives for the cause and silently endured decades behind bars, so that they can get out of jail and enjoy their fortunes."

Juanca said, "If they freed Caro Quintero, it's because they have some job for him to carry out."

Whenever the PRI captures an important drug trafficker, as occurred this summer with the arrest of Zeta capo "Z-40," it is believed by most Mexicans to be either because U.S. government authorities have pressured them into it, or because it's a strategic move that benefits other rival figures and groups. Many who voted for the PRI in the summer of 2012 did so with an acknowledged belief that only a pact between the victorious PRI and one powerful cartel, or with a group of cartels, might restore peace to the country: an end to violence, if not to corruption. Though the violence rages on, maybe, one day—according to this optimistically pessimistic scenario—if ever an alliance of criminal organizations and the PRI successfully takes hold, its rivals vanquished, the narco war will wane. Then the PRI and those crime groups, and their economic allies, can rule over and under Mexico together. In my mind it would be something like Putin's Russia, though probably with a more complex and combustible prescription of politics, crime, and money than in Russia.*

More ominous in this context than the absolving of Salinas Gortari and the freeing of Caro Quintero was the

---

* As this book was going to press, the Sinaloa Cartel capo, Joaquín Guzmán, El Chapo, was captured. Please see Appendix note for more on this.

news, in August, that PRI members of Congress had voted to roll back federal laws regarding transparency and access to information—laws enacted twelve years earlier, during the hopeful period following the "overthrow" of the PRI by President Fox's election. National and international anticorruption and human rights groups credit the laws with having ensured significant advances in Mexican society in those areas in the years since. The laws aided and protected the team of *New York Times* reporters who won a 2012 Pulitzer Prize for their investigatory pieces on Walmart and its bribery of officials in Mexico. They're gone now, those laws.

Given what we've seen so far, I don't understand how anybody could still be credulous enough to buy any of that garbage about a "new PRI."* However, I live in the DF, where people are used to thinking of the PRI as Mexico's problem, not theirs. Inside that bubble, I'd for years maintained my own bubble. But by last summer, that had begun to change, and I undertook to learn what I could in a short time. I know that some of my newfound convictions can be somewhat adolescent if only for being so passionately held. Some of the innocence has been drained from my way of living in the DF, but innocence isn't something that at my age I have much use for. Though I suppose there is also a kind of innocence at the heart of my knight-errant spirit in the summer of 2013, a fantasy ambition to "save the city from Death!" But the city's resilience and energy, its iconoclastic individual and community spirit, aren't dependent on me or my perceptions; that's something the city famously discovered about itself in the immediate aftermath of the devastating 1985 earthquake, and has sustained and built on ever

---

* *Time* magazine hailed Peña Nieto's presidency in those words on the cover of its November 30, 2012, issue. But "new PRI" babble was all over the U.S. media.

since. The Distrito Federal is the one true bastion against the complete restoration of the PRI and its "perfect dictatorship." All over the city I hear people saying so, in one way or another, nowadays, and many use precisely this phrase: "the last bastion."

Sunday night, August 18. I come home a little before midnight. The lobby is dark, the television is off, and only one of Ebrard's *guarura* is present, sitting up wide awake on the couch. I probably shouldn't reveal which *guarura* he was. We speak awhile, first about the Heavens case. He says he's heard that the twelve kidnapped were clean; and regarding their possible involvement in criminal activity, all there is against them is that two of the kids are the offspring of imprisoned narcos. I say that so far this is the sense I have of it too. I ask how his boss, the former mayor, is doing, and the *guarura* says that it's a dangerous time. Ebrard, he says softly, has been the only one really *chingando* Peña Nieto. AMLO too, I think, but everyone expects fiery populist opposition from AMLO; I suspect the intelligence and even the reasonableness of Ebrard's criticisms cut deeper.

The danger to which the *guarura* is referring doesn't have to be elaborated on. I think immediately of Donaldo Colosio, the urbane PRI presidential candidate assassinated in 1994 just when he was gaining traction as a national figure by unexpectedly campaigning as a reformist who spoke of Mexicans' "thirst for justice." Carlos Salinas de Gortari surely hadn't expected his appointed successor to wage a "thirst for justice" campaign, certainly one of his least favorite political agendas. This is a reason it is commonly believed in Mexico that Salinas was behind the killing, which is also a reason that the reviled former president, for all his continuing offstage power and influence, has been forced to lead a nearly clandestine life. Carlos Salinas, of course, is routinely described as Peña Nieto's "political godfather." What lessons does the godson take from the godfather? Political assassinations of nationally low-profile but locally influential opposition figures were a PRI electoral tactic in the 2013 summer elections. To assassinate the widely beloved AMLO would instantly spark a violent national uprising. Ebrard, like Colosio, doesn't yet inspire that kind of national devotion. His recent outspoken combativeness may be part of a strategy to overcome an image as an effete DF progressive. But with the controversies over the reform of Pemex and the PRD leadership's role in the "Pact for Mexico," Ebrard has been winning enemies not just within the PRI but within his own party as well.

"*Esto se va a poner cabroncito,*" says the *guarura*. "This is going to get heavy."

On August 9, the Procuraduría, the DF chief prosecutor's office, had announced a significant breakthrough in the Heavens case. Finally one of the "seventeen kidnappers" caught on the video outside the *after* was arrested: Ricardo Antonio Méndez Muñoz, "El Negro," twenty-nine, admitted belonging to La Unión, and claimed that during the operation his role, for which he said he was paid a little over two hundred dollars, was to keep an eye out for police. But soon afterward, he said, he was sent to Coatzacoalcos, Veracruz, to stand guard in a safe house where three of the kidnapped—two males and a female—were being held. All three, he told his interrogators, had been killed there, the men executed with firearms, the woman suffocated. El Negro also said that the kidnappers were demanding a ransom of fifteen million pesos, which strengthened the Tepiteño families' beliefs that the missing, or most of the missing, remained alive. His capture seemed by far the most important break in the case so far, though Chief Prosecutor Rodolfo Ríos warned the press not to draw conclusions, because the three bodies still had to be found. Veracruz authorities joined DF and federal police and forensic experts in a search for corpses in the general area identified by El Negro, and found seven. Over the next suspenseful week or so, forensic testing revealed that none of those corpses belonged to the missing Tepiteños. El Negro was quickly forgotten, his testimony a puzzle that soon prosecutors, police, and their spokespersons no longer even alluded to in their statements about how steadily the investigation was proceeding.

On August 19, the DF's anti-kidnapping police announced the arrest in Toluca of "El Chucho" Carmona, a bar owner and presumed member of the faction La Unión Insurgentes, which had employed, according to some news reports, the drug dealer murdered outside the bar Black in the Condesa. Prosecutors now affirmed that the Heavens *levantón* was tied to a *narcomenudeo* turf war between La Unión Insurgentes and La Unión de Tepito.

August 20. At a party in our apartment, Nayeli, a news editor who is Meño's boss at the newspaper he reports for, *Más por Más*, as well as his girlfriend, tells us about an adventure she recently had aboard a party bus. She and a girlfriend who writes for the monthly magazine *Chilango* were invited to a publicity cocktail party aboard a party bus so that they could write about it in their respective publications. Two young men outfitted in designer shirts unbuttoned to expose their chests, gelled hair, etc.—a pair of typical *mi reyes*—tried to pick them up. Nayeli went to the washroom, leaving her drink by her stool, just as her friend went to the bar carrying her own glass for a refill. A while later, she began to feel strange, and said she wanted to go home. Hey, said the *mi reyes,* we'll drive you home. Come on, let us take you home in our car. Why would you rather take a taxi? Taxis aren't safe for a beautiful young woman at night, let us take you home, *ándale.* But Nayeli shook them off and caught a taxi. She felt a frenzied panic coursing through her body, and also hot flashes. By the time she got home she had so much energy she was practically bouncing off walls but then, suddenly, she fell into unconsciousness. When she woke hours later she understood that those two *mi reyes* she'd met on the party bus had drugged her drink. Needless to say, the party bus company received no publicity plug.

Gonzalo and Pia have brought a huge pot of tamales to the party. We've planned a party jam session in my apartment, a sort of encore to last summer's more spontaneous *tocada,* when their adolescent son Jero got to play guitar with his hero Juan Cirerol at the annual Aura hamburger cookout, which we decided not to hold this year. Juan Carlos Reyna, the Nortec guitarist, said he was going to bring other musicians, including Quique Rangel, the Café Tacuba base player. Cirerol is off touring somewhere. In Paris, Jero has been fronting bands with musicians several years older than he is. In a few weeks, in Paris, he'll be starting his first year of high school, but he says he wants to go to college in the DF, at the UNAM, because he'd rather play with Mexican than French rockers.

Jero has brought his acoustic guitar. But Reyna turns up empty-handed. In his apartment, he says, he has only an electric guitar. And Quique Rangel has had to cancel because his girlfriend has fallen ill. So there will be no concert, unless Jero wants to give us a solo show. A gawky and shy fifteen-year-old with braces, and ears sticking out, Jero stands stiffly against a counter in the kitchen emphatically shaking his head no.

A number of the guests are Mexico City reporters and the talk among them tonight is especially about the teachers' strike against Peña Nieto's and "the Pact's" educational reforms. It's one of the Pact's necessary reforms, most people tell me, but there is sympathy for the teachers too. It seems unfair that underpaid teachers, especially those who work in extremely underfunded rural schools, should have to sacrifice their job security to evaluation exams when no one else on the federal payroll has been required to do the same. Some sixteen thousand teachers from the national teachers' union, mostly from Oaxaca and Guerrero, have poured into the city, blocking and tying up traffic, especially in the center, and they have surrounded both the Senate and the Congress, preventing legislators from entering. They've set up a tent city in the Zócalo. Both Mancera and the PRI seem paralyzed by the protests. So far neither dares use force to try to disperse or control the protesters. (The teachers' so far fruitless protests, marches, and occupations will grow in the coming weeks, and endure well into the fall.)

It's a good party, maybe the last we'll ever have in this apartment. A lot of conversation and laughter, plenty to drink, lots of tamales. Eventually, well past midnight, guests begin to leave. Jovi goes to bed. The approach of dawn finds Reyna and me up alone, still drinking, listening to music on YouTube; only this one aspect of the night and dawn is an exact reprise of last summer. At about six a.m. a new girlfriend phones Reyna; she's coming to his apartment, so he has to leave. I finally go to bed. And then it's about two hours later and Jovi is frantically shaking me awake. There's an earthquake. Sirens are wailing. She runs to stand inside a doorframe. She's furious because it took so long to wake me, too long for us now to be able to run downstairs. Disoriented, I think I am in Guatemala. I'm still drunk. I stand watching her, feeling confused about where I am and what is happening, and then I get it, and run to squeeze into the doorframe alongside her, but she tells me to go and stand under my own doorframe. The earthquake, measuring 6.2, is one of the strongest in the unusual series of quakes the city has experienced over the last year. This one also lasts nearly two minutes, I learn later, but I've been awake for only the tail end. People say it's a good sign that we've had so many quakes recently, that tectonic plates beneath the earth are shifting and making adjustments, relieving pressures that might otherwise lead to a massive killer quake. On the living room floor are the telltale splotches of crumbled cement that shake down from the ceiling only when the swaying of our building has been especially forceful and sustained. The walls and floor begin to tremble again—it's an aftershock—and Jovi and I run outside and scamper down the six flights of stairs to the lobby, and out onto the sidewalk.

August 22. It's a little past nine in the morning when I sit down at my computer and, as I routinely do, open up SinEmbargo.com. Only a few minutes before, Martin Moreno has filed a breaking story about the Heavens case. Bodies thought to be those of the abducted young people have been discovered by federal police in a concealed grave near a small farmhouse in a wooded area of the México State municipality Tlalmanalco, about fifty-five kilometers outside the DF, near La Mesa ecotourism park. Moreno's sources say police and others from the PGR (the federal attorney general's office) have been excavating the grave since last night, and that thirteen corpses are buried there, twelve those of the victims abducted outside Heavens. AnimalPolitico.com carries the same story, though it says seven bodies have been found, and only that they are possibly connected to the Heavens case. A few hours later it is reported that DF chief prosecutor Ríos has told Radio 98.5 that so far five bodies have been found in the grave, and that it will not be possible to identify them until DNA testing, which should take two days, has been performed. Ríos says that it is possible there are more bodies; later he tells a television station that there are seven. The lawyer for the families of the abducted young people, Ricardo Martínez, says that according to his PGR, PGJDF, and México State sources, the bodies are indeed those of the missing Tepiteños. Moreno files again to report that according to his sources the thirteenth corpse is that of a young man from Guadalajara, who before wasn't counted among the abducted because nobody had filed a missing person report on his behalf. Moreno reports that the families had told authorities about him—a youth they knew by the name "Alancito"—from the very beginning.

Chief Prosecutor Ríos tells the media that finding the grave was a result of collaborative work between his PGJDF investigators and the federal PGR. That claim is contradicted hours later when the federal attorney general, Jesús Murillo Karam, says that the discovery of the grave was accidental. Federal police had gone to the remote *rancho* to investigate a possible safe house where arms were stored, he said, and had found the grave nearby, covered with lime and asbestos and a lid of cement. Two unnamed men taken into detention there are described as *lugareños,* locals.

But perhaps this too will turn out to be a false alarm, like El Negro's declaration that three of the dead were in Veracruz. It will be at least two days until the DNA testing is completed, according to federal authorities. But when I wake the next morning, Saturday, it's to the news that five of the corpses have already been identified. Three of the five—Guadalupe Karen Morales, her husband, Alan Omar Atiencia Barranco, and Rafael Rojas Marines—are related to the three families Pablo de Llano, the *El País* reporter, and I had visited in the Tepito *vecindad* apartment a month before. Only Alan Omar Atiencia, whose brother Juan had met us at the subway stop and walked us over there, had been identified by DNA. Ana María Vargas's daughter, Guadalupe Karen, had been identified by a tattoo of entwined dolphins on her hip, and Rafael Rojas, Ruth Marines's son, by the metal plates in his arm and his new prosthetic teeth. Also identified were the corpses of Gabriela Ruiz Martínez and Josué Piedra Moreno.

Pablo de Llano had returned from his vacation in Spain the same night the grave was discovered, though he didn't know that when he went to sleep. He was awoken by a phone call from one of his editors the next morning—that was yesterday, Friday—who gave him the news. Then he'd spent a long day and night reporting the story, much of it with the families; at the Bunker, the prosecutor's office; and at the PGR's DF headquarters. During the day he'd also gone out to Tlalmanalco, and to the isolated *rancho* called La Negra that held the grave, where PGR police, forensic experts, and earthmoving equipment were at work. The area was cordoned off and he hadn't been able to get anywhere near the grave, but he was able to speak to police coming out from the site, who told him that the scene there was extremely grisly and that the stench was horrible. Pablo told me that the wooded area was very remote, an "in the middle of nowhere" kind of place. It seemed hard to believe, he said, that the PGR had found the grave there by accident. The DF chief prosecutor's and the federal PGR's first statements about the grave had been published and broadcast in the media before any of the family members had been informed of the discovery. Later that Friday, though, the families had been summoned to an afternoon meeting at five-thirty with Chief Prosecutor Ríos at the Bunker. But at four-thirty the PGR held its own press conference. María Victoria Barranco was on the subway on the way to her meeting with the city's chief prosecutor when she received a text message on her phone saying that her son Alan Omar's corpse had been identified. "We'd agreed that we were to be the first to find out, and it wasn't like that," she told a reporter. "I need to see the body of my son. What if they give me a body that isn't his and I bury it? My son had tattoos. I want to see those tattoos. The authorities didn't do anything; we had confidence in them at one time, but we've been deceived. I found out on the metro, and if the prosecutor knew it was my son, why didn't he have the decency to tell me, his mother, first. Why my son? What did he ever do to them?"

That afternoon's meeting in the Procuraduría with Chief Prosecutor Ríos and Raúl Peralta, the chief of the investigative police, in charge of the investigations in the Heavens case, was contentious. Afterward the families went to the federal PGR's DF headquarters for another meeting that lasted until one in the morning. Outside the PGR, family members and friends gathered while others were speaking to officials inside. Pablo saw Danae Téllez, Gabriela Téllez's teenage daughter, sobbing. When he saw Jacqueline Robles, Jennifer's sister, arrive he thought that she looked typically composed and cool. Only a few seconds later, he told me, he heard a pained shriek, turned, and saw Jacqueline doubled over, wailing, and a male friend holding on to her.

Saturday afternoon, August 24, Pablo and I return to Tepito, once again to the *tianguis* owned by María Teresa Ramos, maternal grandmother of Jerzy Ortíz, son of El Tanque. The stall is full of family members, four generations in all, middle-aged women, younger women, men, children nestled in their mothers' laps. They greet Pablo warmly. "We should have waited to eat these *quesadillas* until you got here, Pablo," says a woman behind the counter, gesturing at the paper plates and take-out containers in front of her. Of all the reporters covering the Heavens story, only Pablo has devoted attention to the families and tried to tell their stories. That day's *Reforma* blatantly "copied" without crediting Pablo's *El País* piece of photographs and short word portraits of the missing young people, reducing the latter to snippets of two or three sentences. María Teresa, the elfish matriarch of the clan, sits behind the counter. Compared with the last time I saw her, her feisty vitality seems depleted. Her lids look swollen and narrowed, as if it is a struggle to hold them open, and her gaze is listless and a bit frightened. She seems lost inside her own sadness and crushed hopes for her youngest grandson. But the younger women project a bustling family solidarity. Jerzy's mother, El Tanque's wife, Leticia Ponce, is speaking to another man at the back of the stall. She'd had a blue diamond tattooed onto her wrist shortly after her youngest son's disappearance to match the one he had in the same spot. Lying atop a pile of John Lennon T-shirts in the shelving along a wall is a copy of that day's *Universal*, open to an inside page, and above the fold there is a headline, *Identifican a cinco del Heaven en fosa*—"Five Identified from Heavens Grave"—and a color photograph showing Leticia from behind, her long blond hair loose and wild-looking in the camera's flash, the blue diamond tattoo like a butterfly perched on her wrist as she reaches out to embrace a woman whose face is contorted in a sob. The man Leticia has been speaking to at the back of the stall holds her in a long hug, and when they part I see Leticia composing herself, wiping tears from her eyes. She comes over to speak with us. Today her hair is tied back, and she wears a yellow long-sleeved pullover shirt with one of those 1960s huge-eyed waif girls printed down the side. She is light-skinned, in her late forties, about five feet three inches, her facial and physical features pleasantly rounded, with a nearly unlined face. She seems almost a Scandinavian type of woman, sweet natured but hearty and strong. Pablo has told me that the other families regard Leticia as their leader, and I can see why. She projects spontaneous warmth, an air of soft manners that is without timidity. She looks you right in the eye, and speaks directly. The notorious capo's wife. The family, prosperous by Tepito standards, clearly belongs to the barrio's upper strata. María Teresa has college-educated grandchildren, the grandson who knows about "communications" but who studied art and became a performance artist, the granddaughter who is a chef. I can't help thinking of the mafia family portrayed in *The Sopranos,* their middle-class mores and aspirations.

Leticia tells us about the meeting with the chief prosecutor at the Procuraduría, the Bunker, the previous evening. She says that in their prior meetings, she and the families had held their tongues, always ceding the benefit of the doubt to the authorities. They hadn't wanted to say anything that could put their abducted relatives or the hoped-for goodwill of the investigators at risk. The meeting last evening, Friday, was different. "The families aired their anger and complaints," she says. Julieta, Jennifer's "mother," the one who sews *Monster Inc.* figures, usually so quiet and stern, had opened the meeting pugnaciously, warning the authorities, "Don't take us for *pendejos.*" Chief Prosecutor Ríos was nearly speechless throughout the meeting, Leticia says. We ask what his demeanor was like. "Stone faced," she says, but also "shaken, no, very consternated." She says, "I wanted my son alive. Just give me back my child and I'll be gone, I don't care about the rest." That used to be her attitude, she says. "But now the situation has changed. I want the people who did this behind bars. This is just the beginning. I want them in prison so that this can't happen again. I don't want this to happen to anybody else."

The families have no faith left in the chief prosecutor and his investigators and police, who over three months of constant assurances that the investigation was advancing failed to provide answers or results. And they are skeptical of the PGR's claim to have found the grave by accident. Nor do they even trust the PGR to correctly identify the corpses. Like María Victoria Barranco, Leticia asks, "What if they give me a body that isn't my son's?" She and the other family members are demanding that Argentine forensics experts be brought to Mexico to verify and complete the autopspies. I think, for a moment, that the families' insistence on Argentine experts is a way of postponing their acceptance of the inevitable. But then Leticia, clutching the sleeve of another woman who is leaving the stall, declares, "A mourning is starting, and I want Jorge to be here." Jorge is El Tanque. Leticia's face crumples, and she begins to cry. El Papis too, she says, referring to Said Sánchez's imprisoned father. "I want them to be here for the reception of the bodies." She is petitioning, she tells us when she turns back to us, for her husband and Said's father to be transferred to a prison in the DF for the funeral. They won't be allowed to go to the funeral, but she wants the caskets brought to them.

Later I think that the vocal distrust of the PGR to correctly identify the bodies, the insistence on Argentine forensic experts, is a way for the families to deny the authorities the opportunity to claim that this one grimly final job has been competently done and executed in good faith when nothing else has been.

A pretty, dark-haired little girl is clutching Leticia's leg. This is her granddaughter, four-year-old Karewit. "*Mi vida*," Leticia coos cheerfully, embracing the girl. "Yes, we're going soon," she tells her. She introduces Karewit to me, and I lean down so we can exchange kisses on the cheek. Karewit wants to go to the fountains at the Monument to the Revolution, which has an esplanade with shooting jets of water. Leticia wants to go too. "I want to get wet, I want to scream," she says emphatically. Her smile is almost embarrassed and contrite, as if she thinks I might regard what she has just confided as odd. Then she says that Karewit gets nervous when she hears people talking about Jerzy. He was Karewit's favorite; she called him, though he was her uncle, *el chiquito guapo*, "the little handsome one." Karawit's father has filled his bedroom with pictures of his brother Jerzy. The father is there in the stall too, and Leticia asks him to hand her his cell phone. She shows us a close-up of a wall covered with a collage of color photos of Jerzy. Karewit leans over the phone and touches one of the images and says, "That's the best one." Leticia asks, "What do you call Jerzy, Karewit?" The little girl smiles and responds shyly, "*El chiquito guapo*," and dances away.

Leticia's cell phone rings, and when she answers, she says, "*Mi amor*." It is her husband, phoning from prison. After a moment she passes the phone to Pablo, who has interviewed El Tanque in the prison in Hermosillo, Sonora. "Jorge says that God is with us," Leticia tells me. "That only God knows why these things happen." When Pablo gets off the phone, he tells me that El Tanque has told him that he wants to be able to touch his son's coffin.

"*Ya cambia todo*," Leticia says to me. Everything has changed. "It changes your life, and it's not fair." She briefly succumbs to tears again, collects herself, calls for Karewit, and says, "Let's go." Saying good-bye, I embrace Leticia tightly; I can't help myself, and I feel as if I don't want to let go. The imprisoned narco's wife. The warm physical life in my arms encloses the shattered mother inside her. I want to tell her, Believe me, I know, I understand—but I don't say anything like that. Go and get wet in the fountain, go and scream! A memory of riding my bicycle in the countryside, screaming Aura's name at the top of my lungs. I remember too, from the first days of death, this mix of manic sociability, shock, displays of "strength," sudden tears, the impulse for magic rites, to get wet and scream. As Leticia is leaving, holding Karewit's hand, Eugenia gives her sister a hard slap on the rear, like a football coach sending a player into a game.

María Teresa's husband, the gray-haired, fit-looking man who, last time we were there, was sent to fetch a T-shirt, is at the stall too. His nickname is "Alain Delon," because the family thinks he resembles the actor. Well, I think, with his soulful eyes and suave demeanor, he resembles Alain Delon more than Mancera resembles George Clooney. Later Pablo tells me that he's a workout freak and long-distance jogger. He uses a long pole to bring a Guns N' Roses T-shirt down from a hanger for a customer.

Eugenia, in a loose beige blouse and jeans, is darker than her sister, and has a similarly gentle and direct manner; it must be a family trait. But right now she looks a little stunned. She has just received a text message on her cell phone, she calmly tells us, that her nephew Jerzy Ortíz's corpse has been identified. The family has a source in the PGR, she tells us. She shrugs helplessly. "Who knows if it's true," she says. Until the Argentines confirm it, she will not accept it. She pauses a long moment, and then says, "If it's not them, then where *en chingados* are they? It's almost worst, if it's not them. Then where are they?" From the very beginning of the case, there has been mistrust between the families and the city's justice authorities. "We told them there were thirteen who were missing," says Eugenia, "but they didn't believe us. It was eighteen days before they even accepted they were there [in Heavens]. Oh, they're just out partying, they told us." It was the families, Eugenia said, who had brought prosecutors and police a witness, a youth from the neighborhood, who knew the identity of at least some of the kidnappers. It was that witness who'd led police to El Negro, the La Unión gang member who admitted to taking part in the kidnapping, but who'd misdirected investigators to Veracruz. That same witness, Eugenia told us, went on a drive around the Condesa with the investigative police chief Raúl Peralta. "He saw a van circling the neighborhood," said Eugenia, "and said, 'That's them! Grab them now or you'll never get another chance.' But Peralta said, 'No, we need an arrest order,' and then he never did anything more about it."

Eugenia is the family note taker at meetings with city prosecutors and investigators and the federal PGR, and she produces two of her notebooks. Pablo wants to get the exact sequence of what was said at yesterday's meetings. The PGR was asserting that some of the bodies had been identified by the clothing they had on, says Pablo, but hadn't they said earlier that the bodies were nude? Hadn't they discovered the clothing in bags nearby? "Yes, nude," says Eugenia. "No, wait," she says, "no." She flips through her spiral notebook, and then lifts her hand to her forehead. "I don't know," she says, flustered. "I was in shock, I think. I missed things. I couldn't keep track of everything."

We go back over the meeting at the Bunker with Chief Prosecutor Rodolfo Ríos and Raúl Peralta, in charge of the police investigation. It's important to Eugenia that we get it right because it was the first time, she says, that the families spoke out and said what they thought. She tells us that at the meeting Leticia had said, looking directly from one official to the other, "Whoever is behind this, whoever falls, whether it's you, Rodolfo, or you, Raúl, I want them captured." Eugenia says, "But they had no responses to anything."

Betty, aunt of Monserrat Loza Fernández, was always the most supportive of the investigators at their meetings, says Eugenia. "She was always tossing them bouquets, saying, 'Oh, thank you, we have so much confidence in you,' but yesterday she stood up and demanded, 'We want answers.' The chief prosecutor ignored her. 'I'm waiting for you to answer me,' she said. She repeated it three times before the chief prosecutor finally turned to her."

"All Ríos said was, 'We're going to capture those responsible,'" says Eugenia. Chief Prosecutor Ríos is a balding man with deeply pitted shadow-encircled eyes, flaccid cheeks, and a large jutting chin that exaggerates the smallness of his thin-lipped mouth. But I've seen him only in news photographs.

"Then Peralta," says Eugenia, "got into an argument with Rafael Rojas's brother. 'Let me finish,' he kept saying, raising his voice." The room erupted angrily, she says, with family members accusing the police chief of speaking like a *grosero*, lacking respect. "Peralta apologized. He said that he'd raised his voice only so that everyone could hear him," says Eugenia, wryly.

Gaby Ruiz's father, who had come from Veracruz, said, "If this was narcos, if there are narcos in Mexico City, it's because you permit it, maybe not you specifically, but you knew. And now you put on this little theater."

Eugenia said, "My daughter Penelope never talks at the meetings. She listens, analyzes, passes me notes on pieces of paper. But yesterday she stood up and raised her hand. Peralta passed her over three times to call on others. But finally he called on her and she said, '*Buenas noches*, I'm Penelope Ponce, the cousin of Jerzy. My question is: Is this case still your responsibility?'"

Penelope is there in the stall too, and Eugenia calls her over so that she can tell us exactly what she'd said. Penelope, who resembles her mother, and seems to be in her late twenties, is the chef. She sits down with us, clasping her hands between her knees. Her expression and dark brown eyes looking grave with concentration, she softly and methodically begins to recount what she said at the meeting. Yes, she'd introduced herself just as her mother said she had, and had asked Ríos and Peralta if the case was still their responsibility. Then she'd said, "If it is, as for me at least, I don't think that's good news. You didn't find them alive, or dead, and you haven't found the people responsible for this. This is just like the other twenty-seven thousand disappeared in Mexico," citing the official number given by human rights groups for the number of disappeared during President Calderón's *sexenio*. "In all these cases, the same thing happens. First you deny that it happened. You say that they weren't even there. That there weren't cars and then that there were cars. Then you criminalize the victims. Because they were out at that hour. Because they're from Tepito. You did the same with Virtual Mix"—another club, from which five young people had disappeared earlier that year—"but there it was because the victims were gay. You try to fill the families with doubts. Maybe in some cases you find them alive, or you find them dead, or you never find them, but you always close the case without finding the guilty ones. But this case isn't finished."

"Twenty-seven thousand, that's just a number," Chief Prosecutor Ríos responded.

"Twenty-seven thousand times the results have been just like in this case," Penelope retorted. "Your incompetence is visible from kilometers away."

With that, the meeting ended.

Penelope couldn't have drawn a truer or more pertinent analogy. Twenty-seven thousand times in Mexico. Only once in the DF but only in the sense that the capital had so far not experienced a *levantón* of so many, like this one. Twenty-seven thousand, and more, cases of government incompetence and malfeasance, and of impunity. The shadow over Tepito and the shadow over Mexico are the same shadow. That shadow has spread over the DF.

As Pablo and I walk out of the Tepito market, a small boy in front of a stall selling fragrances adroitly sprays each of us on one hand with cologne. The strong sweet smell of undoubtedly counterfeit cologne fills the taxi we share back to Colonia Roma. Pablo says the families' lawyer, Ricardo Martínez, told him, and is publicly stating, that he has information—undoubtedly from the PGR—that about thirty men were involved in the kidnapping from Heavens, and that they'd been armed with assault weapons, and had come and departed in vans. This is similar, of course, to what the three young witnesses fortunate enough to escape by fleeing onto Heavens' roof had told authorities. But it is information that Chief Prosecutor Rodolfo Ríos has willfully ignored, and hidden. Pablo and I think we know, more or less, what the Mancera government is so desperate to hide, the presence of assault weapons and vans lending credibility to the witnesses' declarations and what can be inferred from those declarations. But it may be just a matter of time before the truth begins to come out. The federal government, the PGR, now seems to hold the cards in the Heavens case and, in Pablo's words, "is marking the paces," deciding what comes out, and when. The Heavens case, to paraphrase Pablo's source, still has a long way to go before all its political capital will have been spent.

August 25. Five more corpses have been identified: those of Jerzy Ortíz Ponce, Said Sánchez, Jennifer Robles González (Jacqueline's sister), Arón Piedra Moreno, and Monserrat Loza Fernández.

August 26. *Reforma* and other newspapers report that nine of the thirteen bodies were decapitated. Such decapitations are a signature of organized crime. The manner in which Heavens' owner Dax Rodríguez Ledezma and his female companions were murdered—and their bodies tortured, burned, and transported from Guerrero to Morelos to be found there—also bore the grisly symbolism of a narco cartel. The former head police investigator—Raúl Peralta's predecessor—of the DF chief prosecutor's office (PGJDF) told *Reforma*, "The DF isn't a bubble. If they don't sound the alarms, we're going to find ourselves with a grave security problem."

The PGR attorney general, Murillo Karam, seems to be retracting the story that the discovery of the grave was accidental. Now he has told AP that federal investigators were acting on a tip that the bodies might be in Tlalmanalco. Near a cemetery in the area, they spotted an armed man, standing watch, who fled at their approach. The federal investigators proceeded to the ranch with an order to search it. They found bags holding clothes; a box of cell phones; and two "locals" who worked as watchmen there, one of whom, while being questioned, told the investigators that bodies were buried there. And an unidentified PGJDF source has leaked to the press the information that approximately twenty-five men had arrived at the *rancho* at around one in the afternoon that Sunday—less than two hours after the Heavens *levantón* had occurred—in various vans, and ordered the watchmen to leave. Ricardo Martínez, the families' lawyer, tells the press that the thirteen abducted young people were then murdered and buried almost immediately. They were decapitated and dismembered. The killers probably used chain saws.

August 27. Newspapers headline Chief Prosecutor Ríos's announcement at a press conference on Monday that the After Heavens mass kidnappings and murders were a *narcovenganza* by La Unión de Insurgentes against La Unión de Tepito, a settling of accounts for the slaying of the drug dealer Horacio Vite Ángel outside the bar Black in the Condesa. Ríos is sticking to the scenario that the crime was nothing more than the result of a turf war between two local drug-dealing gangs. The chief prosecutor insists, "We're not talking about any cartel, or about organized crime." Ríos announces that there are now three members of La Unión in custody: El Negro; El Chucho Carmona, an associate of Heavens' owner El Lobo Espinoza; and another man recently arrested in the DF, Víctor Manuel Aguilera García, who, according to the chief prosecutor, was involved in bringing the abducted victims to Tlalmanalco. Given the record so far, it seems possible that those La Unión detainees, like Heavens' imprisoned owners, won't confess much more than their own involvement in the crime, or will even, as in the case of El Negro, give disinformation. If that is so, it could be because they fear the consequences of being truthful. Another possibility is that authorities are suppressing, at least for now, other information the detainees might have given. The involvement of the gang being called La Unión Insurgentes certainly could be and probably even is an essential part of the story, but this only highlights the many questions that remain unanswered. Today, at least, the major Mexico City newspapers are striking a critical and even derisive tone. They cite a series of experts who speak about the telltale signs of organized crime in the case and its implications for the city, and *Universal* insists that the "intellectual authors" of the mass kidnappings and murders, not just those who might have been involved in carrying them out, need to be identified. *Reforma* closes its front-page story by reporting that Attorney General Murillo Karam "admitted that [the PGR] has information on the case, but he refused to reveal it because the case is in the hands of the capital's chief prosecutor's office." In *El País* Pablo de Llano, for the first time, wrote about what his own highly placed off-the-record source had told him about the "criminal empowerment" of gangs "protected" by corrupt police agents. This reality seems to be what the city government of Miguel Ángel Mancera doesn't want to acknowledge and is determined to hide: not only that organized crime has brazenly asserted a presence in the DF under his watch but, furthermore, that the city's organized crime problem is rooted in its police.

Neither the chief prosecutor nor anyone else has yet to provide proof that any of the thirteen kidnapped and murdered young people were involved in a *narcomenudeo* gang or even in minor drug dealing. None has yet been linked even circumstantially to the murder of the drug dealer outside Black. There is only a taint by association regarding two of the murdered adolescents: the offspring of Tepito narcos imprisoned ten years ago. Nor has the chief prosecutor, or anybody else, suggested a rationale for why a local gang would kidnap and murder twelve or thirteen seemingly innocent young people in retaliation for the murder of a single drug dealer. At the Monday press conference, Ríos said, "It's what the witnesses have told us. We can't provide a personal opinion about why this has happened." The chief prosecutor has no information—nor even a hypothesis—about why so many people were abducted and killed, or about why those thirteen were chosen.

The PGR seems to be watching the DF's mayor twist silently in the air while deciding when to give him another whack. The president, meanwhile, has kept completely silent about the Heavens case, not even uttering a few politician's platitudes of solace to the families directly affected by this unprecedented act of criminal violence in Mexico's capital, nor offering any words of support during what is clearly, or should be, a trying moment for his friend Mayor Mancera. My source, a month ago, had reflected that if only Mancera would come out and openly acknowledge that the DF now has an organized crime problem—even if his organized crime problem includes his city's police force—and declare that his government is determined to combat it, "then the city would applaud him." And it would! Mexico City likes a fighter, and seems repulsed by the specter of a mayor about whom people are always saying things like, "Someone or something has him by the balls, but who or what?" So why doesn't Mancera do that, and try to rally the city behind him? Instead the mayor triumphantly announces to the press, "The Heavens case is nearly closed."

The spectacle grows more alarming and shameful day by day. We may not be sure of what the *jefe de gobierno,* Miguel Ángel Mancera, is hiding, but, as now seems starkly apparent, he is hiding something in plain sight.

At the end of August, I received an e-mail from Nelly Glatt. She'd read about my book in a magazine for Mexico City's Jewish community. She just wanted to say hello and to know how I was doing. I hadn't seen Nelly since the beginning of the summer of 2012, when, during a therapy session, I'd told her about my driving project, and she'd interpreted it as a means of taking control of my life. A few days later, on August 30, I went to see Nelly again at her cozy office in Las Lomas where, only a week or two after Aura's death, I'd first come to see her. When I arrived I took my seat on the familiar plush leather couch, across the room from where she sat, as regal and beautiful as always. The mood was different, more effusive and friendly than during all those past sessions, even if we adhered to our roles, me speaking about myself, Nelly commenting. I told her about what had happened in my life since that last meeting; in other words, I retraced my steps through the time frame of this chronicle.

Circuits within circuits: February's collapse, the recurrence of trauma symptoms, which I'd pulled myself out of by starting to write this chronicle of that summer. Nelly asked if I still thought about Aura every day. Every day. She's a permanent part of me, I said; it's as though I always know exactly where she is inside me and where to find her whenever I need her. If those words were hyperbolic, it was only to a degree. Every day Aura makes me smile, I said. Or she challenges me. And nearly every day there are also moments when I feel overtaken by her loss and struggle to comprehend it: terrible moments from her last hours come rushing back, and send gutting gusts of dread and confusion through me. Or I encounter somebody who unexpectedly shares an admiring or stirring memory of Aura, which may bring brief tears and, again, that piercing sense of baffled loss, mixed with something sweeter. Enduring love, I suppose that's what it is. The moments pass. Though I will never be able to comprehend Aura's death, I do think I live with it now with less resistance, less corrosively, with less inner panic than before. Aura has her place inside me now, I told Nelly, though I hate that phrase and its false impression of gardened cemetery neatness. What is Aura's place?—death and memory, never neat or orderly, always a forest and an ocean.

"You've learned about death in an important way," said Nelly, "and I imagine it is what you will want to write about from now on. Everyone thinks he or she knows death and almost everybody does to at least an abstract degree, but you know it face-to-face and have lived closely with it in a way that not everybody has." Nelly said that after Aura's death it became a pattern with me to need to come face-to-face with the imminent possibility of my own death in order to wake me up to life again. The time I was hit by a car, and the party bus assault I'd just told her about—both of those incidents had somehow made me pull myself together and get going again. Nelly said that she hoped I was through with needing or looking for that kind of jolt. It didn't surprise her that I'd become so involved with the After Heavens case. She suggested that I was compelled by a wish and even a sense of obligation to be of help—wasn't that true? Somehow I'd known all along, right from the start, what drew me to the case. Of course there was little, if anything, I could do to be of help or solace to the Tepito families, but the "wish" to, yes, that was true. I'd also felt a compulsion to draw closer to, to get to know a little better, this Mexico of violent death and trauma.

Nelly likes parables, or stories that resemble parables. Some are drawn from her years of practice and others from her Jewish faith and Jewish religious writing and tales. She shared a few during that visit. One was a story she'd read in the same magazine in which she'd come across that piece about my book. A rabbi had written about his first visit to Jerusalem many years before, and to a strange little synagogue there that was founded by Jews who'd emigrated from Africa. Embedded in the wall next to the ark holding the Torah, specially illuminated by lamps, was a coffin. He'd never seen a coffin displayed in a synagogue. That the coffin held the remains of an ancestor was inconceivable. Traditional Jewish law, Nelly explained, prohibits the Kohanim—members of the tribe of Levi, the priestly family descended from Aaron, who have a ceremonial role in synagogue prayer services and other special duties—to have contact with or even to be in the same room as the dead. But in this congregation, Jews were encouraged to pray with their eyes fixed on a lamplit coffin. When the visiting rabbi asked the synagogue's rabbi what was up with the coffin, he answered, "You come from a drop of semen, and you go to the tomb, and in the end you must justify all the actions in your life to the Creator. The consciousness of mortality is the most important truth we can engrave within ourselves in order to be able to live life to its fullest."

The coffin as a seemingly heretical visual symbol was an affirmation, not of death, the rabbi wrote in the article Nelly had read, but of the power that the knowledge of the inevitability of death has to transform lives. It reminded me of what the Tepito merchant policeman had said as we walked over to Doña Queta's shrine that day about the Santa Muerte not being "the worship of death itself." The coffin, wrote the rabbi, "requires introspection from whoever observes it" and should direct the observers' thoughts not to death but to life.

Rather than a therapy session, it was more like a valedictory ceremony. Later I thought that our conversation had been somewhat like the ending of the movie *The Wizard of Oz*, when the wizard, in "giving" the Tin Man his heart, the Scarecrow his brain, and the Lion his courage, extols virtues they already possess or have recently won. The wizard's gift is that they finally recognize those virtues in themselves. Nelly—unlike the wizard, in no way a charlatan—gave a meaning to my progress through grief. It was, in many ways, the same meaning that I'd been trying to put into words during the months I'd spent writing this chronicle.

Almost on the same day as my visit to Nelly, Jovi and I had good news. Dr. Parral, my landlord in the Río de Janeiro apartment, who lives upstairs—a crusty but elegant seventy-year-old cardiologist who smokes cigarettes—didn't want us to give up the apartment. To persuade us to stay, he lowered the rent considerably. I was then able to find a subletter within days, a young Frenchman who used to work for Pfizer and now wants to open a bakery in the DF. I had to agree to rent it to him until next July, a couple of months longer than ideal, but what a huge relief not to have to pack everything up and put it away in storage.

The night before we flew to New York, I met Pablo de Llano for drinks in the little bar near the plaza. He told me that the families were refusing to acknowledge that the bodies in the PGR morgue were those of their relatives until foreign experts performed the DNA testing. Many, thought Pablo, were clinging to the belief that the dismembered bodies found in the grave in Tlalmanalco were not actually those of the missing young people, who might still be alive somewhere. Such was the mistrust the families felt for the authorities now, believing them capable of lying even about that, and also of being too incompetent to do the testing correctly; but surely some family members were simply refusing to accept death until it was irrefutably and "scientifically" proved. Ruth Marines had told Pablo that she'd received a message from her son Rafael—a candle flame taking the visible form of an angel and then of a heart—which she interpreted as meaning that he was all right where he was now and that she shouldn't worry about him. When Pablo asked if she meant still alive somewhere in Mexico, Ruth responded, "I know that Rafa is no longer with us here on earth; he's in that other place."

Yet Ruth Marines was still among the relatives who refused to accept the remains that the authorities said they had identified as those of their murdered young people. Those remains had by now been moved from a PGR forensic morgue to the DF justice system's Institute for Forensic Sciences. There a new round of DNA testing, city authorities said, had reconfirmed the identities of the bodies, and the families were summoned to receive them. But only four families had complied, including the family of the thirteenth victim, Alan Francisco Daniel Menchaca Bazán, "Alancito." Leticia Moreno, who collected the bodies of her two sons, Josué and Arón, said, "They can say whatever thing, whatever they want; my boys were all about study and work." Nine families refused. "We have no confidence in them," said Leticia Ponce, Jerzy's mother, "because most of the skulls they've shown us [only in photographs] don't even have hair and the remains are just bones, without flesh, which doesn't correspond to the degree of decomposition that should exist." As much as it was an act of denial or desperate hope against hope—after all, Ruth Marines knew that her son had been identified by the metal plates in his arm and by his prosthetic teeth—the refusal to collect the bodies was a defiant and bitter rebuke of both the city and the federal authorities' dishonest and cynical handling of the case. It was a public statement of these relatives' belief in the victims' innocence, and a rejection of the unacceptable scenario that this mass kidnapping and murder, carried out with nearly military organization and precision, was only a result of a conflict between two local gangs. The nine families' refusal to collect the bodies, to hold funerals for and bury their loved ones, left a void in the Heavens case, an emptiness that was an absence of answers and of truth, the emptiness engendered by the impunity that is destroying Mexico.

From New York, I tried to follow the case throughout the fall. The news was being dominated by the ongoing teachers' union strike, which by October was becoming violent, with clashes between protesting teachers, anarchist groups, and the police, and with mass arrests. There were also recurring stories in the press about the Mexican economy's stagnation in the months since Peña Nieto and the PRI had taken power, and consternation over rising violence and crime all over the country. The National Institute of Statistics and Geography reported that Mexicans' sense of insecurity, or feeling unsafe, had risen 77.2 percent in the months of Peña Nieto's presidency. The institute also reported a steep increase in kidnappings throughout much of the country, including the DF, and stated that "police forces were intimately tied to the rise in extortions and kidnappings in 2013." Clearly the restoration of the PRI was leading to a full restoration of the top-to-bottom culture of institutionalized organized crime that this political party has long been associated with.

In October Mayor Miguel Ángel Mancera once again alarmed and baffled the city's residents by canceling the Mexico City book fair, held over a week and two weekends in the Zócalo every October. It was widely reported that he had done so at the behest of President Peña Nieto, who was in any case no fan of book fairs and in this case wanted to deny Andrés Manuel López Obrador the chance to hold an anti-privatization rally in the Zócalo on one of those weekends. The fair, always well attended, is more than just an occasion for bookselling and author presentations; it also turns its center stages over to activists. For example, preceding a minor event that I took part in last year, there was a main event in which a caravan of mothers and other family members from Central America who'd traveled to Mexico to publicize the plight of their missing migrant relatives were joined onstage by a Mexican families of the disappeared group, and by the migrants' most outspoken and courageous defender, Father Alejando Solalinde—a stirring event that received wide press coverage. The DF's writers and intellectuals, especially those who support AMLO and the left, such as Elena Poniatowska, Paco Ignacio Taibo II, and Fabrizio Mejía Madrid, are influential figures in the city, and, as Mancera should have foreseen, they vowed to go ahead with the book fair anyway. What was Mancera going to do—unleash riot police on writers and readers? Mancera backed down, though only partially, permitting the fair to be held on only one weekend, during which AMLO did hold his rally. In late November the PRD finally pulled out of the "Pact for Mexico" over the proposed privatization of Pemex. Soon afterward, in December—with AMLO suddenly sidelined from the fray by a heart attack—PRI legislators, joined by those of the PAN and smaller right-wing parties, without debate, express-approved the Pemex constitutional reforms.

Polls now showed that the proportion of city residents holding a negative opinion of Mayor Mancera's leadership was approaching 60 percent. Increasingly, commentators in the press were sounding the alarm, sometimes with overt derision, about the direction in which the mayor was taking the city. A column in *Más por Más* by Alejandro Almazán began, "Yesterday, on a plane flying to Guadalajara, I ran into an old friend who told me that Mancera had tricked the Chilangos. 'He told you he was on the left, but it looks like you voted for the PRI,' and he grinned through his teeth and I had no arguments to contradict him with." A few paragraphs down Almazán wrote, "Mancera has no idea how to act. If he did, during the days when the teachers were occupying the Zócalo, he would have been able to enter through the front doors of city hall, instead of going through the Palacio de Hierro [the department store next door]. He took the employee elevator all the way up, and went across the roof. They say the flies didn't know what color to turn, they were so embarrassed for him." In the column Almazán also mocked Mancera's subservience to Peña Nieto on the matter of the use of the Zócalo.

AnimalPolitico.com published a widely remarked open letter to Mayor Mancera, in which its young columnist, Antonio Martínez, decried a city government "in free fall," one in which the current mayor has abandoned the style of government that characterized his PRD predecessors. "My preoccupation, believe me, isn't for you personally," wrote Martínez, "but that in truth I believe that the Distrito Federal should survive as a system whose independence stretches the boundaries of public debate. Mexico City, under your leadership, shouldn't succumb to the terrible agenda of the government of the Republic that seems intent on eliminating opposition, undermining dissent, and stigmatizing minorities. If the beacon goes out—if you put it out—then the return of the 'perfect dictatorship' seems inevitable."

In December, Juan Villoro wrote, "In keeping with the Christmas spirit, the popular imagination has found a new nickname for Miguel Ángel Mancera that rhymes with his surname. They call him La Esfera"—the Bulb—"because he's just an ornament." On New Year's Eve, the city government sponsored a free concert on the Paseo de la Reforma, headlined by the cumbia superstars Los Ángeles Azules. When a government functionary, speaking from the stage, attempted to deliver a greeting from Mayor Mancera, the crowd of 50,000 responded with a storm of shrilly mocking whistles—*rechiflas*—and jeers.

*   *   *

Throughout the fall, though, arrests had continued to be made in the Heavens case; by the end of October, nineteen men were in detention. Most of these, as Pablo de Llano described them in *El País,* were "peons," young men who said they'd been employed by La Unión in peripheral aspects of the abduction and murder, and who in all liklihood didn't themselves know who they were ultimately working for. The arrests were quietly announced, little information was given, and the men disappeared into custody, some formally charged, others held for interrogation. The magazine *Proceso* reported that one arrested La Unión youth had told interrogators that he'd been summoned back to the remote ranch in Tlalmanalco hours after the abducted victims had been brought there, and had seen murdered bodies arrayed in a row, but one young man was still alive—he had no idea who this was; "the fattest one," he told his interrogators—and this one was sobbing, and he was ordered to decapitate him, and he did.

Then, in late September, a Mexico City policeman was arrested. He was a Zona Rosa beat officer who took orders from and informed for a La Unión leader known as "El Javis," and the public reason given for his having come under suspicion was that his lifestyle didn't correspond to his salary. Over the next three weeks, three more policemen assigned to the Zona Rosa were arrested in the Heavens case, again quietly, with sparse additional information. But wasn't this a breakthrough? Didn't this begin to expose, as some of us had suspected nearly from the start and as our most trusted sources had told us, that police involvement in organized crime was a crucial element of the case? In an e-mail Pablo de Llano wrote that it wouldn't be such a breakthrough "until a police commander is arrested."

According to Chief Prosecutor Ríos, a twenty-four-year-old member of La Unión arrested in September had told his interrogators that he and other gang members had been sent to After Heavens because "some of the people" who killed Horacio Vite Ángel, the bar Black dealer, were there that night. The others abducted from the bar had been selected for death because they were partying with the targets, or else they were chosen at random. But Ríos didn't identify which young people had been the primary targets, and offered no proof or corroborating evidence that there was any truth to the allegation. Nobody seemed to know yet, and the authorities seemed unable to explain, what La Unión and its supposed factions actually were, or why, as Ríos continued to emphatically insist, their existence and activities were not considered "organized crime." And the authorities, both DF and federal, seemed no closer than they'd been five months before to being able to identify—perhaps because they didn't want to identify—the crimes' intellectual authors, the "Deep Ones" who were the actual powers behind it, or to explain their true motives.

According to an investigative report by Raúl Mongé published by *Proceso* on October 3, the authorities *do* know, but "have been determined to deny it from the beginning." According to Mongé, who seemed to have gathered his information from credible, if anonymous, sources among both DF and federal investigators and police, the "Deep Ones" are the Sinaloa Cartel. The cartel's main operative in the DF, according to Mongé, is Ricardo López Castillo, El Moco (the Snot), the former federal police agent in the PGR and Santa Muerte devotee who in 2010 founded La Unión in Tepito, the barrio of his birth. This was after the 2009 slaying by navy commandos of Arturo Beltrán

Leyva, El Barbas, in Cuernavaca—the Beltrán Leyva Cartel had controlled the Tepito and DF drug market. Since then the Sinaloa Cartel, operating through El Moco and La Unión, had moved to seize that market. Arming some three hundred drug addicts, vagabonds, and teenage delinquents, El Moco took over all the Tepito crime rackets, not only drugs but also contraband, extortion, and fencing stolen goods. As Tepito residents had told Radio Nederland, La Unión controlled the barrio through terror, "killing people just for fun." "Backed by the Sinaloa Cartel and the connections he'd made during his time in the PGR, López Castillo [El Moco] had little difficulty penetrating the capital's police corps," wrote Mongé. El Javis—previously named in connection with the arrest of Zona Rosa police in the Heavens case—was identified as an important subordinate of El Moco. In 2001, El Javis had spent some time in prison after an arrest for drug dealing in the Condesa. Another subordinate, known as "El Antoine," controlled the dealer trade in the bars, discothèques, and nightclubs of the Zona Rosa–Roma–Condesa *plaza*. The article described an imprisoned "godfather" and *santero* who initiated teenage prisoners into Santería and sent them to El Antione to become drug dealers when they got out. The article in *Proceso* said that Horacio Vite Ángel had been an especially valued dealer for the Sinaloa-Tepito organization, and affirmed that the Heavens *levantón* was in retaliation for his murder, but the article didn't say whom the retaliation was directed against, nor did it implicate any of the murdered Tepito young people in Vite Ángel's slaying. It reported that the chief prosecutor's office, the PGJDF, knew who executed the drug dealer outside Black: "a known Tepito extortionist whose nickname is 'El Grande.'" If true, that report contradicted Chief Prosecutor Ríos's recent vague statements suggesting that "some of the people" who had killed Vite Ángel had been among those abducted from Heavens that night.

According to statements given by those so far arrested in the case, El Javis, Mongé wrote, appears to have organized the *levantón*. Wherever El Javis went, he was always accompanied by four veteran *matones*, killers, from Durango, in the heart of the Sinaloa Cartel's fiefdom. The four gunmen, said to be in their forties, were among the twenty-five men who arrived with the abducted Tepiteños in three vans at the *rancho,* La Negra, which is owned by a man from Durango. According to Mongé only the males were immediately killed, decapitated, and dismembered. The five women—Guadalupe Karen Morales Vargas, Gabriela Téllez Zamudio, Monserrat Loza Fernández, Jennifer Robles González, and Gabriela Ruiz Martínez—were promised that nothing was going to happen to them, were placed inside a truck trailer, and were given beer and drugs. After the males had been killed, El Javis, El Antoine, and the others, "as if nothing had happened," spent a couple of hours drinking, dancing, and "amusing themselves with the women," and then the women were slaughtered too.

Apart from the four arrested police, according to the article in *Proceso*, the PGR has informed the DF's SSP police chief, Jesús Rodríguez Almeida, that at least several more of his police were involved in the crime, and that La Unión's network of corrupted officers probably includes the PGJDF, the chief prosecutor's office, whose investigative police unit were heading the investigation into the Heavens case. "Despite having the names of those presumed to be implicated on his desk," wrote Mongé, "Rodríguez Almeida inexplicably hasn't handed them over to local prosecutors." According to Mongé's sources, during the fallout from the Heavens case, El Moco fled to China.

(As most of the *fayuca,* counterfeit goods, sold in Tepito come from China, El Moco would certainly have connections there.) The whereabouts of El Javis, El Antoine, and the four *matones* from Durango are unknown.

The article in *Proceso* was published on October 3. As far as I can tell, following the case from New York, it was met with near silence. Officials didn't comment, not even to refute it. There was little or no follow-up or commentary in the media. But when I read the article, a lot fell into place; it corroborated much of the information that had come to me, in bits and pieces, over the past six months since the *levantón* occurred. Here was more evidence and a partial explanation of the police involvement that Pablo de Llano and I had long suspected. Here, at last, was an identification of the "Deep Ones," the ultimate powers behind the crime: the Sinaloa Cartel. The placement of the corpses of Dax Rodríguez and the two women in Huitzilac, Morelos, inside the Beltrán Leyva's "paradise," made sense as a message delivered by one cartel, Sinaloa—and implicitly, perhaps, by its allies—to another cartel.

Maybe we, the public, along with the families of the victims, will never know what really happened in the Heavens case, or who was ultimately behind it. Later, in the fall of 2013, I had a chance to speak with a group of veteran PGJDF police officers, investigative police, former *judiciales,* SWAT team commandos, and anti-kidnapping police. We were meeting to talk about a separate matter I was researching, but Tepito, the Heavens case, and police involvement in the crime came up. "Tepito is a center of power in this city," one of them told me. A great deal of money is made in Tepito, flows through there, and so it is a center of political power. That was why, the police told me, their units—elite crime fighting units—had routinely been kept out of Tepito and were almost never sent on operations there. The neighborhood was left to the police who were assigned to the police stations there. But it was not those police who controlled or empowered crime in Tepito, they told me. It was the politicians who controlled the police, they said.

On Tuesday, October 22, the Federal Human Rights Commission held a press conference to address the Heavens case and other recent disappearances in the city. DF prosecutors and police were criticized for having leaked information in the Heavens case that put both family members and witnesses at risk, and for the many other "irregularities" of their investigation. And the commission accused the DF's authorities of having deprived the families of their right to truthful information about what had happened to their relatives. Most significantly, the commission called for an investigation into police involvement in the abductions and murders in the Heavens case. "If the police were involved, then we are confronted by a case of forced disappearances," said the commission's interim president, Mario Patrón, "and the murders would become extrajudicial assassinations." Patrón called the Heavens case a "historic occurrence" that had opened eyes to the problem of disappearances inside the DF's vaunted security "bubble."

But who would carry out that investigation? It seems likely that all the relevant justice authorities, in the DF and at the federal level, have something to hide in the Heavens case, or else regard only cherry-picked elements of the crime as useful political capital. A SinEmbargo.com editorial addressed the problem of police involvement in the rising incidence of disappearances in Mexico, including in the Heavens case:

"And the pain, the pain of thousands of families that have suffered from these crimes can't be healed by anything," the editors wrote. "Maybe, just slightly, by a true imparting of justice. But the answers never arrive, or they come in slow dribs and drabs. Meanwhile the criminals, among them police authorities, generate all through their communities more and more suffering."

On December 19, 2013, Mexican news agencies reported that according to "high-level sources within the PGR," the kidnapping and murder of the young people in the Heavens Case was provoked by a dispute between the Sinaloa Cartel and the Beltran Leyvas over control of the Mexico City drug trade—a direct refutation of the scenario insisted upon by Mayor Mancera and Ríos. According to those sources, the two adolescent sons of the imprisoned Tepito gangsters were the operation's target, and the other young people were victims of "bad luck." Left unaddressed was the question of whether or not the *levanton* and mass murder had helped either cartel to achieve its goal. That news report was like the final blips emitted by a missing airliner's black box—since then silence has all but enveloped the case, at least in the media.

On the night after the discovery of the clandestine grave in Tlalmanalco, Israel, the brother of Monserrat Loza Fernández, told a reporter from *Universal,* "My sister didn't deserve this; she was a woman dedicated to her children. She was a young single mother who now and then liked to go out to have fun. Monserrat is a good person, I say that she was a good person. She never was involved in anything illicit and it befell her to die in the cruelest manner that anyone can imagine. These have been desperate months, of anguish, desperation. I didn't know whether my sister was eating or not, or if they were abusing her, or mistreating her. I had a certain hope because I had many dreams, I kept dreaming that she came home."

The cruelty and near hopelessness of the situation overwhelm. Maybe the Heavens case is nobody's cause now but that of the families. They, like tens of thousands of other families in Mexico, have been sent on journeys that they, individually or banded together, will mostly have to endure alone, through that place without solace where the dead often seem more alive than the living.

Appendix Note

On February 22, 2014, Joaquín Guzmán Loera, El Chapo, was taken prisoner—without violence, without a single gunshot being fired—in a Mazatlán, Sinaloa, resort hotel in an operation mounted by Mexican navy commandos in cooperation with U.S. authorities, particularly the DEA. Under President Calderón, in 2009, Mexican navy commandos and U.S. law enforcement had hunted down and killed Arturo Beltrán Leyva, El Barbas, in Cuernavaca. Peña Nieto was carrying on with Calderón's policy of waging war through the capture and killings of major capos—though there was no bigger trophy than El Chapo. But the running of an organization as wealthy, vast, and global as the Sinaloa Cartel doesn't depend on just one person. In a famous 2010 interview with *Proceso*, one of the Sinaloa's other venerable leaders, Ismael "El Mayo" Zambada, said that the cartel was prepared for the possible capture of its capos and had replacements ready; it's long rumored in Mexico that Sinaloa's legendary narco capos work for hidden bosses, men who don't want *narcocorridos* being sung about them—"there is talk of an x- governor," wrote Alejandro Páez Varela, a few days after El Chapo's arrest, in SinEmbargo.com. In a widely quoted interview with the Tijuana weekly *Zeta*, Edgardo Buscaglia, a Mexican security expert and senior research scholar in law and economics at Columbia University Law School, said, "El Chapo is one member of the Sinaloa criminal network's leadership, but let's not forget that Sinaloa is a horizontal network consisting of thousands of franchises that operate according to directions from Sinaloa transmitted through strategic and tactical alliances. Sinaloa doesn't have a vertical structure of command and control, they have regional criminal alliances, and in other countries; so that directorship will continue, [El Chapo] will simply be replaced." Buscaglia said that the capture of the mythologized capo, in a country like Mexico, "with its voids in governance," didn't "even minimally guarantee the dismantling of a criminal network." Buscaglia said, "El Chapo Guzmán and his people in Sinaloa had hundreds of Mexican politicians in their pockets, let's see if they arrest them now." The weakening of the Sinaloa Cartel would become a reality, he said, only if El Chapo's capture was followed by detentions of the corrupt politicians and functionaries at all levels who permitted and aided the Sinaloa Cartel's operation and expansion, and with investigations into the thousands of seemingly legal businesses and properties, in Mexico and the United States and elsewhere, through which the cartel and its associates laundered and invested its billions, and the eventual seizure and dismantling of those entities. As long as the chains of complicity between politicians and cartel capos are not destroyed, he said, "then the war against the narco traffickers can be considered lost."

Phil Jordan, a former director of intelligence for the DEA, created a stir when he said in an interview on Univision, the U.S.-based Spanish-language television network, that "I never thought the PRI would arrest him, because El Chapo invested a lot of money in Peña Nieto's campaign, so I was surprised when I learned that he'd been arrested." Jordan said that his allegations about El Chapo had been "documented by U.S.

intelligence, though I don't have papers I can show you." He said that "Chapo has always invested in politics," just as the capo recently freed from prison Rafael Caro Quintero used to. Jordan made the observation that before the PAN came to power in 2000, "The PRI had a lot to do with drug trafficking and with the godfathers of Mexican trafficking." He told the television network, "Something bad happened between the PRI and El Chapo Guzmán. What I can't tell you now, because I don't know why they arrested him."

There was nothing particularly surprising in Jordan's remarks, other than, perhaps, that he'd made them on television. After all, in Mexico there had been many news reports of Sinaloa Cartel intrusions, especially in Sinaloa state, into the 2012 and 2013 summer election campaigns. But spokesmen for the PRI and Peña Nieto's government responded as if with shocked indignation over Jordan's interview. The DEA and the U.S. embassy quickly released statements disassociating themselves from "the opinions" of the former DEA intelligence chief.

A U.S. news agency, AP, had been the first to announce the capture of El Chapo. Mexican government officials did not confirm it until hours later. Over the next week, the Mexican media was filled with analysis and speculation about the arrest; many conspiracy theories—many sounding not at all farfetched—were aired. There was a consensus that the U.S. government had instigated the arrest, and there were reports of U.S. drones having been used. "If one believes that both governments often knew where [El Chapo] was and that he was allowed to operate freely for many years, as I do," wrote the Mexico City–based director of the Americas Program of the Center for International Policy, "the question is why now? Why capture him at this particular time?" Another former DEA agent, Héctor Beréllez, told the EFE news agency that El Chapo's capture was related to the recent freeing from prison of Rafael Caro Quintero, now ready to reassume his position as "capo of capos." El Chapo, according to Beréllez, knew he'd lost his protection and that his arrest was imminent; that he may even have negotiated his arrest was an opinion shared by several other experts in the Mexican press, and was not discounted by Buscaglia, the security expert from Columbia University. The Sinaloa Cartel is widely perceived to have enjoyed its greatest protection and growth under Calderón's PAN government; the Sinaloa Cartel's greatest rival, the "unspeakable" Zetas, has been especially entrenched in PRI strongholds such as the states of Tamaulipas, Veracruz, and México; thus another expert saw behind the strategy to "strike and weaken the Sinaloa Cartel," an effort to "fortify the group 'of the last letter.'"

In a later interview with SinEmbargo.com, Buscaglia said that the Sinaloa Cartel might have come to perceive El Chapo as a liability—he was too notorious, he drew too much attention—and that that might be how he'd lost his protection. He explained that when one cartel or another is described as "protected," this doesn't mean that someone at the top, a previous president or the one Mexico has now, has given such an order, but that the protection is something the cartels create themselves, from the bottom up, from a base of regional police and politicians and so on and moving upward, nationally, internationally, weaving their net of corruption, secret deals, and protection. But then something can change, a decision is made, a drone flies through the weave just like that, and down goes the capo. The capo goes down, but usually not the cartel.

Of course El Chapo has been in prison in Mexico before, from 1993 to 2001—he famously bought his way out, escaping in a laundry cart—years during which his cartel's profits and growth were hardly impeded. If Mexico decides not to extradite him to the United States—and for now, Mexico seems determined to keep him, just as El Chapo and his lawyers seem determined to stay—and he remains in prison there, he can probably maintain some degree of command over his cartel. During his previous prison stint, El Chapo had a lavish lifestyle. A young Televisa-contracted actress I spoke to at a dinner party two years ago told me about a Televisa *telenovela* star who earned six-figure sums—in U.S. dollars—for her prison assignations with El Chapo. Following his arrest, the capo spoke with his captors during the helicopter flight to the capital. El Chapo freely admitted to responsibility for two or three thousand deaths, though the number of those murdered by the Sinaloa Cartel—including many innocents, and maybe even including the Heavens thirteen—during his years of command is far higher. El Chapo boasted to his captors that he was just a narco trafficker, not a kidnapper, extortionist, or human trafficker like his rivals in "the group of the last letter" indeed are. El Chapo is a family man. When asked why, having barely evaded capture in Culiacán barely a week before—escaping through a tunnel network leading from the bathroom of one of his mansions—he hadn't returned to the safety of the mountains, and had gone to Mazatlán instead, he said it was because he "hadn't seen his girls," and wanted to—his twenty-two-year-old wife and their two small daughters, the youngest of his sixteen children, who were present at his capture. It was also reported in the Mexican press after his capture that, according to police authorities, a woman named La Michelle had the job of bringing the capo, every three days, a girl between thirteen and sixteen years of age, "who received a hundred thousand pesos for a day of sexual labor."

The journalist Diego Osorno told me, "This is the situation now. Peña Nieto has decided that there's going to be no other capo of capos but himself."

Postscript: January 2015

One afternoon in mid-December 2014, Pablo de Llano, the *El País* correspondent, and I went to visit Ana María Vargas in the same apartment in a Tepito *vecindad* where we'd spoken with her in June 2013, almost exactly a month after her daughter, Guadalupe Karen, and her husband, Alan Omar Atiencia, had been abducted along with eleven other young people from the Heavens. Two months later, on August 21, the thirteen bodies, mutilated and decomposing, were finally discovered by police buried in a clandestine "narco grave" in the México State municipality of Tlalmanalco.

Now, with Christmas approaching, the downtown streets surrounding Tepito and those of the ancient market barrio itself were teeming with mercantile activity, the traffic stalled. Forced to abandon our mired taxi many blocks from Tepito's center, I followed closely behind Pablo, who knew the way much better than I did, through those nearly impassable sidewalks whose crowds and energies made me feel both hyperalert and elated.

Pablo hadn't been in touch with the Heavens' families for several months. Mexico was now subsumed by a crisis provoked by another mass kidnapping and apparent murder of young people. During the night of September 26 and in the first hours of the 27th, in the small city of Iguala, Guerrero, uniformed municipal police, along with a handful of other gunmen, had

carried out a series of armed attacks on five buses transporting students from the Ayotzinapa Normal School and another
bus, having mistaken it for a student bus, that was carrying a
soccer team. The police and other gunmen shot and killed six
people, wounded more than twenty, and abducted forty-three
students. Those students were part of a larger group from the
school who were traveling in buses they had commandeered to
transport them to the annual October 2 march in Mexico City
that commemorates the 1968 massacre of student protestors
in the Tlatelolco plaza by the PRI government of Díaz Ordaz.
Hijacking buses for this and other logistical reasons is virtually
a traditional practice at the underfunded and proudly leftist
college, which trains students to become schoolteachers in impoverished rural communities.

The following morning, the body of one student was found
in a field, eyes gouged out and facial skin completely torn away
from the skull, the signature of a Mexican organized crime killing. The other students had not been seen since, though the
search for their bodies had turned up so many narco graves
filled with the remains of murdered and dismembered victims,
exposing one of Mexico's greatest not-so-secret secrets to the
shocked eyes of the world: With well over an estimated hundred
thousand disappeared victims of the narco war in recent years,
Mexico was now considered one giant narco grave. According
to the Mexican government, which so far had arrested dozens
of the Iguala municipal police and others in the case, the police,
on orders of Iguala's mayor, had handed the students over to the
members of a local drug trafficking group known as Guerreros
Unidos. But in truth, the mayor, the police, and the narco gang
were one and the same; all over Mexico, local authorities have
become integrated with organized crime. Federal police and

military troops stationed in Iguala, who were certainly aware of what was happening in their immediate territory on the night of the 26th, did not intervene to protect the students, and may have even collaborated in the crime, though, so far, the government has ignored all calls for a full investigation into the federal police or army's role.

In a nationally televised press conference on Friday, November 7, Mexico's Attorney General, Jesús Murillo Karam, announced that the missing students from the Ayotzinapa Normal School had been executed and incinerated in the Cocula municipal dump, the few recoverable remains too badly burned for even the Argentine forensic experts advising the PGR to identify. They had instead been sent to a specialized DNA lab in Austria. Many came to feel that this news conference was a cynical ploy to smooth over President Enrique Peña Nieto's exit from the country to attend an economics conference in China, as well as a government attempt to project an image of control and competence. Many Mexicans were infuriated too by the callousness shown to the Ayotzinapa families by publically claiming that the students had been horribly murdered in this way before any of the remains had even been forensically identified. In the ensuing weeks, scientific experts from the UNAM, as well as other journalists closely reporting on the situation in Guerrero, cast serious doubt on the physical and chemical plausibility of totally incinerating forty-three bodies on a rainy night in the small Cocula dump. It would have required 33 tons of wood, or 995 automobile tires, and 53 kg of gasoline per body; the area of the dump would have needed to be ten times larger, and the column of smoke would have been visible for miles.

The case of the Ayotzinapa students had been preceded by another massive human rights violation in June, when federal

troops had massacred twenty-two youths in a warehouse in Tlatlaya, México State; human rights groups and journalists exposed
the attempted cover-up of that crime. The crimes unmasked
the emptiness and deception of President Enrique Peña Nieto's
reform and supposedly modernizing agenda and the aggressive
international public relations campaign waged on its behalf that
publically, as a matter of calculated policy, ignored and sought
to disguise Mexico's direst realities, including rampant organized crime throughout much of the country and corruption
and impunity at every level of the state, realities which left the
population, much of it mired in poverty, ever more exposed to
violence and utter lawlessness.

Throughout that fall of 2014, called the "Mexican Autumn"
by some, Ayotzinapa provoked protests throughout Mexico and
abroad. Those protests in Guerrero were sometimes furious
and violent; the marches in Mexico City for the most part stir-
ringly massive and peaceful. The fact that Mexican corruption
and impunity are embedded at the very top of the Mexican
state would be vividly illustrated in the coming weeks, when
separate investigative journalists would expose the financing
of expensive mansions for Peña Nieto and his wife and for his
cabinet's influential economics minister, Luis Videgaray, by a
contracting company, Grupo Higa, that has received lucrative
contracts from Peña Nieto's governments, both now that he is
president and before, when he was governor of México State.
In the congress, the PRI and other political parties blocked all
attempts to grant a new anticorruption prosecutor autonomy
from the federal government. "I don't think anybody doubts,
at this point," Alejandro Paéz Varela wrote at SinEmbargo.com
on December 29, "that it just stops there: that Grupo Higa
hasn't bought more high-ranking federal officials and various

state administrations. I don't believe that, given the previous examples, that anybody doubts anymore—at least that's the perception—that this government is drowning in corruption." After just two years in office, Enrique Peña Nieto had been, both nationally and internationally, spectacularly stripped of any image of competence or credibility, and his government was plunged into a seemingly unprecedented crisis. No president has been more unpopular, has received lower approval ratings, since Ernesto Zedillo in 1994–95, the years of an economically catastrophic devaluation of the peso.

I was temporarily living in New York again during the late spring of 2014, when Pablo de Llano attended the funerals of several of the Heavens victims after the families had finally and reluctantly gone to SEMEFO, the city's judicial forensic morgue, to retrieve the human remains identified as those of their relatives by Argentine specialists. One of the funerals he'd attended was for Ana María Vargas's daughter, Guadalupe Karen, and her husband, Alan Omar. He told me how he'd stood atop a pile of freshly shoveled dirt overlooking the grave into which Karen's coffin was about to be lowered, and how from there he'd watched Karen's beautiful younger brother Brian throw himself upon the coffin, sobbing and screaming and refusing to relinquish his grasp of it, until he fainted. When the coffin was finally lowered a barely revived Brian sat slumped, in a spent daze, in the dirt beside the grave.

Now we sat with Ana María in the same small living room, crowded with orphaned children and Chihuahua dogs, where we'd last spoken well over a year before. The room was decorated for Christmas, including with a small white artificial tree adorned with pink bulbs and tinsel trimmings. And the beautiful Jessica, Brian's younger sister, was there too, holding in her arms her recently born son, who wore red-and-white Santa pajamas and cap. She no longer lives with her mother. Ana María, pretty and delicate, sitting next to me on the couch, had a new tattoo on her wrist: Karen's name entwined with an infinity symbol. A large studio portrait of Karen now hung on that wall commemorating the family's other dead young people, near the photos of Ana María's murdered late son, Cesar Adrian, and of Nayali, the twenty-year-old relative killed by a stray bullet in Tepito. Now, along with Karen's, there were three new photos on the wall: one of Alan Omar, of course, and of two more young male relatives who'd died since I'd last been there—one, the son of one of Ana María's uncles, shot dead during an altercation in Tepito, and the other prematurely felled by cancer.

Nineteen months after her daughter's abduction and murder, even though some twenty-five suspects have been arrested in relations to the Heavens case so far, Ana María still has no idea as to why the crime happened—who was really responsible for it, or why her daughter had been victimized—than she'd had when we'd last spoken. Though the Mexican justice system can be a murky labyrinth, she has tried to follow the case and went to one of criminal hearings, held in a courtroom affixed to the prison, el Reclusorio Norte, in which the imprisoned suspects were led through a dark tunnel to stand before a door of steel bars, like the door of a prison cell, in one wall of the courtroom. Ana María said the prisoners were not allowed to turn and look at the small audience of Heavens family members in the courtroom; still inside the tunnel, the prisoners, apparently, were made to stand with their backs to the bars while a judge and lawyers on the other side of those bars conducted the hearing. Ana María said that the case appears to still have a long way to go before it gets to the judgment and sentencing stage. The defense lawyers were filing one delaying motion after another. And, according to the prosecutors, important suspects still remain at large. "Who knows if all twenty-five of the suspects detained in the case so far," said Ana María, "are actually even guilty?"

Back in early June 2013, during the first weeks after the abductions, Rodolfo Ríos, the city government's chief prosecutor, had told the families that the "Tepito gang" that came into Heavens and carried out the abduction was looking for two people, though Ríos never identified which of the thirteen those two were. Neither Ríos nor any other government investigators ever offered the families any new insight into the crime after that. They never even offered a theory as to why the other young people were taken. "If they were only after two," asked Ana María, "why did they do the same to all the others?" Before, the families at least had the ear of the city prosecutors. "Now they don't tell us anything," said Ana María. The families never had any faith in the city government's investigation of the case, which from the start ruled out any involvement by "organized crime." Attorney General Murillo Karam and the PGR, she said, also insisted that there was no organized crime involvement in the case, which was why they'd refused to take charge of the investigation. "But with twenty-five already arrested," said Ana María—including a number of arrested police—"how can they say it's just ordinary crime?"

Every aspect of the official handling of the Heavens case had left Ana María filled with suspicion and doubt. She wasn't even convinced that the remains she'd buried were actually those of her daughter Karen. The remains found in the grave had retained human skin, but the families were given bones. Ana María and her family had also been given a small bag of what they were told was Karen's hair. Ana María did not trust even the Argentine forensic specialists—the same team working now on

the Ayotzinapa case—simply because of their association with
the PGR. Recently she'd run into Jerzy Ortiz's mother, Lety,
who told her, "My heart tells me he's not dead, that they lied."
Ana María said that her personal message to the parents of the
missing students from Ayotzinapa would be "Don't believe what
they say. Keep looking for your sons."

   She told a story about a Tepito neighbor whose twenty-
eight-year-old daughter had "disappeared" fourteen years before,
leaving her four small children without a mother. Her neighbor
had searched for her daughter relentlessly, going to morgues
and to police and finally human rights authorities, who told
her that if her daughter had been missing for so long, she was
probably in a *fosa común,* a clandestine common grave, by now.
She searched for her daughter spiritually too, visiting a seer and
santeros who "brought *la muertita* down from the other dimen-
sion." In a dark room where the *santeros* conducted the séance,
Ana María's neighbor saw her daughter descend a staircase midway and stand in the shadows. She then heard her daughter
speak in her own voice. She told her mother that although she
was dead, and indeed buried in one a *fosa común,* that she was
well and at peace, and that her mother should be too. And then,
after fourteen years, the long-missing daughter tracked down
her own oldest child on Facebook and began to communicate
with her. It turned out that, like so many other "disappeared"
women in Mexico, she had been kidnapped into sexual slavery.
Her kidnappers had put her to work in many different places
around the republic, until finally, Ana María told us, she had
been rescued by "an impresario." The impresario took her to live
with him in a big house somewhere in México State. One of his
conditions for saving the girl from her "bad life" was to prohibit
her from communicating with her family. This sounded not so

unlikely, I thought: The "impresario" may well have been type who had plenty that he needed to keep hidden. But when the daughter fell ill with cancer, she could no longer resist finding and getting in touch with her family. He was paying for all her cancer treatments, said Ana María. She'd run into the daughter's mother just that Sunday during the pilgrimage march to the basilica of the Virgin of Guadalupe pilgrimage. "Don't lose hope," the woman had told her. "They told me my daughter had gone to the other place, and I heard her speak—even in my dreams my daughter spoke to me and told me that she was dead. And look, now I've found her."

Ana María had been deeply affected by her neighbor's story. "It unnerves me," she said. "It's caused me a lot of anxiety. I haven't been able to sleep."

There are some strikingly obvious similarities between the Heavens case and that of the forty-three abducted students from the Ayotzinapa Normal School. In both, authorities and complicit media attempted to criminalize the victims, to make them seem to blame for what had happened. On November 18, 2014, in the newspaper *La Razón* Carlos Alazraki, an advertising executive and veteran PRI insider who has worked on PRI presidential election campaigns, published a typical disinformation smear in an editorial: "Forty-six days ago two bands, of students and Iguala narcos, got into a brawl . . . There are varying versions of what happened . . . That they were two bands who hated each other to death. That one were guerrillas and the other narcos. One or the other wanted to control the whole region." In both Heavens and Ayotzinapa, despite the numerous arrests, including of police, in each case, months went by without those suspects

providing, at least without any publically known justice consequences, reliable news concerning the whereabouts of the missing
or any full and credible accounting of the crimes. In both cases
the federal PGR and Attorney General Murillo Karam seemed
to be putting political damage control ahead of transparency
and the urgency of justice. As Pablo de Llano wrote in a piece
published in *El País* comparing Heavens and Ayotzinapa, in
both cases the victims' families publically came to coinciding
conclusions about the federal PGR: "We don't have an ounce of
confidence in them," a spokesperson for the Ayotzinapa families
had declared. "We have a TOTAL lack of confidence in the
work of the PGR," read a communiqué released by the Heavens'
victims' families in the summer of 2013.

There are stark differences too. Attempts to criminalize the
missing young people from Tepito largely succeeded, though no
proof was ever provided that any were, around the time that the
crime occurred, involved in any criminal activities whatsoever.
As a result, there were never any "mega marches" in the streets
of Mexico City calling for justice in Heavens case or for the
missing Tepito young people to be returned alive. The Ayotzinapa Normal School's young students were well known in
Guerrero state, and surviving students and the families of those
missing had quickly organized into effective spokespersons. So
many well-reported accounts of the school and its students had
appeared in the Mexican media that don't collude with the PRI,
or in the foreign press, that Mexican government officials, at
least, realized that innuendo and smears against the students
were backfiring, and so eliminated them from their public and,
for the most part, even "off-the-record" statements.

There is one possible direct link between the two cases. Dax
Rodriguéz, one of the owners of Heavens, fled to Guerrero, to

that same small city of Iguala, where he was later abducted along with his teenaged girlfriend and a female cousin; their murdered and burned bodies turned up in Huitzilac, Morelos, territory of the narco capo Hector "H" Beltrán-Leyva, with whom the Iguala narco gang Guerreros Unidos had been associated. Guerreros Unidos essentially ran Iguala—it certainly ran its mayor and police. When I spoke to Marcelo Ebrard, the former Mexico City mayor, in January 2015, our first conversation in nearly a year, I asked him what he thought about the Heavens case now, and he immediately mentioned the abduction of Dax Rodriguéz and the two women in Iguala and the subsequent discovery of their remains in Huitzilac. Ebrard regarded that as an indication of organized crime involvement—of both Guerreros Unidos and Beltrán-Leyva—in the Heavens case too. "They're linked," he said. "It shows that these groups have been operating here in the city for some time. Here in the official version they say [the Heavens case] was just local drug-dealing gangs, but that isn't credible."

H. Beltrán-Leyva, on the run and posing as a business-man, was captured in October, the latest in a series of older, seemingly redundant capos to fall. Some of the narco cartels and alliances seem to be fragmenting into smaller groups. They seem to have realized that they can operate without the burden of being attached to or taking orders from the notorious capos who attract so much attention and keep so much of the money. They can take over local governments and police, municipality after municipality, on their own. Politicians provide their protection.

"Political corruption is the mother and father of the expansion of organized violence in Mexico," Edgardo Buscaglia, a legal

and security expert on Mexico and senior research scholar in
law and economics at Columbia University Law School, told
the newspaper *El Universal* this fall. He reminded the newspaper
that Carlos Navarrete, the current president of the PRD, had
publically admitted that "there is a tacit pact of impunity among
politicians in Mexico." Politicians don't investigate politicians
in Mexico. The State doesn't investigate the State. Last February, following the ballyhooed capture of "most wanted" narco
capo Joaquin "El Chapo" Guzmán, Buscaglia told the press,
"El Chapo Guzmán and his people in Sinaloa had hundreds
of Mexican politicians in their pockets, let's see if they arrest
them now." Eleven months later, Mexico is still waiting to witness any such arrest of one El Chapo's politicians. According to
Buscaglia, some 77 percent of Mexico's municipalities are currently controlled by narco cartels, with local state and municipal
forces and politicians fully subsumed by them. "The police aren't
autonomously corrupt," he said. "They have their patrons, and
whenever you follow a diagram of corruption . . . you always
arrive at the political class, one way or another."

No major politician, and certainly none of the main parties, has escaped the taint of Ayotzinapa. The PRD governor
of Guerrero, Ángel Aguirre Rivero, was forced to resign. He'd
previously governed Guerrero for the PRI, but was reelected
governor in 2011 in a last-minute "marriage of convenience"
with the PRD; he is a longtime PRI heavyweight and a friend
of President Peña Nieto. The PRD now seems on the verge of
disappearing, destroyed, in part, by its connections to Iguala
and the missing Ayotzinapa students. Iguala's narco mayor, José
Luis Abarca, belonged to the PRD and was reputedly close to
at least one of the two PRD political leaders known as "Los
Chuchos," Jesús Zambrano. When the PRD's fully discredited

current leadership rejected calls for their resignation by the party's founder, Cuauhtémoc Cárdenas, perhaps the only universally respected politician left in Mexico, Cárdenas resigned from the party instead.

Mayor Mancera is by far the most unpopular Mexico City mayor in modern memory. Alejandro Paéz, during a conversation we had in October, said of Mancera, "He's the most gigantically ridiculous politician the left has seen, and he's put at risk the left's control over the city." Without any political power or capital of his own, said Paéz, Mancera has become utterly dependent on "Los Chuchos." Over time, Zambrano and Jesús Ortega had gained utter control of the party—handing out posts and jobs, handing out money, essentially, said Paéz—and moved it close to the PRI. Los Chuchos had no rivals and were going to be able to pick the next PRD candidate for mayor in 2018. Essentially, said Paéz, they were going to turn the city over to the PRI. The loss of the city, said Paéz, "would mean the end of a dream." What dream is that? I asked. "That in this country an island can exist where the PRI isn't in charge and can't corrupt. A place where the citizenry can have a say in decisions." But now Los Chuchos and even their party seem destined to disappear from the national political scene. Perhaps the DF has been saved.

Inevitably, the aftermath of Ayotzinapa also saw a PRI-orchestrated media campaign that tried to pin the tragedy of the missing students on their traditional rival, Andrés Manuel López Obrador, AMLO. Following his 2012 presidential loss, AMLO had broken with the PRD to form his own party, MORENA. Given the discredit now being heaped upon the traditional political parties—including the PAN, unforgiven for having begun the disastrous narco war and for abetting so much corruption in the first place—perhaps AMLO and his party were in a position to improve their seemingly marginal national political prospects. So there, on TV and on the front pages of newspapers, the PRI had rolled out its heavy artillery, the leaders of the lower and upper chambers of Congress and its national party president, seated together, gesticulating and grimacing, demanding that AMLO come clean about his relations to Abarca and Aguirre, and calling for the PGR to interrogate him. On social media a #LielikeAMLO hashtag barrage was launched, and Chucho Zambrano, of all people, was tweeting that AMLO is a liar, a coward, and a demagogue.

Marcelo Ebrard, considered by many to be the most talented and forward-looking politician of his generation, certainly on the left, is another who might have been in a position to step into the vacuum of political leadership left in the wake of Ayotzinapa. But the once-esteemed former Mexico City *jefe de gobierno* had a rough 2014. Engineering malfunctions had forced the closure of the 12 subway line, the "Golden Line," that had been seen as one of the signature achievements of Ebrard's mayoralty. In this day and age, repairing flaws in a subway line's tracks should not seem beyond the capabilities of any city government, but as of this writing the line remains out of service, and it seems little is work is being done on it; trains have not been replaced by the company that built them, as required in the original contracts. Instead, at least according to some observers, Mayor Mancera and PRI allies in the mainstream media, especially on Televisa, publically exaggerated the subway line's problems and whatever city government decisions may have been at fault in order to damage Ebrard and his future political prospects. Now Ebrard seems likely to be even further damaged by his association with Ángel Aguirre, whose campaign for the PRD governorship of Guerrero he'd supported. Throughout the autumn of 2014, Ebrard maintained a seemingly willful and perhaps strategic public silence. Ebrard readily admitted "I promoted Aguirre" when, during our conversation in January, I brought up the subject of his support for the former governor and its possible political repercussions. "But I did nothing that I need to be embarrassed about," he said. "I have nothing to hide. I've never had any business dealings with Aguirre, and besides, he has to take responsibility for his own decisions. I thought he should be our candidate because he had a better chance of winning than anyone we had. I wanted to prevent the PRI from winning. But it was Ángel who decided to align himself with Los Chuchos, and to become close to the government. All along I said that the PRD had to change, that it had to reclaim its opposition role—don't sign that pact, let's put forward our own ideas—in forum after forum, I said that. Nobody can say that my position has changed."

Ebrard, like so many other observers, does not expect the PRD to survive its current crisis. Mexicans, he said, have lost faith in all the political parties. "Our institutions have lost their authority." The community consensus, he said, from which political institutions draw their legitimacy, doesn't exist anymore. "We're reaching the end of a cycle," said Ebrard, "of a historical period that lasted a quarter of a century, of an idea from the past that is becoming exhausted—let's call them the liberal reforms [the Salias Gotari government's privatizations, NAFTA, etc.]—of which the energy reform is the last chapter. In all that time the country hasn't grown, we're no better off, and social inequality is static. They have this idea that evidence doesn't matter. But the basic problem is that Mexicans know that no matter how hard they work and how much of an effort they make, they're not getting ahead. The surprise is that we don't have even greater social protests." After twenty-five years, said Ebrard, the Mexican poverty rate hasn't shifted—it is still at 53 percent. By comparison, he said, since the end of the Pinochet dictatorship, Chile has lowered its poverty rate from 40 to 14 percent, years during which parties from the right and center-left have governed. "How the new cycle begins, that's the big question. But that we're coming to the end of a cycle, I have no doubt. "

Ebrard said that Mexico's looming 2015 elections are unlikely to lead to change. Voter turnout will be low, he said, both due to organized campaigns to abstain or nullify ballots, and general indifference. But those elections, he said, will also send a message—"Your system doesn't interest me anymore, we're tired of this system"—that the political establishment will probably miss. "The people are drawing a line, saying they've reached their limit, but they're also giving a warning: They're saying *Change this.*" Once the 2015 elections are past, he said, will be when the left will "have to gather our dead, begin to recuperate our forces, and propose a new vision for this country." Looking ahead to 2018, Ebrard said that he believes Mexico's diverse and growing civic movements are likely to find a way to unite outside of any organized political party, with its entrenched and closed bureaucracies, its entitled castes and hierarchies. "A new movement," he said, "but not a party."

Attorney General Murillo Karam had ended the November 7 press conference, in which he'd put forth the government's theory that the forty-three students had been burned by three now captured members of Guerreros Unidos at the Cocula municipal dump, by saying, "*Ya me cansé*": *I'm finally tired,* or, more colloquially, *I've had enough.* Indeed, he was tired, not having slept, he said later, in forty-eight hours, but he'd inadvertently provided Mexico's burgeoning civic protest movement with a new slogan and name that would spread as quickly as, two years before, #YoSoy132 had. That same night of the press conference, #Yamecansé was all over social media, summoning people to a march in Mexico City the next night: #Yamecansédelmiedo. *I've had enough of fear . . . I've had enough of Enrique Peña Nieto. I've had enough of impunity. I've had enough of the narco state . . .* and so on. The permutations seemed infinite. "The state is dead" is a popular chant at the marches that have been filling Mexico City's streets over the past months. Another is "Peña and Mancera, the same *chingadera*"—betraying his city's citizenry's right to peaceful protest, Mancera's Mexico City police were committing many brutal and arbitrary acts of violent repression against the marchers. On November 15, five days before a "mega march" scheduled for November 20, President Peña Nieto gave an ominous speech in which he said of the Ayotzinapa protests, "They appear to be responding to an interest in destabilizing, to generate social disorder, and above all to attack the national project that we've been constructing." And he warned—echoing the very words he'd used at the Ibero in 2012 to defend the violent police repression at Atenco, words that had ignited the #YoSoy132 student movement that almost derailed his presidential ambitions—that the State is "legitimately empowered to employ force."

In the late afternoon hours of November 20, people began to gather at various spots in the city for the march that would converge in the Zócalo, the main plaza of Mexico City. I went with friends and some neighbors from our building. By the monument El Angel, I saw an elderly woman holding a hand-drawn sign that read YES, I'M AFRAID! I TREMBLE, SWEAT, TURN PALE, BUT I MARCH! FOR AYOTZI, FOR ME, FOR YOU, FOR MEXICO.

As Ayotzinapa family members and students and other members of their Guerrero contingent were led to the front of the march, people chanted, "You're not alone." One of the Ayotzinapa group was a young woman, holding a swaddled baby, and she was sobbing as she walked forward. There were machete-wielding peasant farmers from Atenco mounted on horseback. I saw many middle-class families, including children and young parents pushing baby carriages. Raucous contingents of university students were there too, of course. It seemed as if every imaginable group and subgroup, large and tiny, that exists in Mexico City was present. For a while we marched between a contingent from a capoeira school and a marijuana legalization group. I saw a nearly seven-foot-tall, long-haired, blond young man marching in the nude and holding up a sign that read SWEDEN IS WATCHING. Many shouted counts of one from forty-three, followed by "Justicia!" #YaMeCanse was scrawled on countless signs, followed by whatever that marcher had "had enough of." #YAMECANSE OF THE WAR AGAINST THOSE OF US RAISING OUR VOICES, THE CRIMINALS ARE THE POLITICIANS! Many chants were inventive or cheerfully obscene. The larger contingents, of universities and secondary schools, cordoned themselves off inside rope barriers against infiltrator provocateurs. People shouted at marchers wearing masks to uncover their faces. The masked marchers were presumed to be members of small anarchist groups, or else professional provocateurs, who, as had happened at previous marches, would provide the police with a justification for responding with violence against all the marchers.

Usually the main significance of a march, large or small, is simply that it took place: that people took the time to walk in support or against this or that because it felt like the right outlet for indignation, or for support. But sometimes a march makes concrete a moment of collective cultural expression that can be harder to put into words. This was an expression of Mexico City, of a way its residents like to think of themselves, in full flower. But it was also representative of a discernible something that seems to be happening in many other parts of Mexico. When a friend said that at the march he "could feel Mexico on the move," he didn't seem to me to be exaggerating. Some said that 200,000 marched and some said more, though I don't know how any accurate count could be made. We didn't reach the Zócalo until about three hours after the first marchers had. By then the podium where Ayotzinapa family members had addressed the rally was dark and empty, and I saw no sign of the giant effigy of Peña Nieto that was set aflame there, photos of which were featured the next day in media reports all around the world.

As had occurred at the end of the previous march, a small group of "anarchists" had clustered in front of one door of the National Palace, apparently battling a line of armored riot police. From the distant, opposite end of the vast plaza, we could hear and see explosions and flashes, presumably from Molotov cocktails, perhaps also of tear gas canisters fired by police. Between us milled a dark mass of thousands still in the Zócalo, many slowly moving toward the surrounding streets exiting the plaza. The reporter in me wanted to get a closer look at the conflagration in front of the palace, but the people I was with didn't want to go any nearer. I left them waiting, and I'd walked perhaps about fifty yards when I suddenly heard loud bangs and screams, sensed a panicked surging in the crowd, and turned around, walking back as swiftly as I could to where I'd left my group. When I reached them, Nayeli, a twelve-year-old girl who is our upstairs neighbor, grabbed my hand. All around us, people were now running out of the plaza, faster and with growing panic. The situation was rife with all the dangers of thousands of people stampeding. We made our way through the darkened streets, navigating down the blocks that seemed emptiest, and finally we found a taxi.

It wasn't until the next morning that I began to learn about what had happened at the Zócalo and in the surrounding streets, including those we'd fled through, that night. A large number of Mexico City police had suddenly emerged from the shadows on the Cathedral side of the Zócalo and charged the protestors. Then, all around the plaza, they'd blocked off streets, trapping thousands inside a circle that, it turned out, we'd just escaped. Eventually eleven protestors were arrested, but many more were beaten, clubbed, and kicked. It seems that none of the eleven who were arrested were among those who'd been attacking the palace, hurling Molotovs or otherwise battling police in front of the National Palace. Some were arrested while fleeing the plaza and others in the streets around it. Some of the arrests were filmed on smartphones by witnesses, often companions of the arrested. Most were university students. Swept up in the panic, most of the students and others in the crowd had started to run from the Zócalo. Liliana Garduño Ortega, thirty-one, who had been photographing the protest, fell down in the stampede, and in the next moment she was being clubbed and kicked in the head by police, and then arrested. Hillary Analí González Olguín, twenty-one, an UNAM student, was also beaten and arrested after falling down. Atzín Andrade, a twenty-nine-year-old art student, had become separated from friends and was waiting for them by the flagpole when police grabbed him. Luis Carlos Pichardo, a fifty-five-year-old filmmaker, and Laurence Maxwell, forty-seven, a Chilean doing postgraduate studies in the department of philosophy and letters at UNAM, were among those arrested. None of the eleven had any previous criminal records. Turned over by Mexico City police to federal authorities, they were formally accused of "attempted homicide," "criminal association," and "rioting," and transferred to federal prisons in Veracruz and Nayarit. Later it would be reported that the evidence for the accusations of criminal association included police observations that some of the arrested students called each other "compa." None of the arrested was among those who'd actually battled with police, but during the tumult in front of the National Palace one anarchist type had managed to pull a policeman to the ground and had kicked his helmeted head. According to human rights organizations monitoring the case, that incident had been used to justify the attempted homicide charges against the others, because "everybody knows that a blow to the head can cause death." According to their lawyers and human rights groups, the eleven were beaten, tortured, and denied the guarantees of due process.

José Alberto, a twenty-one-year-old merchant, didn't even know there were going to be protests in Zócalo that night when he arranged to meet his wife, Tamara, there. They became caught in the crowd charged by police. Both were beaten, though he especially was, by at least ten police; he was taken to a police bus, beaten some more, and received ten or fifteen shocks, he said, from an electric prod, after which he lost consciousness. He was found lying unconscious in Corregidora Street in the early morning hours and taken to a hospital. "Because of the beating, I don't remember the sequence of everything that happened," José Alberto later told a reporter from the digital news site Animal Politico. "But there is one thing that I remember exactly, and that is in the moment that I reached the police bus, where they pushed me down onto my knees, there were about fifteen other people there in civilian clothes. Five were being beaten, like I was, but another ten were just there, sitting, resting, among the police . . . From what I could tell, they were the ones who'd provoked the rioting . . ."—i.e., the so-called anarchists and "*encapuchados*" who'd attacked the National Palace.

The day after the march, President Peña Nieto thanked Mexico City's Mayor Mancera and his police for their cooperation with federal authorities in upholding order in the Zócalo. But exposure in the media and on social networks of the arbitrary arrests and violence against peaceful protestors and bystanders mounted, and the hapless Mancera once again found himself subjected to a storm of criticism and repudiation. A few days later, his police chief, Jesús Rodríguez Almeida, submitted his resignation. On Saturday, November 29, a federal judge freed the eleven people arrested on November 20, saying there was absolutely no evidence to support any of the charges against them. It was a sharp rebuke to the government and a victory for all those who had protested against and denounced the arrests.

On December 1, the second anniversary of his presidency, Peña Nieto was greeted by a poll showing his national approval rating at 39 percent, the lowest for any Mexican president since 1995. Since then, his government's crisis and impression of ineffectiveness have only deepened. Mexico is living an historic and unprecedented moment in which its entire political class, all politicians, all parties, have lost credibility. This void strikes some as dangerous, others as an opportunity. Some see it as an opportunity to create a new kind of political leadership outside of the established parties, an opportunity for radical reform achieved through the ballot box; others hope for a genuine grassroots-led revolution that will reinvent Mexico, already manifesting itself in the spread of community police and other civic self-governing initiatives throughout the country in which civilians have assumed the roles of ousted or discredited local authorities.

I don't pretend to know what is going to happen in Mexico. Undoubtedly, though, Ayotzinapa has provoked resounding expression of the frustration, anger and desperate yearnings for change of millions of Mexicans. Those calls for change and shouts of protest speak for the tens of thousands of Mexican disappeared and for the suffering of their countless loved ones, for the victims of so many previous massacres and killings—not only Ayotzinapa but Tlatlaya, Aguas Blancas, Atenco, Acteal, San Fernando, the ABC nursery fire, Heavens, and so many others—and of the infinite abuses suffered by Mexicans every day in a country where the powerful almost never have to answer to justice. Who can predict what Mexico will be like in 2018, when the country is scheduled to next hold its presidential elections? Will there be a new political party or parties or even a new form of civilian organizing? When I spoke to Father Alejandro Solalinde—the prominent Catholic priest and human rights activist—in Oaxaca in the fall of 2014, he said that be believed that two sectors of society in particular will drive change in Mexico: youth and women. "These two, each on their own side, have been the most punished, abused, infiltrated, massacred, disappeared," he said. "People are going to give their all. This movement isn't going to stop."

Acknowledgments

The Interior Circuit is a book inspired by the friendships that have marked and sustained my life in Mexico City, especially in the aftermath of July, 25, 2007. I'd like to thank more people than I'll be able to here, but without these front line *cuates*, this book would not have come to be: Juan Carlos "Juanca" López, Yoshua Okón, Juan Carlos "Fresa Salvaje" Reyna, Martin Solares, and David Lida; Fabiola Rebora; Naty Pérez, Sam Steinberg, and my goddaughter, Aura Steinberg-Pérez; Pia Elizondo, Gonzalo García Barcha, and Jaime Navarro; Jon Lee "Saqui" Anderson. I've learned from the work of so many journalists in Mexico, many of whom are also good friends: Alejandro Almazán, John Gibler, Nayeli Gómez, Sergio González Rodríguez, Manuel "Meño" Larios, Mónica Maristain, Oscar Martínez, Diego Enrique Osorno, Guillermo Osorno, Alejandro Páez Varela, Marcela Turati, Neldy San Martín and Magalí Tercero. I'm especially grateful to my guide to Tepito, *el joven* Pablo de Llano.

Abrazos grandes also to: Alejandra Frausto, Yuri Herrera, Tanya Huntington, Brenda Lozano, Valeria Luiseli, Luisa Matarrodona, Mauricio Montiel, Ruth Mungia, Luis "Brazi" Muñoz Oliveira, Laura-Emilia Pacheco, los Rabasa, Quique Rangel, América Sanchez, Paola Tinoco, and Mariana Vargas. Nelly Glatt, you are in a category of your own. The Premio Aura

Estrada, given every two years at the Oaxaca International Book Fair, has become an essential part of my life in Mexico, and I'm especially grateful to my partners in running the prize: Guillermo Quijas y Vania Resendíz and the wonderful Almadía/FIL Oaxaca family; and collaborator, juror-for-life, and beloved friend, Gabriela Juaregui. My thanks also to all the writers who've served on our juries—they've now chosen three winners, Susana Iglesias, Majo Ramírez and Verónica Gerber—and also those who've so generously come to Mexico to present the Cátedra Aura Estrada: Vivian Abenshushan, Daniel Alarcón, Paul Auster, Luis Jorge Boone, Carmen Boullosa, Alvaro Enrigue, Margo Glantz, Siri Hustvedt, Mónica de la Torre, Junot Díaz, Richard Ford, Rivka Galchen, Alma Guillermoprieto, Nicole Krauss, Guadalupe Nettel, Cristina Rivera Garza, Colm Toíbín and Alejandro Zambra; and also to those who've helped sustain the prize in other ways: Sharon Dynak, DW Gibson, Sandra Lorenzano, Ernesto Zeivy, Carolina Ferreras and the Mexican Cultural Institute of New York, Gabo and Mercedes, and my dear friend Beatrice Monti von Rezzori.

Outside of Mexico, and especially in the darkest times, I could always count on Barbara "Panda" Epler, Bex Brian and Vanessa Manko; also Andrew Kaufman, Esther Allen, Calvin Baker, Rachel Cobb, and, of course, for decades, Chuck, John and Mary; also, Annie Proulx. Kim R., a profound thank you. Fabulous Sarah Wang was the first to give an encouraging read to parts of this book. Trinity College helps to keep me afloat, and so does the espirit de corps of my colleagues in the English department, including my friend, hall of fame prof and scholar, Paul Lauter, retiring this year. Warm gratitude too, for their crucial critical reads, support and efforts, to my agent Binky

Urban, and to my other family at Grove Atlantic, including my good friend Morgan Entrekin; my editors Elisabeth Schmitz and Katie Raissian; Amy Hundley, Deb Seager, and Charles Woods. Thanks also to Rachel Kushner.

Jhoana Montes Hernández, *mi* Jovi, you are the resurrection and the light.